# WHAT
# DID
# I DO
# WRONG?

**Also by Lynn Caine**
*Widow*
*Lifelines*

# WHAT DID I DO WRONG?

Mothers,
Children,
Guilt

## by Lynn Caine

ARBOR HOUSE
NEW YORK

Copyright © 1985 by Lynn Caine
All rights reserved, including the right of reproduction
in whole or in part in any form. Published in the
United States of America by Arbor House Publishing
Company and in Canada by Fitzhenry & Whiteside, Ltd.

Manufactured in the United States of America

10   9   8   7   6   5   4   3   2

This book is printed on acid free paper. The paper in
this book meets the guidelines for permanence and
durability of the Committee on Production Guidelines
for Book Longevity of the Council on Library Resources.

Library of Congress Cataloging in Publication Data

Caine, Lynn.
What did I do wrong? Mothers, children, guilt

1. Mothers—Psychology.   2. Parenting—Psychological
aspects.   3. Mother and child.   4.Guilt.   I. Title.
HQ759.C255   1985        306'.8'743        84-24513
ISBN: 0-87795-623-5 (alk. paper)

*To my mother and to Eleanor Friede,*
*the mother of this book*

# Contents

# Acknowledgments

I am grateful to the hundreds of people who contributed their encouragement, advice, and inspiration to these pages.

First, I should like to thank Valerie Moolman for her expert editorial guidance, intelligence, and good humor. I should also like to thank Jeanne F. Bernkopf and Carolyn Stallworth for their important editorial contributions.

I am indebted to all of the mothers and friends who contributed to this book in one way or another. Special thanks to Carmen Azcuy, Patricia Bertrand, Lisl Cade, Toby Chiu, Judith Cohen, Marvelle S. Colby, Frances Dory, Mary Chichester Dunetz, Marilyn Fenton, Christine Filner, Jean O'Connor Fuller, Janice Gustavson, Anita Halton, Irma P. Heldman, Laura Hirsch, Zigrid Kornhaver, Kathy Mandry, Bonnie Maslin, Marian Heath Mundy, Lawrence and Connie Pray, Dorothy Rabinowitz, Nancy Shuker, Nikki Smith, Carol Weiss, and Patty Zarate.

My thanks to the authorities who contributed not only their precious time, but also their encouragement and advice: Ronnie Diamond, Dr. Willard Gaylin, Edith Gould, Elaine Heffner, Dr. Ronee Herrmann, Ilene Lefcourt, Dr. Virginia Pomeranz, and Leah Shaefer.

To my agent, Peter Skolnik, I should like to express my thanks for standing by during the difficult times. And, finally, my deepest gratitude to my children, Elizabeth and Jon, without whom—to be sure—this book would not have been possible.

# CHAPTER ONE

# The Imaginary Mother

I AM standing at the corner of Fifty-eighth Street and Ninth Avenue in Manhattan, looking for the Emergency entrance to Roosevelt Hospital.

It is midnight, Christmas night. Buffy has collapsed on the sidewalk, unable to catch her breath. She has bronchial asthma and I think she is dying.

A nurse passes by, barely glancing at us.

"Please help me," I plead. "Help me get my child to the Emergency Room before it's too late."

"You're on the wrong corner," she replies. "You've got to walk a block west to get a wheelchair."

"What? Are you crazy? Leave my daughter here alone and helpless?"

But the nurse has hurried on.

Then I see an ambulance coming up the block.

I run into the road.

"Stop!" I yell. "I've got to get my child to the E.R."

"This is an eastbound street, lady. You're on the wrong corner."

Wrong corner be damned. I am furious.

"I'm not moving. I'm standing right here in front of your fucking ambulance and I'm not moving until you help my child."

A small, wild-eyed woman yelling obscenities can be quite effective.

11

We are in the Emergency Room.

Three paramedics and two doctors later my teenager is out of danger and breathing normally. She cares very much that I am with her and holding her hand.

She clutches tightly. "Don't leave me."

As if I would.

I relax as she sleeps. The episode is over.

But instead of relief, I feel guilt. The bad mother tape in my head begins to play: "If only you'd been a better mother, Buffy wouldn't be here. If you hadn't been mean to her, if you hadn't yelled at her and frightened her, she wouldn't have had this attack. Everybody knows that asthma is a psychosomatic disease. It's all your fault."

I stop the tape. The message is familiar. Ever since my children were babies, I have been tormenting myself in this way. I've always been afraid of damaging them, of not knowing enough as a mother, of not being good enough, not patient enough, unselfish enough . . .

Now wait a minute. I know better. Why am I doing this to myself? Why should I feel this way? I'm not a perfect mother, but I love my kids and they know it and I do my best.

Yet I always blame myself. And almost every mother I've ever met blames herself when anything happens to her children. It's an occupational hazard. And the way we feel has nothing to do with reason, with what we have or have not done. We automatically, endlessly, flagellate ourselves.

I am still thinking about this when we get home.

Why should mothers feel this burden of guilt? Even for circumstances over which we have absolutely no control?

Because we have come to believe what we have been told.

As Betty Friedan observed some two decades ago in *The Feminine Mystique*, popularizers of Freudian psychology suddenly discovered in the 1940s that mothers were to blame for almost everything wrong with the American family and people. "In every case history of troubled child," she wrote, "of alcoholic, suicidal, schizophrenic, psychopathic, neurotic adult; impotent, homosexual male; frigid, promiscuous female; ulcerous, asthmatic and otherwise disturbed American, could be found a mother."

Modern medical and psychological research tells us that this sweeping mother blaming is nonsense. But the damage was done, and the wounds remain. Mother has been judged and found guilty, just as I have judged and blamed myself.

To be a mother in America is to occupy an ambiguous position. For babes in arms and tiny toddlers, mom is the universe. For preteens she is—in a two-parent family—the lesser of two security figures, a source of necessary comforts, some emotional support, and considerable frustration. For teenagers, she's an over-the-hill female who knows nothing, understands nothing, is largely in the way, but can be counted on to do most of the household chores.

As growing children see their mothers, so does the nation. When the nation was young, mother was revered. Rightly so, because mother was a pioneer in a harsh and frightening world. We Americans invented Mother's Day to pay tribute to the first woman in our lives, the symbol of nurturing security and the model of unselfish love. Mother was the very essence of hearth and home, and our worship of her was touched with a healthy respect bordering on fear.

But we were deluding ourselves. In fact, Wonder Mother was the idealized heroine, the woman who never was, an impossibility on a pedestal. Real mothers staggered under the weight of their superimposed perfection and the inadequacies they recognized in themselves as they tried to fulfill the invented image of *mom.*

Then, inevitably, came the backlash.

The first popular attack on mothers was launched in 1942 by writer Philip Wylie in his book *Generation of Vipers,* a collection of essays on American manners and mores. The most malicious and most frequently quoted chapter dealt with a subspecies of American mother on whom the author blamed everything from the pasty look of American men to political corruption. *Momism* became a buzzword for excessive devotion to mothers who dominated their offspring with a smothering love. Wylie's conclusion: "Gentlemen, mom is a jerk."

That did it. Thereafter, mother was fair game, particularly for sons who had read a little Freudian psychology and thought they understood it.

After a series of relatively feeble antimom salvos, *Vipers* was followed by Dan Greenburg's *How to Be a Jewish Mother*, an overnight hit that became the top best-seller of 1961 and the book responsible for bringing the term "Jewish mother" into everyday speech.

Greenburg's attitude toward Jewish mothers became unpleasantly familiar to us all. "Underlying all techniques of Jewish motherhood," he said, "is the ability to plant, harvest and cultivate guilt. Control guilt, and you control the child."

The Jewish mother caricature became a metaphor for all mothers—a sad irony, when it was mothers themselves who were suffering under the guilt of their inadequacies.

Then, as if this were not enough, mom woke up one morning and found that she was not only a possessive jerk, but a laughable one, a figure of scorn typified by Mike Nichols's observation upon having trouble with a new play: "We have to exploit mothers in the first act. Audiences always go for jokes about mothers."

Since the beginning of the assault on mothers there have been innumerable examples of books, movies, and television serials portraying the stereotypical mother as icy, hard, controlling, manipulative, and bitchy. There are many other equally unattractive mother pictures to be discerned, among them the wimp mother, the one who does nothing right because she is an ineffectual, indecisive person who is in thrall to her family and her children. Desperate for help, she seeks the counsel of analysts and child psychologists, only to have her worst fears confirmed in a series of conflicting signals: she *is* doing everything wrong; she has lost control altogether and is seriously damaging her children; she should have sought professional help before; the last person she consulted was out of step with current thought or didn't know what he was talking about; she shouldn't have listened to any advice at all but trusted her own instincts.

Under the combined pressure of economic need and the feminist movement, legions of women have been leaving home to go to work. Nearly half the married women in this country with children under six work outside the home as well as in it. Nearly one family out of five is a single-parent family like mine. And that parent, more often than not, is a woman, responsible not only for the care of the children, but for part if not all of the family income.

These are today's women—modern mothers.

But they're not. These same women in their role as mothers fall right back to the prefeminist era. They accept without challenge the blame that was heaped on them generations ago and the scorn perpetuated by much of modern fiction and popular psychology. They are beset by feelings of guilt and raise their children with doubt rather than with pride. If anything goes wrong in the family, from a cut finger to a drug bust, they feel they must have caused it in some way. Fathers rarely castigate themselves. Mothers do it all the time.

In every other area, women have made enormous strides. And yet, as mothers, they still seem paralyzed by guilt and fear, casualties not only of antiquated momism but of women's crusade for equal rights outside of the home. For all of the great gains achieved through the women's liberation movement, there has been little change of perspective on the special problems and responsibilities of mothers. What special interest group speaks out for us, rallies and encourages us? Not one.

As a practicing yet not notably admirable mother, I do not

and cannot set myself up as a model. But after many years of talking to thousands of women all across the country, I have learned that there are certain universals in motherhood, and that most mothers, no matter what their age or background, identify with the frustrations and despairs and triumphs I have experienced. I know that a New York widow with two children has much in common with a Kansas mother of seven, because I know that woman and she knows me. However different our situations, we all seem to go through the same kinds of trials and joys and fears.

Partly through my own children, partly from other mothers, and partly from researchers I respect, I have found a growing body of evidence to suggest that mother may have only a limited influence for good or bad. No one can predict or determine the way a child is going to turn out. There are very few useful rules on how to bring up healthy, well-adjusted children, and even when these few rules are followed there is no guarantee that they will prove effective. Even experts have disturbed children. Offspring who look like sure losers turn out winners; early winners turn out losers in the long run. Adversity may hurt children, strengthen children, or have little to do with their development. Children are far more resilient than we have been led to believe by quasi Freudians and well-meaning experts who give us prescriptions for raising our families; and we do not understand why it is that some youngsters scar easily and others, miraculously, do not scar even under apparently devastating conditions.

But one thing is clear: emotional well-being does not depend on mothers alone. I do not mean to minimize the mother's role in shaping her child. But there are many other factors involved in personality development and character structure, including of course the father, position in the family, genetics, temperament, health, intelligence, peers, teachers, society, economics, and just plain luck.

After their father died in 1971, my own children developed in ways I could not have predicted. My son, Jon, now twenty-three, of whom I so often despaired, has grown into sturdy young manhood in spite of my failings and his crises. He himself is largely responsible for what he has become, but I believe that if I have given him one thing of value it is the image of woman as a person of diverse interests—not a domestic cliché, but a busy wage earner, author, public speaker, mother, fighter, music lover, cat fancier, popcorn addict, opinionated individual, and occasional wit. He is not going to go through life disparaging his mother, other mothers, women in general—or himself.

My daughter, Buffy, now nineteen, is going to be stronger and freer than I ever was. I have shared my strengths with her and acknowledged my weaknesses (which she is quick to point out, should I neglect to mention them). She does not fear her sexuality as I once feared my own. When she becomes a mother she will never feel as inadequate as I have, because she has a healthy sense of herself and knows how to communicate. I don't try to teach her anything. Rather, I try to help her understand. We are both pioneers in a world where a woman's role is no longer defined, and we enjoy seeing ourselves change.

I carry the voices of thousands of mothers with me—on tape, in my notes and questionnaires, echoing in my mind—and I know their fears: "Why do I do these things?" "What's wrong with me as a mother?" "I didn't know motherhood was going to be like this!" "Where do I learn about how to discipline?" "How come my kid is the only one who's not in the ninety-ninth percentile?" "I swore I'd be different from my own mother, but every day I get more and more like her." "I'm so angry with my daughter that it scares me." "Why isn't there a school for mothers?"

There have always been schools for mothers—informal ones, comprised of extended families or groups of acquaintances who stand in for the large families many of us lack. And some of us tend to overlook these vast resources. I say, don't knock them; seek them out. When my children were small I used to take them to Central Park, where I'd sit on a bench almost cross-eyed with boredom while the other mothers engaged in their particular brand of shoptalk. If only I'd paid attention, I would have realized that what these women were doing was holding little park-bench seminars in mothering, sharing both their expertise and their doubts. It was years before I admitted to the need for a similar support group for myself.

Today, there is a growing movement of mothers reaching out to each other for reassurance and an exchange of information. Throughout the country, mothers' groups are forming and addressing themselves not to the needs of their children, but to their own needs as parents. The fact is that women who become mothers don't necessarily come to motherhood knowing how to mother, and they need to find this out before becoming swamped by their own ignorance and the prejudices of the mom baiters.

The mother schools of the 1980s in which women of all backgrounds have come together to share information, fears, experiences, problems, and solutions, have moved beyond the park bench to a more formal structure. Throughout the country there are mother centers and workshops of virtually every affiliation, offering companionship as well as education. What they teach varies. In a mothers' center I attended in Dutchess County, I was intrigued to note that they held workshops for mothers in everything from thumb sucking to extramarital affairs.

The overall impact of these groups is that mothers are beginning to let go of fear and are developing more self-esteem. These are two giant steps. Out of my own experience of mother schools, mother talk, and confidence classes I teach, I have learned how mothers have taken these steps even without the guidance of a formal mother school—by learning that the child-development experts give us criteria, not guidance; and that, for all our doubts, we are our own experts.

I have sought guidelines through interviews with mothers,

psychologists, educators, physicians, fathers, and daughters. I have used my lecture platform and my workshops as a laboratory and my own life as a vehicle. And in the chapters that follow, I incorporate my findings into the case history of an imperfect but loving mother—myself—and of a couple of terrific children. Mine.

# CHAPTER TWO

# The Unfit
# Mother of the Year

YOU may remember me: the shattered widow, coping with the problems of earning a living and with the raising of two children whose needs I could not meet.

Martin and Jon and Buffy and I had been the perfect little family, secure in our happiness with each other and our lives. Then Martin became ill, and for fourteen months we watched him die of cancer.

He was gone. It was a shocking blow, made worse by long anticipation. But the nightmare was not over. My husband's death had left me not only emotionally but financially ill equipped to be the strong parent figure I felt my children needed. For a time my grief and fear were incapacitating. Helplessly, I worried about money, about my own feelings of resentment toward the husband who had abandoned me, about my many shortcomings as a mother. I was sure that I was doing nothing right, that I was damaging my children for life.

The fact is that I was, in a way, neglecting them. I earned our keep, came home, collapsed with the exhaustion of unhappiness, and yelled at them for disturbing me even while I brooded about their future. My misery was more real to me than they were. Friends, neighbors, and my mother filled in for me as much as they could, not realizing—because I couldn't bring myself to tell anyone—how lost and insecure I felt. They thought I was tough. I wasn't. I simply wasn't admitting weakness. I couldn't let myself cry out for help. I didn't know how to take action, or what action to take. It was easier to do nothing.

The realities of life were suddenly brought home to me when my son was asked to leave the most permissive school in the East, possibly in the nation. He didn't work, his absentee record was appalling, and he was disruptive when he did show up. Worse: he was using drugs.

I had known it. I'd caught him at it with his street friends. But it took his expulsion from school to bring home to me how serious his situation was.

At the same time, I realized that I knew even less about my daughter's problems than I knew about Jon's. She had never mentioned any. I had never asked. Her school had never complained. For all but the most practical of purposes, she had not had a mothering mother since her father's death. And yet she seemed to be content. So I felt remorseful but relieved and let myself concentrate on making arrangements for Jon.

With any luck at all, the three of us would now get back on track. It was high time we did. I could not cry by myself forever. Nor did I.

But even as I moved past my agony, helped by reaching out to other widows, feeling that I could help them in their pain, I continued to flagellate myself as an incompetent mother. It took me years to realize that I was not unique, to understand how much I am like other mothers and other mothers are like me. We all make mistakes and blame ourselves—excessively—for them.

With that revelation, I turned a corner in my life and at last, gradually, began to develop into a mature mother, no longer consumed with worry and self-pity and guilt.

It was a lengthy process.

Meanwhile, mourning time was over. We had settled down to the business of living.

Jon, a wiry, street-smart near-fifteen, was away at a prestigious boarding school. Buffy, soon to be a precociously feminine eleven, was home with me in our apartment in Manhattan. An unaccustomed peace reigned in the household.

I missed Jon. Sometimes I wondered if I'd been right to send him away, but we'd agreed there was good reason. An adolescent boy doesn't care to have his life run by a female parent. He'd told me often enough that he needed a male role model, and since I wasn't about to marry one for his sake, it had seemed sensible to send him off to an all-male school. His school's academic standards were high, there was a good sports program, and we had liked the location and the staff.

My main purpose in sending Jon to boarding school had to do with his physical safety rather than his academic needs. I wanted him out of town, out of reach of drugs and drug dealers and the druggie street kids he'd been hanging out with. Away from me and the city, I felt he was bound to shape up.

His letters to me were infrequent but happy. It was a pity that his report cards weren't better, but I wasn't ready to start breathing over his shoulder about his grades. For the time being it was enough that he was healthy and content. And safe. The dean's list could come later.

Buffy was no great scholar either, but she was a diligent worker. She seemed to have found her academic niche— slightly above average, I was happy to see—and was sticking to it. She was quiet and self-contained. I felt I could rely on her.

I kept watching this amiable little girl to see if she showed any signs of busting out the way Jon had done before he had gone away, but no one could accuse her of being a behavior problem. I didn't always have to be after her to do this or that, or stop doing this or that. I never had to worry about her homework. It was always done. She was polite and obedient. Her room was neat. But she wasn't quite the docile girl child I used to think she was. It slowly dawned on me that she was an expert at staying out of my hair and doing exactly what she pleased.

What pleased her most was horseback riding. She had fallen in love with horses at her first summer camp, when she was seven, and she spent every afternoon at the riding stable. Years before, my pediatrician, Virginia Pomeranz, had urged me to make sure that Buffy excel in something, whether it be swimming or playing the recorder, and Buffy had made her choice. Sometimes I wished she had chosen a less expensive hobby, but after all the years in which I felt I had left her to her own devices and done so little for her, I couldn't deny her this great pleasure. It wasn't just a luxury. Several summers of riding camp and her afternoons at the stable had done her a world of good. She had developed an almost mature, though tentative poise. And yet she was still an endearing child who loved being surrounded by family.

That wasn't easy, because ours was a very small family and Jon wasn't often home. But Buffy was deeply involved with my mother and spoke to her often on the slightest pretext. It was the same with the neighbors in our apartment house and on our block and in the next block, and with my friends as well. They formed one big family, as far as she was concerned.

Patty was at the core of this informal family. Patty was our live-in student who, like Buffy, had been adopted, and had pulled us all together when we needed her most. It amused me to see how Buffy was using Patty to build up her network. Patty, as magnificently beautiful as an Aztec princess, was like a magnet for kids of all ages. The younger ones flocked around because she would sing and draw and help them with their homework. A lot of Jonny's friends came to visit her because she had become their friend.

And at first Buffy gathered them all around her, as if they were her visitors, her very own extended family.

I felt, at times, that I was neglecting her terribly, because my work as a publicist for a Boston-based publishing company involved long hours and frequent out-of-town trips, leaving me little time at home. But seeing all those kids coming and going, with Buffy the little queen in the center and Patty by her side, made me realize that my resourceful daughter had built herself a good, strong support system. The apartment was a haven to her even when I wasn't there.

To my amazement, she seemed to have very little hurt in her after our years of turmoil. Or little that she was willing to admit to. Every incident of my rejection or anger that I dredged up she countered with an excuse.

"I always knew you didn't mean it," she said. "After you screamed at me, you'd always take me out and buy me an ice cream the next day. I knew you were sorry."

If I'd been sorry then, how sorry I was now. Imagine thinking I could square her with an ice cream cone!

I told her that I had always felt guilty when she had awakened in the middle of the night screaming with fright. I thought her nightmares were a reflection of how scared and unhappy she had been during the day. "But you always came and took me into your bed when I was frightened," she told me.

Another time, I said that I had felt truly awful about not spending more time with her and Jon right after their father's death. "It's no way for a mother to behave," I said, "coming home at night and throwing herself on the bed and telling her children to go away and leave her alone."

Buffy refused to let me feel guilty.

"You were very upset," she said earnestly. "You didn't know what you were doing." I was astounded. It was as if our roles had been reversed. "You missed daddy so much you were a nervous wreck."

I could hardly believe the charity of this child. How could she be so understanding and forgiving? This, paradoxically, made me feel guiltier. Buffy should not have to defend and comfort me. Grown-up as she might be, she was still the child. I was the mother.

That winter of Jon's first year away Buffy began taking over some of the household chores with great goodwill and competence. She loved shopping for groceries at the supermarket, to spare Patty or me a trip, and was careful to point out what good buys she had made. I was very proud of her.

I gave myself little credit for her development. If she had been timid and nervous, a problem child, I would have taken the blame. "It's all my fault," I would have said. And been convinced that I was right. But she wasn't timid and she wasn't nervous and she wasn't messed up. She was an outgoing, even-tempered preteen, a pleasure to have around. It seemed to me that she was building a healthy little life for herself and she had a pretty good idea what she wanted to do with it.

But I wasn't so sure what was going to happen with Jon.

What I saw of him was not very promising.

So long as he was away at school and out of sight—out from underfoot, I told myself guiltily—I could persuade myself that he was all right. But I felt less than encouraged when he came home for holidays. At first he sought out his friends, the street kids. Then he started going to a lot of concerts in Central Park, which seemed to me an innocuous and even admirable pastime until I realized that he was hanging out with a group called the Parkies, a band of tattered post-hippies who attached them-selves to every musical group that played the park. Jon's ambi-tion was to be a roady—the fellow who carries the music stands around.

Wonderful, I told myself silently. And your father was a law-yer. But I wasn't seriously concerned that his roady phase would last very long. I was more concerned about where it might lead.

He didn't seem to be learning much at school, but he had started accumulating a thrift-shop wardrobe that astounded even his peers. Each time he came home he reminded me of nothing so much as a Halloween beggar. He didn't believe in buying clothes or wearing them. He acquired costumes. One of his favorite costumes was a tailcoat, much too large for him, which he wore with torn jeans, a T-shirt, and an utterly repel-lent pair of sneakers. He also, on occasion, sported a bowler hat with his tails, or a pair of peacock-feather earrings. For special occasions, he had a wonderful flowing brocade robe in black and gold and various shades of dirty red, a combination I liked very much, except for the grime.

I knew he was out to shock and irritate. Shocked I wasn't, because I found him too funny, but I couldn't let him know how truly comical he was in his efforts to assert himself. I was a little irritated that he should be making such a clown of himself, and yet I didn't really mind his act. I accepted it as part of the process of growing up. A lot of boys his age were acting out in very much the same way.

But not at school. Jonny's headmaster and teachers were not amused. Nor were his grades very funny. His report cards got worse instead of better. They were terrible, *terrible*, TERRIBLE. And it wasn't just in his studies that he was slipping. "Jon is a bright boy, but he is not using his potential. . . . He does not come to class. . . . When he does he is disruptive. . . . He falls asleep. . . . He doesn't do any homework. . . . He is a behavior problem. . . . He is failing."

I went to his school for a conference. I was very charming to the principal and guidance counselors. Nobody was going to be permitted to think that I was not a polite, well-brought-up mother. Jon, in his turn, was charming to me in his somewhat bizarre way. Somehow, it was us against them; we both felt that the people at this school were very stuffy, and we fell into a kind of conspiracy. They were nice but they were very conscious of running a fine, beautiful, classy boarding school for scions of the best families. Clean-cut scions, preferably. Jon and I were both amused that they had let in a kid like him in the first place. They had known what they were getting. They had interviewed us both, and Jon had certainly not been on his best behavior or in his most appropriate costume. They knew he had been thrown out of his last school, the permissive one. I suppose they thought they could reform him and I hoped they could—but their rules, the old rules, didn't seem to be working for kids like Jon.

When I left, nothing had been resolved.

I kept hoping that things would change, but with every report card my hopes were dashed again. Jon wasn't getting anywhere. And the price was high. Why was I spending all this money just for him to mess up his life? I didn't begrudge the cost of the best schooling I could get for him. I've always considered my children's educations among my major responsibilities. But the savings from my book *Widow* weren't going to last forever. Sooner or later my son was going to need a scholarship; but Jon's conduct was such that no school, except maybe reform school, would ever give him a scholarship.

I didn't know what to do. Even I could see that Jon was incorrigible and that the school couldn't do anything for him. He was the school maverick. *My kid* was the school maverick, with his ridiculous ponytail and his terrible clothes—this, at a school with a dress code. And he was stoned much of the time. I don't know how long it took for me to realize it, but I finally did.

After my initial shock, we had a moderately reasonable discussion about what he used and how he got it. I admitted my naive assumption that, at his out-of-town boarding school, he would be out of reach of drugs and drug dealers. He looked at me pityingly and explained that users can always find suppliers, and vice versa. The richer the kids, he pointed out, the more drugs available, including the expensive ones, like cocaine. He, of course, only smoked pot.

I wondered. I also wondered what I had accomplished by sending him there. I'd removed him from the Central Park drug scene and dropped him down in a more genteel one, where he happened also to be exposed to learning—if he felt like doing any work. Which he didn't. I had briefly bought some peace of mind, and that was all. I'd been wrong to believe that any school could, or should, do the parents' job. My job.

So I'd been wrong again. Somehow, as a parent, I was always wrong. My heart sank to a new low. And yet I still had a glimmer of hope that something in his life at school would turn my son around. He was still loving and caring. He was too intelligent to throw himself away. He had the right stuff and he'd shape up.

But I was deluding myself. Before Jon came home at the end of his school year I was informed that he would not be "invited back," as the headmaster put it in his gentlemanly way. My son had not worked out, had not applied himself. He had a serious behavior problem and was not benefiting from school. Which in turn was not benefiting from his presence.

I panicked. What was going to become of him? Buffy, to whom I had paid so little attention, was turning out to be more or less a model child. Jon, the indulged one, had become a major problem.

When Jon came home for the summer he was defiant and defensive. Our shared amusement was gone. It was impossible to discuss his behavior at school or his future plans. All I knew was that we would have to find another school for him by fall, and that he'd have to go to summer classes in order to qualify. It took days of concentrated effort to convince him that he had to go to summer school. Having agreed, he kept flaring up with quick adolescent anger. He flung himself out of the apartment and stayed away for hours. When he came home he went to his room and slammed the door.

Summer was hell. Buffy had gone happily off to camp, looking forward to mucking out stables and riding for hours and hours every day. Jon and I were alone again, but I rarely saw him.

We had found another school, this time in the city, where he could be close to me, but meanwhile he had to apply himself at summer school and pass his courses or he wouldn't be admitted.

All I could do was tell myself what I had been telling myself for years: life will be better in the fall. When Jon is at his new school, a permissive school where he will be understood, everything will be all right. He will like it there and hit his stride. I just have to sweat it out until then.

But fall was many weeks away. Things got worse. I saw less and less of Jonny. When I got home from work, he'd be gone. I had no idea where he was, or with whom, although I knew he spent a lot of time hanging out in his tailcoat and jeans at the Band Shell in Central Park with his incorrigible groupie friends. The few meetings we had usually took place around 4:00 A.M. Communication between us was impossible. When we did speak to each other our exchanges were hateful, abusive, and painful for both of us.

I'd scream at him and he'd scream back, both of us out of control. I felt like the unfit mother of the year, convinced that his behavior was the result of my inability to cope.

I could feel the fear like shooting pains.

What was I afraid of?

What is every mother afraid of? That her kids will turn out to be no good and that it will be all her fault. Buffy was all right, but Jonny was well on his way to becoming a juvenile delinquent, if he wasn't one already.

Somehow we got through the summer. The first day of the new school year arrived. He went off that morning with the surly growl I had come to expect, and I offered up a small prayer that things would be different this time.

My little girl was home, taller by now than I, subtly changed as adolescent girls do change in the months of summer. I was determined to spend as much time with her as my job permitted.

But after a time I found, when I came home late, that Buffy was coming in even later. Not really late enough for me to become concerned, but late enough for me to want to know where she was.

"Hey, mom, it's all right. I was just at Chess City."

"Chess City? What's that?"

"Gee, Mrs. Caine!" That was Lisa, a pretty little brunette who'd come in with Buffy. Boys and girls were always coming in with or after her. "Didn't you know? Buff's the queen of Chess City."

"I still don't know—"

"It's just a place where a bunch of old guys play chess."

"What do you mean, old guys?" I was alarmed. "And what are you doing with them? You don't play chess."

"Oh, mom. There's pinball machines there too. I play the machines."

"And is she terrific!" said Lisa. Enviously, I thought. "I mean, that's why we call her the queen."

"Wonderful," I said sourly. I remembered the place now. A couple of blocks away, up a flight of stairs, a bit seedy-looking. "I don't want you ever to go there alone, okay? And I'd like you to let me know before you go."

As I went on with my mother lecture it occurred to me that Buffy's royal visits coincided with Patty's absences. Is this what the kids did when Patty was out on business of her own? Did Patty know, or was this going on behind her back?

Next day, I came home early. The house was quiet. Patty was alone, studying. I asked her about the queen of Chess City.

Patty looked at me quizzically. "Sure, all the kids go there. They go in packs. Buff's usually home by nine. At least, when I'm here. But I told her I was going to be late last night."

"Hmm. Is that where she is now?"

"No, she's baby sitting for Zigrid," Patty said. A little hesitantly, I thought. "You remember, she asked you if that would be okay."

I remembered. Zigrid was a really nice, beautiful German woman with two little girls and a couple of enthusiastic dogs, all of whom lived in another wing of our building. Buffy, I knew, had been doing a lot of baby sitting and dog walking for

Zigrid and other immediate neighbors. She must be making a small fortune. And spending it on the pinball machines?

"She saves most of it," Patty said, reading my thoughts. "But, um, she doesn't really do it so much for the money as for, well, I guess, the company."

"The company? Dogs and babies? When *you're* home?" Patty must be kidding.

But Patty wasn't kidding. "The mothers," she said.

Buffy, it turned out, had been checking out all the women in our building and had adopted a couple of them as surrogate mothers. Myra, whom I didn't like much, was one. Zigrid, whom I did, was another.

Surrogate mothers. I let it go for a while, watching, and then I talked to Buffy.

"I know I'm not around a lot of the time, but what about Patty? She's here for you, you know."

Buffy turned on me, eyes blazing. "Oh, is she? Lisa's here, Angela's here, Betty's here, Bobbie's here, everybody's here, and they're all around Patty. She's always paying attention to all of them. Nobody's here for *me*. She isn't, and you aren't. But she's *supposed* to be here for *me*."

I had never seen such a look of resentment on her face. Such a look of jealous rage.

"Buff, she is here for you and only for you. You always liked having the other girls come around. They're your friends, your good friends."

"No, they're not! They're not here for me any more than you are. They're visiting *her*."

I was astounded. So much for my illusions about her happy little family.

"But you like having them around," I said weakly.

"How would you know? You're always somewhere else. All you do is work and go to those *business* parties all the time. You're never here for me. You're always with other people."

"Wait a minute! Who do you think I'm doing it for? I'm

the breadwinner in this family. I can't be in two places at once. What about me? Do you think I'm having fun?"

"I *really* don't know. Now, if you'll *excuse me*," she said with vastly exaggerated politeness, "I have a baby-sitting date. Good-bye."

And out she went.

I did not quite know what to think. Buffy's jealousy was a revelation to me. Beneath that self-contained exterior was— what? A kid with normal early adolescent hangups? A deeply angry, needy child?

I mulled it over and kept an eye on her.

Whenever possible. Increasingly, it seemed to me, she was baby sitting or otherwise hanging around Zigrid. The two little girls, Buffy remarked pointedly, were like sisters to her. Much more like family than the loutish, disagreeable brother, Jon, who shambled in and out at odd hours and snarled at her.

She stopped just short of saying Zigrid was like a mother to her.

Did she wish she were? And was I jealous?

At first I was more relieved than envious, happy that Buffy had found someone with whom she felt loved and safe and to whom she felt important. And Zigrid, when I talked it over with her, seemed genuinely pleased to have Buffy around.

But the more I thought about it, the less I liked it. Obviously, my kind of mothering was not enough or not right for Buffy. I had failed in some very basic way. She shouldn't have to reach outside the home for someone to love.

I was struck with the incredible thought that I was losing my daughter to another mother.

# CHAPTER THREE

# Jumping Ship

MY son with the feather in his earlobe may have been a behavior problem to me, but he was regarded with something like awe in selected younger circles. Hanging out at the Band Shell in the park, chief Parkie among a group of Parkies, had given him a kind of celebrity status that brought home to me something of the adolescent underground there was in New York.

I went to a New Year's Day party at around this period. Jon wasn't with me. I think he would have died rather than be seen in public with his mother. But there were some kids there, nice kids. Any one of them, I thought, might have been a suitable friend for him if he had been a suitable friend for them.

A phone rang through the hubbub. My hostess answered and called out, "Jon Caine's on the phone." And a young girl said, "Not *the* Jon Caine!"

*The* Jon Caine? I didn't like to ask precisely what he had done to earn this breathless recognition, but I did wonder. Was it just his crazy clothes? I hoped so.

I knew I had given him a ticket back to Central Park by enrolling him in a city school. But, as he had pointed out, you can take the kid out of the city, but you can't take the city out of the kid. City habits flourish wherever city kids go. If he wanted to hang out, goof off, and get high, he could do it anywhere. He might as well be near me. I liked the idea of having him around, although God knows we didn't see much of each other and it wasn't exactly fun when we did.

We—mostly I—had chosen his new school with difficulty

because the choices were getting fewer and fewer. Not many schools care to take on a student who has been asked to leave two others. An academic school was certainly not going to take him. Neither was an institution with a religious affiliation. A public school wouldn't be able to give him the needed attention. But there had to be someplace that would not only accept my son, but be able to help him.

The fact is, I was looking for a school that could fix my kid. Obviously, *I* couldn't. I'd already screwed up and made a mess out of him. And of course it was my fault and only mine, because no one else was responsible for him.

Yet I had no faith in my own ability to put Jon back on the track. I'd lost all influence over him, if I'd ever had any. Somebody or something had to bail me out. Surely, some school could provide what I was unable to provide or didn't know about. I had to turn the boy over to professionals.

I had asked around and been told about a school I will call Greenwood. Parents with hard-to-handle children, I had already discovered, keep casting about for different approaches. We don't know which one will work, but we're willing to try anything that seems to offer hope. This school, which claimed to be tailored for "bright underachievers," seemed to have a different approach from that of the staid and establishment boarding school of the year before. Its philosophy was what its prospectus called "permissive," which sounded pretty good to Jon and me, and its policy was to exclude parents in order to engender trust in the children—which seemed to appeal to Jon.

"No parent-teacher conferences?" I asked the principal.

"None at all. They destroy the child's confidence in the school."

"No dress code?"

"No dress code. What the student wears is up to him."

"Any form of discipline?"

"Not, of course, the traditional punitive methods."

He never did tell me what methods they did use, if any, and

somehow I felt I had no right to ask further questions or I would be seen as challenging the principal's authority. I had never felt comfortable in encounters with authorities, especially educators.

I hoped what they were doing was right. The principal seemed capable, even impressive. The children were from all kinds of backgrounds, which I liked, and the classrooms seemed airy and pleasant enough—although I did think I detected a faint whiff of smoke.

We settled into the rhythm of our days. As I saw the routine, I went off to my job in publishing, Buffy went to her school, Jon went to his, I came home early whenever possible to spend as much time as I could with my daughter, and Jon came home later. Much later.

I observed no signs of homework. Perhaps bright underachievers weren't expected to do any. I asked Jon about it one weekend when he happened to be home and up. He laughed at me and went out. School, park, wherever he went—sometimes Buffy saw him hanging out at Chess City—he was still using his own dress code. It was beginning to get to me. Sometimes I wished I could shanghai him and send him to military school for a haircut and a good suit.

Mornings before going to work I'd wake him and Buffy. Later I'd look in and find he'd gone back to sleep. I'd rouse him again.

"Aren't you getting up? Don't you have to go to school?"

Moan. "Cut it out, mom. I don't have a class until ten."

Or eleven. Or twelve. Or three. Amazing how he'd arranged his hours. You'd think he was a graduate student. I thought he smoked too much and told him. I wasn't sure what it was, but I didn't like it. Fifteen, and he had smoke coming out of his ears whenever his eyes were open.

"Hey, we smoke in class. Everybody smokes. It's okay."

"It may be okay for the others, but it's not okay for you."

A short expletive from Jon, and out he went.

I wondered, did the kids really not have any homework?

What time *were* Jon's classes? Was it true, they smoked in class? The worst of it was that I couldn't find out. I wasn't supposed to have any contact with the educators. It would destroy my little darling's trust in his school.

For a while Jon seemed fairly good-humored, except for shouting at Buffy whenever he happened to notice her, and I thought perhaps the change of school was gradually beginning to have some effect on him. Maybe permissiveness was what he needed for a while.

But, as for myself, I was no longer happy with what my friends referred to as my "glamor job." The hours were long and the pay was inadequate and the glamor had worn off. I didn't really like what I was doing anymore.

I was also going out of town even more often than before, giving lectures and workshops for widows and other single parents on how to find lifelines, develop coping mechanisms, and regain their zest for living. These projects had nothing to do with my more than full-time job, but I was afraid to turn them down because I was always worried about money. I was the only security my children had, and I felt I needed the extra income. At least for my peace of mind. But I had mixed feelings about those lectures and meetings. They paid well, which was good. But they took me away from my home, which perhaps wasn't. Jon didn't give a damn, but Buffy openly resented my absences. Once, on coming home, I had found a note from her, carefully picked out in the red ribbon on my typewriter:

```
MOM   I   WAS   SICK   THIS   WEEK
AND   I   DIDN'T   WANT   YOU   TO
   LEAVE   BUT   YOU   HAD   TO   AND
I   UNDER   STAND   HOW   HARD   YOU
   WORK.   I   MISSED   YOU   ALOT
   AND   I   HOPE   YOU   DIDN'T
   CRY.   I   LOVE   YOU   VERY   MUCH
   and   i   Hope   you   don't
   Leave   agen.                    LOVE
                              BUFFY CAINE
```

It would have been a hardhearted mother indeed who did not feel moved and remorseful.

Yet I liked the lectures and was beginning to have the sense that I didn't need a nine-to-five job to support us and even to feel I had something to say that people would listen to. I felt burned out on the job, but alive and involved when I was sharing my personal experiences with others. Workshops and lectures gave me the sort of human involvement I didn't have in my job. And if I made them my career, I would have much more time at home.

I decided to leave the company.

Terrified with that decision, I decided to stay.

Somebody in this family, I told myself, has to be fully employed. It isn't just the paycheck. It's the fringe benefits. The family medical insurance, the life insurance, the paid vacations, the sick leave, the pension plan. We needed that security.

Oh, the lure of those fringe benefits, those seductive benefits. It is hard to strike out on your own after being supported by a paternalistic corporation. And it was also difficult for me to leave what had become a sort of haven for me, a familiar place where there were familiar faces. People I was accustomed to, situations I understood. I couldn't get up the nerve to take the plunge.

So I stayed on and cursed myself for being gutless.

The queen of Chess City clearly relished her supremacy, although it took me a while to elicit any information from her. I had a closer look at her favorite hangout and found it dingy but not threatening, a seedy neighborhood meeting place whose primary attraction was the games and a sort of camaraderie. Old men sat at grimy tables, hunched over chess and backgammon, and kids hammered away vigorously at the pinball machines, drinking canned soft drinks.

"So tell me again how you found this place," I said to Buffy one evening as she and I and Patty sat down to dinner.

"Oh, mom, it's not hard to find! It's practically around the corner."

"I know that. But what prompted you to go in?"

"I went with Susan one day, I told you. She was getting people for the ASPCA membership club and money and stuff, and we joined as paying members and that's how I found out about this place that had pinballs and everything—"

Patty and I exchanged looks of dazed bewilderment. I never got that story straight. *Never.*

"—and I played one game and I got so hooked on it, I loved it. And so I just kept playing and playing and it's like a game that gets your money out of you."

"Your money?"

"No, really, mom, once you start it's really hard to stop. You know, kids hanging out there. So I started coming around with Angela and Susan first, before going on my own. They have hero sandwiches and stuff and everything, and it's really a lot of fun. And then I started going on my own, and I started getting known. And everyone knows Jon, too," she added, with less enthusiasm.

"He still goes there?" I, of course, would be the last to know.

"Oh, sure, sometimes. Later than me, mostly. Anyway, I play chess too now. And I started beating everybody in chess and checkers and pinball machines, and they all think I'm great. It's a lot of fun, mom. They call me the pinball wizard."

I looked at my eleven-year-old pinball wizard, famed queen of Chess City, porcelain-featured and delicate-boned, eyes glowing with self-esteem. Were we going to wind up at Gamblers Anonymous? Somehow I didn't think so. She was enjoying the recognition of her peers. Surely that couldn't hurt.

"I love that!" I said as warmly as I could. "Buffy the pinball wizard!" I hesitated, not wanting to spoil the moment. "I hope you're not gambling away all your money."

She looked resigned rather than resentful. Of course her mother would go and say a dumb thing like that.

"It's my *baby*-sitting money."

I supposed that was an answer.

It was true that she had been doing a lot of baby sitting and dog walking lately, mostly for Zigrid. I knew she always managed to have some money tucked away, even when everybody else seemed to be broke. Through her, I'd come to know Zigrid quite well during the previous few months. In fact, Zigrid was about the only mother I ever talked to, and I liked her tremendously. The surrogate situation had become less alarming to me. It seemed to me that Zigrid, far from being a threat, was a healthy influence in Buffy's life. Something like a loving aunt, perhaps.

Buffy had rapidly become almost a member of that family. The little girls called her big sister. Zigrid did a lot of cooking and baking, which I did not, and Buffy thought of her as an ideal mother. She wanted me to spend more time in the kitchen and on domestic things, the way ideal mothers are supposed to. That touched me, and I felt ashamed of my inadequacy. But I could have no objection to her adopted family. It was a very happy group. I could see that it was a key relationship in her life, and it was one I thoroughly approved of.

The fact that Patty was part of it too made it even better. She was friendly with Zigrid and loved the little girls. Zigrid and her husband had a fairly active social life, and Patty quite often took over for her as substitute mommy when Buffy wasn't available to baby-sit. My warm thoughts about Buffy's extended family flooded back. She *did* need a sense of family, and she had put that need to work. There are little jealousies in every close relationship, and that's why she had flared up at me about Patty "being there" for everyone else. I could not fault her need to be part of a warm support group.

What did disturb me was Buffy's continuing relationship with Myra. I didn't think there was any harm in the woman. I just didn't like the way she would fawn on me one minute because I could get people on television, and the next minute make me feel like a neglectful mother because I was out all day. Poor Buffy felt lonesome, said Myra when I met her in the lobby one evening, and that's why she kept dropping in.

"Oh, I don't think so," I said coldly. "She comes to see Andy. She's very fond of children. Anybody's."

Andy was Myra's adopted four-year-old, and Myra seldom failed to remind me that *her* adopted child received her full-time loving care, which, as everybody surely knew, was what adopted children needed to make up for their lack of nurturing during those crucial infant hours and weeks and months . . . and so on and so on.

I *know* that, damn you, I would say silently. I'm doing the best I can.

Something else that bothered me deeply was Buffy's open displeasure at Jon's return to the city. She had just loved it when he was away. Never mind that he only came home to sleep. Even that was too much. He was around, and he had a share of my attention, and she didn't like that. In fact, she didn't like Jon. He hated her, she said. She hated him.

By this time Jon and I had started to yell at each other again. Life was not better this year. His new school had worked no miracle for him. Or for me. We couldn't get through to each other. There was no communication. Buffy was wrong. He didn't hate her. She was just a person in the house. A slob, he said. He had no real contact with her at all.

He was coming in as late as ever, freakish in his clown clothes. The 4:00 A.M. encounters had started all over again. His eyes were funny. They were glazed. I hated the look of them. They frightened me.

"Where were you? What were you doing?"

"Out! Nothing!"

"Is that supposed to be funny?"

"I was just hanging out."

"And taking drugs." At this point I would be icy, but getting loud. "God knows what you're using, but it's freaking you out worse than ever."

"It's only pot. Everybody smokes pot."

"*Only* pot. You chain-smoke pot. You're stoned every night—"

"I am not!"

"What're you doing with your life? You know it's dangerous. What's going to happen to you? You're out all night, I never know where you are, how do you think I feel?" By this time I'd be yelling and he'd be yelling back.

"How *you* feel, how *you* feel. It's always how you feel. You want to know what's the matter with you? You're nuts. I mean, you're crazy. The hell with it."

Slam-bang into his bedroom. One night he kicked in his door. Left four holes in it. Smashed the lower panels.

Okay, I was nuts. I felt alone and sorry for myself. Not for the first time I felt that Martin would have coped a hell of a lot better than I was, that he would have been a better mother. It was a thought that recurred whenever I felt particularly inadequate and guilty.

I was afraid. I really didn't know where my son went or what he was on. I was scared that something would happen. That he would get run over and killed. I was fearful for his life, afraid of what I heard about experimenting with drugs. It was a time when acid was easy to get, and I'd heard dreadful stories about bad trips. Fatal trips.

*Only* pot? God, I hoped so.

It was fear of the unknown that got to me, as much as anything.

I couldn't understand why we should be having such a hard time. Sure, Martin had died and that had been terrible. But I'd thought we had come through it. Could this mess be a delayed result? It must be more than that. There had to be something I didn't know or my kid wouldn't be this much out of control.

To me, the situation, his behavior, seemed very extreme, and I felt completely unable to cope.

So, apparently, did his school. One day, to my astonishment, I got called in to see the school therapist. And this was the school that didn't want to see parents. However, I wasn't to confer with the principal, or a guidance counselor, but rather a psychologist. My first chance to talk to anyone at Greenwood since Jonny started there. I looked forward to the meeting, but I found the prospect very intimidating. What it meant to me was that I had been tried through my child and found wanting. Their methods weren't working, so it must mean that I was doing something wrong. It means that *you* screwed up, mother, otherwise your child would not be goofing off and we wouldn't have to have this little talk with you.

I arrived at the school feeling like a child myself, called on the carpet to explain my poor behavior. Thinking, too, that Jon must have done something really gross to precipitate my summons. On the other hand, perhaps the psychologist could be of help in suggesting a course of action.

Slightly cheered by this thought, I went into the psychologist's office and was given an instant preview of Jon's first-year report card. It was in columns, listing subject and grade. All the way down the grade column I read, "no credit, no credit, no credit," until at last, at the bottom, a solitary B-plus. I didn't even see what it was for.

I looked up from this pitiful list.

"Why all these no credits?"

"Because he doesn't attend class often enough to get any credit, Mrs. Caine. That's what I'd like us to talk about."

We talked. I was bewildered by the conversation. *There was nothing there.* He mouthed jargon, empty words, veiled accusations; I defended myself as if I were a guilty schoolgirl. There was no meeting of ideas and concerns, no suggestion of a common interest. I said I would do anything to help my son—anything. Did he have any suggestions or guidelines? The question slid right past him and evaporated. He just sat there, passive and impassive, stonewalling me, a lofty expert admitting implicitly that the school had called me in because it was failing with my son—and failing because I hadn't done my job.

He didn't know any more than I did. Or if he did, he wasn't telling. I felt impotent, at the mercy of people who didn't want to talk to parents until they were ready to blame them. All they had done was pull me in and make me feel inferior. And grade me: no credit, no credit, no credit.

I slunk home. The meeting had been useless. The only result was that when I next saw Jon I started a quietly reasoned discussion with him that ended in another screaming match. This time it was, "We can't afford this! I'm spending five, six thousand dollars a year to get you educated, and you can't even drag your ass to class."

"Money! You're always talking about money. What about all the money from the books? And the movie? You've got a job, you do lectures, you—" His young face was twisted with rage. "If it's so hard on you, why did you have to send me to that school?"

End of discussion. Funny, how mother never had the last word.

Curiously enough, Greenwood did not disinvite Jon for the coming year. Perhaps they thought there was still a chance for my son. Or perhaps, I thought cynically, they liked getting my five or six thousand dollars.

Sometimes Jon and I talked to each other almost like human beings, although not very often. Once in a while he'd drop by with one or two of his less disreputable friends to visit Patty and any of the girls who might also have dropped in. I was very happy when they were all there together. Buffy was not. Once I mentioned how pleasant I thought it was.

"Oh, sure," she said sourly, "he wants to be with the girls, of course."

And it was true that he seemed no more a part of the immediate family than the rest of the visitors.

In those relatively calm moments I could see Jon more objectively. Now almost sixteen, he was the quintessential, the ultimate, teenager of his time. The costume, the hair, the obsession with rock music and sound amplification, the hanging out, the don't-give-a-damn hours—all this added up to teenager. It was just a developmental stage; like all kids his age, he was insane.

Still, I was seriously concerned that he was more insane than most. I felt completely unable to cope. Like many Upper West Side New Yorkers of my time, I took my sad story to a shrink. Exploring my feelings did not help me to approach my practical problems. Jon refused to see the psychiatrist I tried to send him to. More than anything else, I felt I had lost touch with my child. It seemed that all I could do was feel afraid for him and worry about his future. If he had one.

So far as I could tell, Jon's second year at his antiparent school was going about as well as his first. I knew he showed up there occasionally because of the contemptuous comments he made about the staff and some "stupid lecture" or other. And once, when we were having one of our regular discussions about him hanging out and getting stoned instead of going to class, he laughed and said, "Oh, everybody gets high in school. You can smoke in the classroom. I told you that. It's easy to get high there. One particular class, the teacher smokes with us. That class, that's practically all we do."

I'll bet it is, I thought. It's probably the one he got a B-plus in. And though I was appalled, I was somehow not surprised.

I began to feel that I was marking time. Something was going to happen, and I had better be ready for it.

I ran into an old friend at a publicity function for a client. Jeff and his wife, Sue, had been among our friends when Martin was alive, and I hadn't seen much of them lately. No rift, just the usual reshuffling of the social group when one member leaves it.

He greeted me warmly and we caught up with recent events. Inevitably, he asked about the kids. To my surprise, I found myself telling him about my fears for Jonny. In spite of the fact that I'd always—and still—had a large circle of warm friends, I'd never been in the habit of confiding my deepest concerns to even those closest to me. But Jeff was neither shockable nor judgmental. I suddenly felt ready to talk.

His face was very serious when I mentioned the Parkies and the Band Shell.

"That's a bad setup," he said. "Remember Charlie Harris and his wife, Lil? Their older kid used to hang out there, whole days and nights. Tommy. Completely ran wild. Charlie couldn't get him home."

I could well imagine the Harrises' feelings.

"What happened?"

"Well, as a matter of fact," said Jeff, "I went in and got him."

"*You* did?"

He shrugged. "Just as a friend. I know my way around a little bit better than Charlie."

Jeff is tough. He grew up on the South Side of Chicago and he does know his way around.

"You have no idea what that Band Shell is," he said. "Dope dealers, delinquent gangs—it's armed warfare. I was brought up with a lot of lowlifes, and I've never, never, seen anything like the park scene. Anyway, I got him out. Seems he'd broken a few laws and he wound up behind bars at the precinct. Followed by Family Court, followed by a rap as a juvenile delinquent, followed by a probation so tough he can't sneeze in the subway without winding up in the slammer. And Lil and Charlie will let him go, if they have to. They can't handle him. Maybe doing time will shape him up."

I was horrified, not so much because my old friends were prepared to let their son go to jail, but because they must feel so desperate, so incapable of controlling their boy. And I couldn't help thinking of myself and my own son.

Jeff was watching me, apparently reading my mind.

"I don't think Jon is quite such a hard case," he said. "You remember Joey, the Harrises' younger kid? She was shaping up to be a real handful, too, and they sent her to some school in Maine where they don't believe in this permissive psychological garbage you get at Greenwood. It's more of a 'tough love' approach—tough on the kids and the parents both. She's really turning around. Matter of fact, they tried Tommy there too, but he couldn't take it, or wouldn't. Ran away."

"To end up in the slammer," I observed, unimpressed.

"It doesn't work for everybody. The kid's got to have some motivation himself."

And Jon didn't have any, I thought. Where was he going to find it? I was beginning to think that no school could do anything for him. Maybe the Foreign Legion would take him. Maybe they'd take *me*.

Probably the school was working for Joey because she was a girl.

Several days later I had an unexpected phone call. I'd been thinking of calling Lily Harris and saying something sympathetic about Tommy, but I couldn't think of anything to say to a mother whose son might even then be in the lockup. Now she was calling me. Stabbed with guilt as I so often was, I managed something.

To my surprise, Lil was brisk and cheerful. She'd heard from Jeff that I was concerned about Jon and thought perhaps I might be interested in the Hyde School. The change in Joey had been astounding, just in a few months. Not only that, Tommy had asked to go back there and had been readmitted. It was too soon to tell how he was doing, but just having him back in school was a plus.

She asked about Jon, and I told her, with a graphic description of Greenwood. She snorted.

"One whiff of grass at Hyde, and it's a tough work detail, starting before the birds get up. It's a very physical place. Plenty of exercise, fresh air, and hard work. Stringent rules. Academically, it's excellent. Offbeat, but excellent. And they insist on parent participation. They don't just encourage it. They demand it. They *coerce* you to participate."

It sounded interesting, but it was, after all, just another school. More than anything, I was touched by Lil's call. One troubled mother reaching out to help another. This was something rather rare, in my experience, and I realized I had not done much reaching out myself. The human contact over a shared problem was, I thought, at least as valuable as the advice.

I wasn't at all sure that trying yet another school was what Jon needed, and I was even less sure that I could persuade him to go. But Greenwood wasn't doing a thing for him. Damn it! My kid was in trouble and I didn't know what to do! Obviously I wasn't handling things very well. If I had been a better mother, Jonny wouldn't be hanging out on the street and we wouldn't be having these problems. Even the support of friends like Lil didn't make up for the fact that whatever I had to do to bail us out, I had to do alone. Nobody was going to do it for me—not my boss, not the school psychologist, not my friends or neighbors. Yet a woman shouldn't have to do these things alone.

And again I would curse Martin for having left us so unceremoniously. I was completely baffled, isolated, angry.

Lil called again. And again. She pursued me with missionary zeal. "You've got to get on top of this," she'd say. "You don't know, I don't know, how this'll pay off, but it's a chance. Take it!"

I sent for the Hyde School prospectus and brochures. To my astonishment I found the material impressive. Yes, there was a lot of high-flown talk about character, courage, and integrity, but there was just as much about curiosity, leadership, discipline, maturity, responsibility, student potential, committed teachers, and open discussion between children, educators, and parents.

Perhaps it would be worth our while to take a look at the

school. Maybe not right away, but sometime. I phoned Hyde and spoke to the headmaster, Joe Gauld. He sounded like someone who cared about children and knew the true meaning of discipline. I began to hope.

The Greenwood psychologist called me in a couple more times. I said the school was far too permissive, that they let the kids get away with whatever they wanted to do. He countered with comments about Jon's home environment. I said there was nothing wrong with his home, it was just that he was never in it and that I had hoped my son would receive some guidance from the school's trained psychologists. He said he talked to Jon whenever he saw him, which would be more often if more effort were made to have the boy attend. If the school had anything to offer, I said, Jon would be there learning.

We sparred pointlessly. I left feeling even more resentful and defeated than before. Jon and I were both being ripped off. What I was being told was, "He's attending this wonderful school, he's flunking out, we can't do a thing with him, now *you* take over." And it seemed to me that this showed a lack of responsibility on the part of the educators.

When Jon's second annual report came, it was completely blank.

Fine, I thought. Clean slate. We start again.

"What would you say, Jon," I began carefully, "about not going back to Greenwood next year?"

"Great! Terrific!" And he actually laughed. "Did you think they'd want me?"

"They're not begging for you, but this time we're going to make the choice." Now for the hard part. "I've been making some inquiries about a school called Hyde, up in the Maine woods. It's not the preppy kind of school at all, not like anything you've been to before, real country living in our kind of countryside."

Maine itself was my big selling point. Jon loved Maine, its ruggedness and the memories it held of summer vacations with his father when we were all together.

"They sent some brochures," I said, putting them into what seemed a reluctant hand. "My impression is that it's really a tough place. No drugs, no booze, no sex, but great teachers and lots of bright kids and you get to join a chain gang if you're caught breaking any rules. I thought we might go up and take a look at it."

I waited for the outburst, as in, "Oh, shit, not another out-of-town boarding school."

Jon said, "Yeah, some friends of mine told me about the place. They sort of said, you should get out of the city, go to school out of the city if you can, you know. And I couldn't believe they said that."

I couldn't either. Who were these wonderful friends of his? But I didn't ask, because he was still talking—really talking—and that was good.

"I thought about it," he said. "I thought, what the hell, I should go, because I'm really not doing anything at Greenwood. I mean, it's a waste. It's pretty bad." He was glancing at the brochures. "Be good to get out of the city again. Maybe we'll go look at it this summer."

This was a wonderfully encouraging response.

We did not speak of Hyde again for several weeks, weeks during which I worked long hours at my job with little satisfaction. It was two years now that I'd been thinking of leaving it. In a way it was like a stale marriage—not good enough to stay with, not bad enough to leave. Always, that damned fringe-benefit tape played in my head. And how could I leave a job when I had no transferable skills?

But I had begun to develop resources I didn't realize I had. I never refused an invitation to speak, to lead workshops, or to teach courses in the category of "women's studies." Finally, I realized that a process had been working, a process that involved transferring the skills I'd used for years in book publicity to my encounters with a wider yet more intimate public. All the research, the imagination, the verbal and written communication, the presentation and selling of ideas—all these I was using when I talked and worked with widowed women throughout the country. Of course I could get out there and stay afloat.

Fringe benefits . . . A voice filtered through my consciousness. Job security? There is no such thing. The firm could be sold tomorrow. A new team could be brought in tomorrow and you could be out on your ear. The present team isn't all that thrilled with you. Your dissatisfaction shows. You're burned out, bored, and the money isn't all that great. You need a break, you need time to review your values.

And I felt that my values were already changing. I was connected to my readers and listeners in a very direct way, a way in which I had never before been connected. Reaching out to others, sharing feelings—something I'd never been able to do—gave me a great deal of satisfaction. In fact, made me joyful. We all need people in our lives. We all need communal energy. And I hadn't even known how closely I was wired into it. Privacy, especially when the one thing you need most is emotional support, is wildly overrated.

Furthermore, I didn't think my wonderful career was particularly healthy for my children.

I must make the break. I must make a change in myself. If we don't change, the people in our lives don't change.

Bracing myself, I jumped ship. And gave myself a short vacation and some time to think about the future before letting myself worry about how cold and deep the water was.

I don't know if I was expecting instant rewards for having taken the plunge, but I certainly didn't get any. My children seemed to have no interest in the fact that I was now home, available, and yearning to be a properly devoted mother. I'd always felt bad about not being there for them, but now that I was there, they weren't. Jon was working as a bicycle messenger in order to earn money to go camping during the summer. He loved camping, and I was glad of that, but he hadn't apparently come to any decision about Hyde, and my reminders irritated him.

Buffy was playing it cool. My thought had been that now I could be the mother she had never really known. I truly felt she hadn't been given much maternal nourishment. But it was only through Patty that I learned she was glad to have me home. Buffy herself was not ready to admit it.

One day she came home from a baby-sitting job and informed me with an extra little flounce that if she felt like it she could go and find her real mother.

Myra had told her so. She, Buffy, had a right to go and search for her.

Myra had told her so. I felt cold with anger. Myra was a dangerous troublemaker. How dare the woman *use* the kid like that!

"Do you think you'd like to do that?" I asked as mildly as I could.

"Maybe someday," said my daughter and disappeared into the kitchen for a snack.

I would have a word with Myra. Buffy's search didn't seem imminent, and yet it was a threat. I must do more things with her. I must get closer to her.

I saw myself at the pinball machines and realized I had to find another way. But I really didn't know how.

Jon came abruptly into my room one day and said, "Well, let's go look at Hyde School."

Delighted, trying not to show how pleased I was, I made a call and set the date.

It was as if something had been unleashed. Instantly, Jon turned as mean and hostile as he had ever been. I couldn't understand it. Did he think I wanted to get rid of him? Maybe, in a way, I did. But his behavior baffled me.

And Buffy went serenely through her days, politely acknowledging my presence.

*This* was motherhood? This was home and family?

I had jumped ship from my job only to find no emotional lifeboat waiting. There was only me—troubled, uncertain, insecure. I certainly had not suddenly become a better mother.

All right, I'd given myself time to think. So *think.*

I was seriously ignorant of the art of mothering. I wondered why, and if other mothers felt the same. Were some just naturally more adept than others? Was I missing something?

I began to look for answers in myself.

# CHAPTER FOUR

# Growing Up

"PLEASE, God, don't let me be pregnant!" The words echoed back to me across the years. "Please, God, I'll never ask you for anything again, not ever. Help me, help me, let me off the hook just this one time."

I was sixteen, and I was terrified.

Reason told me I really didn't have anything to worry about, that my worst fears couldn't possibly be true. But reason wasn't making any headway against my hazy recollection of what had happened that night. I'd had a date with that cute college boy, we had been drinking, and we had—

Oh, Lord, what *had* we done?

I prayed as I had never prayed before.

"Please! I'll give up my right to ever have a child. Please just don't let me be pregnant now."

My father would throw me out of the house if he found out how bad I'd been. And my mother, she'd be devastated. She wouldn't raise her voice. She never did. But she would cry. She cried easily. Never punished. She always turned punishment over to my father. "Wait till your father gets home!"

I agonized and I prayed.

As it happened, I was not to be punished this time. God or my own ignorance or some other mechanism kept me from a fate worse than death—that is, my parents and the world knowing what I had done—and I wasn't pregnant.

Overwhelming feelings of relief and gratitude swept through

me. And then came a different kind of fear. I was afraid of a lot of things in those days, but this was special. I'd made a bargain with God, and He'd keep His end of it. Someday I was going to have to keep mine.

But "someday" was a long way off, and after a while I really didn't think about it much. I just thought about getting through the present, which was tough enough.

I was the oldest of three children. The first three years of my life were heaven. In the beginning it was just me, my parents, my grandmother, and one of my uncles, with frequent visits from my Aunt Julia. Home was warm and wonderful. Everybody loved every little thing I did.

Even my grandmother seemed to think I, her first grandchild, was adorable. I say "even" because she was not a woman who expressed love openly. I don't remember her ever hugging or kissing me, or being demonstrative toward my mother. And yet I sensed she loved me. She played with me, took me places, and laughed when I did clever things. It was later that I found her cold and unresponsive, often critical to the point of being abusive.

It took me a long time to figure out why she became so harsh as I grew up. Grandma preferred toddlers to older children. She liked me until I developed a big, smart mouth, full of questions of my own and sassy answers to everyone else's. My sister and brother were not nearly so fresh. They behaved themselves. Grandma came to disapprove of me because I was not her image of an obedient young girl.

My mother was a gentle, passive person who never raised her voice and appeared to be afraid of people, a very young, unworldly woman when she'd had me; a dutiful daughter easily dominated by her own mother.

She had married a first-generation Russian immigrant, my volatile, self-taught father, who had come to the States as a teenager with his brothers and set himself up in business with them as a manufacturer of some of his own quite successful mechanical inventions. By the time I came along he'd heard Caruso sing and seen Pavlova dance and read every Russian author of note. Later he would insist that I read the classics, and I have him to thank for the fact that I became an omnivorous reader of everything from Tolstoy to *True Romances.* But that was when I was older, and no longer the apple of everybody's eye.

One day I woke up and there was another baby in the house. Suddenly I wasn't so cute anymore. The cooing compliments became, "Quiet, Lynn, you'll wake the baby. Sssshh! You're just doing that to get attention."

Which is true. I was. And I was getting it, but not the admiring attention I considered my due. My brief day in the sun was over. I was a has-been, at the age of three.

My sister, from the outset, was everything a little girl was supposed to be: curly-haired, gentle, even-tempered, sweet-natured, pretty, a picture in pink. Perhaps foreseeing a future as a second banana to a prom queen, I went out of my way to be a tomboy. Even before my baby brother arrived, I was growing up tough and playing with the boys. For a time, I really wanted to be a boy. It was a man's world, my father told me, and I longed to have a piece of it.

As I got older my father taught me about men. He told me to act dumb. "Look pretty and don't let them know you're smart," he said. "Don't talk about yourself, talk about them."

That was before I started coming home with the report cards that showed me as anything but smart. Small but athletic, I was good at sports, which won me some praise both at school and at home. But most of my grades did not.

We were graded on a scale of one down to five. Routinely, I got fives and ones, very rarely anything in between. When I was good I was very, very good, as in art and English, and when I was bad I was atrocious. Arithmetic? Geography? Conduct? Effort? Five, five, five, and five.

We used to eat together every night, from my grandmother

on down to little Donald, and often the subject of discussion would be my dismal performance at school. My mother never said anything to me about my marks. She would just look sad and martyred. At the time this made me furious, but I thought afterward that she just didn't want to add any fuel to the fire. And fire there was.

My father's vocabulary was enormous and so was his rage. He expected a great deal from his firstborn. I had responsibilities! He was always comparing me with my cousins and wanting me to be perfect. *They* were, according to him. Why wasn't I? I was too high-spirited, too headstrong. My wild and passionate nature would have been all right in a boy—was all right in a man like himself—but for a girl it was unseemly.

Why should it be all right for a boy? I couldn't understand this. I was always being told that girls don't do this and girls don't do that; never told why boys could and did. Even bad grades, although not too many of them, were more acceptable in a boy, whose legitimate high spirits might lead him astray once in a while.

Vaguely I realized the unfairness of this while my father banged on the table and seared me with his words. At the height of his fury my grandmother could always be counted on to carry things one step further. It was at the end of one discussion that she first announced, not as a prediction but as a statement of certain doom, "They'll find her body in the gutter someday." So sure of this was she that she repeated the observation often throughout the years, usually at meals.

Yet despite these unsettling sessions, I remember our happiest times as around the dinner table. My mother was an excellent cook and cared that we ate properly. I loved the way she fixed shrimp, loved her pot roast, loved the lamb stew, all very tasty, wholesome things. Grandma was a good cook, too. I think she was at her best in the kitchen, making Polish dishes like potato pancakes and stuffed cabbage.

I was almost never allowed to cook because I always made a

mess when I tried. But on very special occasions I was allowed to lend a small though clumsy hand. I remember Thanksgivings with great joy, staying up the night before and helping to prepare the dressing, cheerfully making my usual mess and not being rebuked at all. That, until I had my own apartment and discovered for myself the great satisfactions of cooking, was about the extent of my domesticity.

Except for one thing. I liked to knit. More than anything in the world, practically, I liked to knit. Somehow it gave me a sense of independence. Perhaps that was because I learned from a friend's mother, rather than anyone in my own family, and I learned when I was very young. Tomboy or not, I wanted to make my own clothes. Wearing something I had made myself was a matter of great pride to me, and within the limits of my allowance I bought yarn and made sweaters and socks until I no longer knew what to do with them.

My sister, Dorothy, had a few suggestions, which I ignored. We shared a bedroom, and it is possible that I may have taken up a little of her space. The room was pretty, all maple and chintz, with twin four-poster beds, a maple dressing table, and flowered wallpaper. Actually, mine was a three-poster bed, because once when my father was mad at me he broke off one of the posts.

By the time I was in my early teens he was angry with me almost constantly. Perhaps it was because my mother could never punish me herself, and he wearied of coming home and being told that I was waiting to be dealt with. It must have gotten almost as tedious for him as it was for me, although it hurt him less.

I waited for my father to get home. I got yelled at and walloped. He took off his belt and he used it. Nobody thought he was abusing me. He wasn't. He was disciplining me. My grandmother helped with her finely honed tongue. I was told I was bad. I believed it. For a while I felt I was the only bad kid in the world, because I didn't see any other kids being punished.

It was only later, when I learned I had company in my badness, that I felt better about it.

The fact is that I was really frightened of punishment. But I was also so afraid of anybody thinking I was afraid that I developed a facade of toughness. And I found I had a hot temper of my own. I still have. I have a short fuse and when it's lit I tend to yell and swear. Does this come with the genes or the home? I don't know. All I know is that my temper is a lot like my father's.

And that the birth of my sister was very disturbing to me after my three years of being everybody's pampered darling. This was a shock that would have been eased, in time, had Dorothy also earned some adult wrath. But neither my grandmother nor my father ever seemed to be angry with her. Nor with my brother, in fact; but that somehow seemed to matter less. For one thing, he was a boy; and for another, he was athletic and funny and I liked him. Also, he was six years younger than I—almost a different generation. Still, I felt unfairly singled out for my father's wrath. He picked on me.

Is this right? Maybe it's a trick of memory, an illusion. Remembering my father, I worry about what my children are going to think of me in the future. I try to make my kids aware that there are both good times and bad, that both good and bad things happen. What makes them better or worse is our perception of them—and our perspective. A few years ago Jon and Buffy and I spent two weeks vacationing in California and had many lovely, memorable times together. What Buffy remembers of that trip is that one time I got mad at her. I screamed at her and threw her watch against the wall. Yes, that was bad and uncontrolled of me. I know it was. But what's happened to the memory of the good times?

So when it comes to my father's anger, I don't know what is the reality and what is what I have chosen to remember. Perhaps he was less angry, or less often angry, than I thought. His enthusiasms were as vast as his rage. He loved company, good food, music, and laughter and was boisterous in his enjoyment of them. Sometimes, in quiet moments, he told wonderfully engaging tales of his youth in Russia. There was a deep well-spring of affection in him, which bubbled up and overflowed when he was in a merry or nostalgic mood. But I feared his dark side, and I rejected his sporadic demonstrations of love.

Meanwhile, I went on doing things that my elders frowned upon and dreamed of deliverance from home and school through marriage. That's what one did: one would grow up to be a mother. It was not a very alluring prospect, because I was getting a message that it was very difficult to bring up children. Especially a child like me. I was self-destructive, smoked and drank in my early teens. If there had been drugs available, I surely would have used them. I wanted to live hard, get high, live on the edge, and die young enough to have a beautiful corpse.

Well, I didn't. End as a beautiful corpse, that is.

Instead, I married Norman.

But that was a little later.

What do I think of, when I think of home and family?

My father's passionate love for the arts, and his gift to me of anger. My mother's sweetness, and her helplessness. She could not deal with me. Having three children seemed at times too much for her. I know she adored us all, and probably equally, but I feel she may have had the problems of motherhood without many of the pleasures.

Fragments of memories come back.

My mother always being there for me when I needed her . . . I remember her putting up my hair in kid curlers because I hated it being so straight. How she would care for me when I was sick, tuck me up in bed, and make a gentle fuss over me. Make me chicken soup, and little chicken sandwiches with the crusts cut off. Fluff my pillows, cover me with quilts and kindness. It was best in wintertime, when I loved being cozy. I suppose she did the same for the others, but I don't remember that.

Occasional discussions of life beyond childhood, and what

was expected of us . . . Little Donald, of course, would grow up to be the head of his own household and a responsible professional man. Dorothy and me? We, of course, would marry. Especially me. My father told me, "I won't be happy until I hear your wedding bells ring."

I left home as soon as I could, went to art school for a while, and then got a part-time job. I was convinced my family was pleased when I left home. I know I was.

When I was still in my teens I met Norman on a subway in New York. He was a worldly twenty-seven-year-old who seemed to have a lot of money, and he knew his way around the city. I was impressed and I fell madly in love. Or something. Within a year we were married. The headstrong but insecure daughter was escaping from clinging family ties and a lowly job into a socially approved situation. Bad Lynn was going to be all right.

No, she wasn't. Norman and I were hopelessly incompatible. I was bored, lonely, and a ridiculously incompetent housewife. The marriage was brief and unsatisfactory. During the course of it we tried to have a baby and couldn't. The worse things got, the more I thought a baby might make them better. Afterward I realized how wrong I'd been to use marriage as an escape and then think that a baby could save the marriage, but I was altogether ignorant of what life was all about and had to learn as I went along.

The time came when I realized that my young mother had also been learning on the job and had done a whole lot better than I.

Norman and I went to doctor after doctor. Then I started going alone to specialists. Norman was all right. The fault lay with me. I could not conceive. Something was wrong with me. Repeatedly, I was told that I could never become pregnant. Whether the problem was physical or psychological or both they could not say, but the fact remained that I could not have a baby.

My bargain with God had come back to haunt me.

One kindly doctor suggested it was possible that everything would be all right if I waited a couple of years and gave nature a chance.

But I didn't want to. I wasn't biologically driven to have a child. I didn't yearn for motherhood. It was just what one did.

Feeling vaguely dissatisfied with myself, I decided that I wasn't going to have a baby, therefore didn't want one, and that was that.

It was also the end of the road for Norman and me. Divorce was a welcome relief.

Everything was different with Martin Caine. A friend from art school introduced me to him one evening after what had become, for me, a typical day of job hunting and making the rounds of agencies in the entertainment and publishing fields. Martin was a lawyer and a bridge player. I wasn't interested in the law and I didn't care for bridge, but I very soon became interested in Martin.

He made it clear from the beginning that I was not his type. I was too exotic-looking, too undomesticated. But he let slip the fact that he liked argyle socks.

I could knit. And I was determined.

It took five years and several miles of yarn for Martin—by then the owner of the world's largest collection of argyle socks—to realize he wanted to marry me.

He waited until a few weeks before the wedding to tell his mother and introduce me to her.

I think she would have hated any woman who married her only child. Certainly she showed an instant dislike of me. She found fault with my having been divorced, though she herself had been divorced when Martin was four. I gathered from Martin that she regarded me as "damaged goods," though she didn't actually use the words within my hearing. Although she had been a working woman through both her marriages, she was displeased that I intended to keep my job in publishing. After her first marriage had broken up, she and Martin had moved back in with her parents and her bachelor brothers, none of whom attempted to create a comfortable home life for the child in their cramped quarters. Yet she objected to me because I wasn't a traditional homemaker. I wasn't much of a cook, I couldn't sew, I was tired of knitting, and I was an unenthusiastic housekeeper.

But worst of all: I could not have a baby. Martin, out of some odd sense of fairness, had warned her not to expect a grandchild. Her prospective daughter-in-law was sterile.

Her bitterness was almost tangible.

My parents were delighted that I was marrying again. I think my father, like Martin's mother but with far more love in him, felt that I was a damaged girl and that I was very lucky to be marrying Martin. He was happy that I was getting a second chance, especially with a nice, attractive man who was too good for me.

To the sound of a second and merrier round of wedding bells, surrounded by loving friends and our immediate family, Martin and I were married. It was a wonderful, happy wedding.

We settled down with each other and two Siamese cats in a four-room apartment in the shadow of the Empire State Building.

Life was fuller than I had ever dreamed it could be. During my years of knitting socks I had found a job I thoroughly enjoyed and taken night courses in copywriting and publishing procedures at the New School for Social Research. As the job grew, it became more and more exciting. It amazed me that work could actually be fun. It was even more fun to come home after long days of shepherding authors around on publicity tours and be with Martin.

Ours was a good marriage. Neither of us had ever known such love, such mutual enjoyment. We had each other, and together we appreciated music, sunsets, laughter, friends, evenings at the theater, vacations in Europe, fine food and drink in the finest restaurants. As a housewife I was the expected flop, but there was neither time nor need for me to be housewifing, so my inadequacy in that regard bothered neither Martin nor me.

What did bother me was my inability to have a child. Martin told me, inelegantly, that if he'd wanted to marry a breeding sow—or was it cow? I don't remember—he would have done so. He had wanted a woman and had married one. But I felt that, secretly, he wanted a child. In unguarded moments he talked about family life, of which he had had so little himself, in such a way that I could not help thinking he was still missing something.

And so was I. I didn't long for maternal responsibility, but I had a feeling of being defective as a woman and a wife because I couldn't have children. I was young and healthy and I could not understand what could be wrong. God does not make bargains—I knew that, now that I was an adult—nor does he punish. It's people who hurt, and people who punish. Often punish themselves.

Again, I went to a New York specialist. The tests came back. So sorry, Mrs. Caine. He sent me to another specialist, a sterility expert. He examined me and ran more tests. So sorry, Mrs. Caine. It seemed that I had an infantile uterus, whatever that meant, and a number of other defects that added up to the single, inescapable fact that I was sterile. Ugly word, *sterile.* Barren. Unfruitful. Incomplete.

Martin's mother lost few opportunities to remind me of what I could not easily forget. "I could die happy," she sighed, "if only I could hold a grandchild in my arms."

I could understand that. But at least she'd had one child. Martin and I could never have any. And we were just going to have to live with that lack.

Five years later.
"That's impossible," I said.

"There's no doubt about it," said the doctor.

I'd started feeling unaccountably queasy a few days earlier and had come in for a checkup, after which I'd been sent to a gynecologist for some tests. The results were in and I was back in his office for another examination.

"But for ten—no, almost fifteen—years now I've been told that I'm sterile." Out of sheer disbelief, I started going through my whole history for him once again.

He smiled. "All the same, Mrs. Caine, you are unmistakably pregnant. About three months along, I'd say."

"How could that be, after all these years? How could it happen?" I was so stunned, I didn't know whether I was pleased or not.

"There's no way to really know. Some psychological trigger, perhaps. Intense desire for a child. It happens."

We talked a little more. He congratulated me, assured me once again that I was in robust health, and patted me on the hand with the fervor of someone participating in a miracle.

I left in a daze. A miracle. Perhaps it was. But surely not because I had an intense desire for a child? I thought I'd put all that behind me years ago. And my wish had never been particularly intense.

I told Martin the news when he came home that night, not quite sure how he would take it after our years of being a chic young New York couple without a responsibility in the world—other than keeping a filial eye upon our respective parents. It had been some time since he'd talked about the joys of family life, and he might very well have lost interest.

He knew I'd been seeing a doctor for what would probably turn out to be just some passing virus, and I hadn't wanted to tell him about the initial diagnosis until the test results were in. So his "Any news from the doctor?" was a casual question.

"He said . . . Yes, I saw him again today. . . . Oh, Martin!"

"What is it?" he asked, with sudden concern. "What's wrong?"

"Nothing's wrong!" I whooped. "I'm pregnant!"

"Pregnant! You're pregnant!" He was unbelieving, almost jubilant, but not quite ready to let go. "Are you sure?"

"Am I sure! The tests came back today!"

He gave a yell of pure joy and his face was ecstatic.

"We're going to have a baby!"

In that moment there was not the slightest doubt in my mind that that was what he wanted more than anything in the world. And in that moment I knew that I had wanted, almost desperately, to have a child not only for him but for myself.

It was a wonderful pregnancy, almost up to the end. Both of us were ridiculously triumphant and happy. My parents were first astounded, then thrilled beyond words. Martin's mother seemed curiously torn between joy at the prospect of a grandchild and resentment that her dreadful daughter-in-law was finally doing something right. All right for you, I told myself childishly. My father will have a grandson to hold in his arms. I will make up for all the years of disappointment that I gave him. My gift to him will be his first grandchild, the firstborn boy he must have hoped for when I came along.

I could see my father in the heart of a large family group consisting of Martin and me, his mother (somewhere on the fringe), my mother and sister and brother and aunts and uncles and cousins, and my father would have his little grandson on his knee. I asked Martin if he minded the prospect of playing second fiddle to grandpa once in a while, and he laughed and said he loved the image of grandpa presiding over a family gathering in which we three Caines would star. He'd never known such a gathering, and he could hardly wait.

It never happened.

My father died of a heart attack seven weeks before the baby was due.

When the time came for me to leave for the hospital I tied a blue ribbon in my hair and went downstairs with Martin to the waiting cab in the absolute conviction that we would have a son. His name would be Jonathan, gift of God. We had chosen the name even before my father had died, and now it seemed particularly appropriate. God giveth, God taketh away.... God giveth.

The labor was difficult and I had to have a cesarean delivery. Martin was with me when I came around. He was almost too moved for speech. "We have a son," he managed.

"Of course we do," I said.

That afternoon, Martin by my side with a besotted look in his eyes, I held Jonny in my arms for the first time. We actually had a baby. A baby boy, our Jon. It was the happiest moment in our lives. If this was not a miracle, it was near enough for me.

The doctor came by next morning to give me the once-over and a little congratulatory speech.

"But thank God the baby's a boy," he added. "I've been delivering babies for years and I've never had a patient who wanted a boy as much as you did."

I felt my eyebrows go up. "What do you mean?" Surely it couldn't be just because of the blue ribbon in my hair. "I don't remember saying anything."

"You wouldn't, Mrs. Caine. Sodium pentothal. Otherwise known as the truth drug. Often used in spy stories."

"Oh, be serious. What are you talking about?"

"I am serious. That's what is was—sodium pentothal. When we were putting you under for the cesarean, you did a lot of talking. That's very common. But it's not so common for a mother to make such a heavy pitch for a boy. Really, I was relieved it wasn't a girl. I don't know how you would have reacted if it had been."

I was none too sure myself. Certainly I had wanted a boy. Don't most first-time—or only-time—parents tend to want a boy? No question, I had yearned to give Martin a son. Something wrong with that?

"I would have been very happy with a little girl," I said. But I was lying, and he knew it.

"Maybe so, Mrs. Caine. Anyway, I guess this is no time to get into a discussion about gender identity. But, you know, you were really obsessed with wanting a boy. So much so that I suspect you don't much like your own sex, or even yourself. You don't value yourself as a woman."

Who, me? Not like or value myself? "Psychiatric clichés," I said sharply, annoyed at him for meddling. "I value my husband as a man. If a woman loves her husband, she wants to present him with a son and heir. It's atavistic."

And that, too, is a cliché, Mrs. Caine, I said to myself after he left the room. For a few minutes I thought about what he'd said. I hadn't been aware that my sexual preference had been quite so powerful or obvious. Of course I hadn't wanted a girl. I hadn't liked being one, so why should I want one? If I were to have a second child, well, maybe that would be different. But this nonsense about not valuing myself as a woman!

Then I thought of what my mother had said.

"You're going to have a boy." She'd been very positive. "I just know it's going to be a boy."

I'd laughed. "You're right. But why are you so sure?"

And she had said, "I just can't imagine you with a little girl."

I had taken the underlying message to be: boys are better.

Or perhaps it had been: you *think* boys are better.

I brushed aside these reflections as I cuddled my baby boy, marveling at his exquisitely formed body and his handsome, masculine little face. He was so well made, so fine and healthy, so much a—a man-child. I was engrossed, beguiled, enthralled.

"You must be careful not to spoil him, Mrs. Caine," the head nurse said to me one afternoon as I was admiring the way my clever baby was tugging at the nipple of his bottle. "A baby is not a toy, you know."

Oh, really, this was too much. First the doctor criticizes me, then the nurse.

"Thank you so much for your advice," I said coolly, and I tuned her out. Nobody was going to tell me what to do with my boy.

The nurse, clearly annoyed, made a few impersonal comments about general postnatal care before leaving me to further reflections about my shortcomings. I was unsure enough of myself as a mother without any well-meant warnings or evaluations.

I was glad to get home with my living miracle. My happiness, I felt, was now complete.

However, I was just a little bit sorry that I had never helped my mother with my younger sister and brother, nor even had any baby-sitting jobs. Babies, I had thought, were yucky. And so I had had absolutely no experience of them. All I knew how to do was to cuddle. Friends had given me baby development books during my pregnancy and advised me to bone up on Dr. Spock, but I, such an avid reader of everything else, was bored by the earnest counsel of the experts. Besides, they contradicted each other. From some I got the message that everything about mothering was a monumental problem requiring minute and constant attention; from others, that I could and should relax. This was welcome advice.

Unfortunately, I found it hard to follow. Jonny was a little pussycat of a boy and I loved every minute of cuddle time. Even looking at him gave me enormous, deeply rooted pleasure. I could sit with him for hours, just looking, not even always holding him, and feel an elemental contentment. But I felt that he and I were living in a madhouse. He didn't seem to mind it, but I did.

We had hired a cheerful and highly competent young pediatric nurse to help make up for my deficiencies as a mother. She was a French Canadian, and in our loftier moments we called her Mademoiselle.

Mademoiselle was instantly devoted to Jon. She adored him. But she hated our two cats, which she claimed would smother the baby. My mother, who was staying with us since my father's death, suggested subtly that the apartment was too small for the lot of us and that we really could manage with an occasional cleaning woman while she, mama, helped to take care of her grandson. Mademoiselle, of course, resented any suggestion of competition for Jonny's care.

In the same four-room apartment of our honeymoon days, we had four adults, two cats, and a baby.

It was driving me up the wall.

For different reasons, I didn't want either my mother or Mademoiselle to leave. What I really wanted was to go back to work, and not just to avoid the hassle of a crowded household. I was painfully restless. This was not my kind of life. I was passionately attached to my baby, and I felt he already knew it. But long days of nothing but him and the two carping women—as I had come to think of them—were not enough for me. My mind and spirit needed more nourishment. I couldn't shake the sense of being cut off from my real world.

My child was only weeks old and already I wanted to go back to work. What would people think? They would think I was an unnatural mother. I'd read enough of the experts of that era to know how vital it was for the emotional well-being of the child that the mother stay home for at least the first two or three years of its life. Personally I thought that Mademoiselle was far more capable of taking care of Jonny than I could ever be. She was not only competent, but warm and nurturing. All I had to give was love.

But how could I argue with the experts or with the nameless, faceless people somewhere out there who would think I was a bad mother if I went back to work? I felt guilty just thinking about it. Imagine how much worse it would be if I actually did leave my baby for my job.

Yet my conflict was greater than I knew.

*   *   *

My boss dropped by to see the baby. We talked shop for a couple of hours and I loved it. I was astonished and almost ashamed, I loved it so much. Ten years of my life had been spent out in that world of bright, stimulating people, and now my life had shrunk down to one overcrowded, baby-centered apartment.

Roger looked me straight in the eye and said, "When are you coming back to work?"

"As soon as the doctor says it's okay," I said, without so much as a pause for thought. "I'll call you when I hear from him. Meantime, I could start working at home right away, if you have anything I can get going on."

"Great. I'll send you some advance proofs. And keep in touch."

Later, stricken with guilt but somehow relieved, I asked Martin how he felt about my going back to my job.

"Do what you want to do," he said. "Do what makes you happy."

So I did.

# CHAPTER FIVE

# Family Life and the Sandbox Set

EVERYTHING worked out very neatly, as if it were meant to be.

Mama, still grieving bitterly for my father—and without much comfort from me, I realized to my shame—decided to go home and sell the house and then look for her own apartment in New York. Mademoiselle declared herself overjoyed to stay on and take full charge of Jonny.

How she could be happy doing nothing but minding a child was beyond me. But she was happy, and wonderful with Jon, which was the most important thing to us. Martin was pleased that I had come to a decision about going back to work, and I felt lighthearted and free.

Yet, even as I was hurrying downtown to the office, I worried that I might not be doing the right thing. That there was something wrong with me. I really liked working better than I liked staying at home, but it seemed selfish and even strange of me to go off and leave my baby. For the most part, my married friends stayed home. They were housewives as well as mothers. Those were their two roles. That was okay. I'm sure that, in most cases, if they'd wanted to work, they would have.

What made me feel torn and guilty was that I could be so bewitched by my little boy and yet so bored with staying at home. At least other mothers waited until their kids were old enough for kindergarten. Not me. I went rushing back when Jon was still an infant.

But damn! I lived for the pace and challenge of the job. Motherhood had ambushed me, caught me totally unprepared.

The fact was that I loved that baby, but I felt very inadequate. From the beginning, Mademoiselle had known I was. The first time she had taken an afternoon off she had called me up to check that the baby was all right. She was probably as relieved as I when I went back to work. And I was competent at work.

But I found it wasn't the same, being back. My attitude was changing. The job became less important to me. It was demanding and it was fun, but I couldn't wait to get home. I'd make dinner and then spend hours in the evenings just looking at the baby. I was mesmerized by him. I would sit there and stare at him in his bassinet and later in his crib, watching him as if he were prime-time television. It was extraordinary to me that Martin and I had actually produced this wonderful, terrific being. The baby validated me as a woman. He was the living, adorable, alert, and cuddly proof that I was not defective. He'd put out his perfect little arms and reach for me and I would reach for him, my heart leaping. I was nuts about that baby.

Mademoiselle lived with us, but she had the weekends off. Her time off was my chance to be a full-time mother. Yet I couldn't always manage it. My expectations had been unrealistic. I'd been unprepared for the claims on a mother's time and energy that a child demands. I was tired after the work week, and doing the cooking and housekeeping, and the weekends brought me more fatigue instead of recharging my batteries as they had in the past.

So, although I adored my wonderful Jonny and took care of him on weekends, I wouldn't always take him out for what Mademoiselle insisted was the fresh air that he needed. Rainy

days were fine. We could stay home and be cozy. But sometimes when the weather was good I would open the window,
wrap him up in a blanket and say, "Here, Jonny baby, here's
your fresh air."

The head nurse, of course, had been right. I did treat him
like a toy. He was my toy. Yet he was much more than that.
Unhandy as I was as a mother, I was comfortable with him
from the moment I first held him in my arms. I felt close to
him in an extraordinary way; closer to him than to any other
human being I had known.

He began to walk at about nine or ten months. I thought he
was a genius. When he said his first word a few days later, I
knew he was. "Cookie," he said.

"Martin!" I screamed out. "The baby said cookie!"

Jonny was so startled by my piercing scream that he didn't
say another word for a month. Not another real word, that is.
He called the cats "babas." Babies. Clever little thing.
Mommy's boy wonder.

I got more and more hooked on the child. But I kept on
working because I had come to feel that the job gave me a crucial identity. No one would have categorized me as a working
mother. I was a married careerwoman who had surprised everyone by having a child—and leaving him home with a nanny.
Only Martin knew how enraptured I was with little Jon. He
laughed indulgently, but like most new fathers he didn't altogether appreciate playing second fiddle. He was proud of his
son but distant from him, as if excluded from our closeness.
His love was not less than mine, but it was different. There was
a kind of awe and incredulity in the way he looked at his boy
and called him "son." Not Jon. He only called Jon "son."

Soon after the baby's birth Martin had said, "If you don't
become pregnant again within the next three or four years,
we'll adopt a baby. I don't want my son to grow up the way I
did as an only child."

He had been a very lonely little boy, a small intruder in a

household of uncles and grandparents, resented by his mother because she felt he impeded her chances of remarriage. When she eventually made plans to marry again, she concealed his existence from her prospective in-laws.

And this was the woman who had yearned for a grandson to hold in her arms. (The grandson who yelled every time he saw her, I noted with guilty gratification.)

I could very well understand that Martin wouldn't want his son to have such a miserable boyhood. Also his feeling that a child does not learn to share if it grows up alone. As Martin saw it, the beginning of sharing is learning to share your parents' attention, and this is an essential part of the growing-up process.

Understanding is not necessarily accepting wholeheartedly. I had very mixed feelings about having another child, however we produced it. But Martin was the decision maker in our family. When I said, "Okay," it was virtually without thinking. Afterward I had one great moment of panic. I was very happy as I was. Our life was marvelous. I found it complete; I had everything I wanted. Why adopt a baby and just complicate things?

Soon I stopped thinking about it. It was not real to me. Jonny was real. Three or four years was a long way away. I had my two men and that was all I needed to think about.

A walking and talking Jon was even more enchanting than Jon the baby doll. I needed to see more of him, now that we could talk to each other. I'd say, "I love you, Jonny." And he'd say, "I love you, mommy." I brought home books—dozens, hundreds of them. *Peter Rabbit, The Wind in the Willows, Just So Stories, Dr. Dolittle, Robinson Crusoe, Great Books of the Western World,* the *Encyclopaedia Britannica.* If he wasn't ready for them all at once, he would be when the time came. Meanwhile, I read to him.

When he was three I decided I would like to work part time. My hours were long and erratic, and even when I was home I was too tired to give him what has since become called "quality time." (I dislike the concept. It sounds so calculating and managerial. "And now, children, I can fit five minutes of quality time for you into my crowded schedule." But I did feel that he was entitled to more energy from me.) The company, however, wanted someone who could be on tap not only every working day, but at various odd times. And so I became a full-time mother.

Mademoiselle departed, full of lamentations. Jon and I did a lot of things together. We went to art museums, where I introduced him to abstract expressionism, which he enjoyed because so much of it reminded him of finger painting, and to the Museum of Natural History, where we both loved the dinosaurs. We stood on street corners together and made street noises, city sounds. When a cab's brakes screeched, Jon and I stopped in our tracks and screeched like the brakes, and when the fire engines sounded, we would wail like sirens. Screech! Howl! Whistle! Wheeo-wheeo-wheeo! We'd hold hands and have a marvelous time.

By this time it had become fairly obvious that I was not about to have another child. I didn't even want to talk about it. But it was always in the back of Martin's mind, and I think that's the main reason we moved to Central Park West into a large, old-fashioned apartment just steps from the park. It was a great family apartment, with big rooms and lots of nooks and crannies for children to play in. Too big, really, for a couple with one child.

Still, Jon needed more than a view of the Empire State Building. He needed a park to play in. Now he had one.

I preferred walking the city streets with him, but I very dutifully took him to the park. Proudly, I observed that he became an instant leader of the sandbox set. He was very aggressive with the other kids, not in the sense that he pushed them around, but in the way he used his verbal skills and body language. He was, in a word, bossy. That amused me. So long as he wasn't mean or hurtful, I didn't mind his being king of the hill.

But I was bored. I didn't need to put him in a sandbox with a bunch of other kids to give myself the thrill of watching him. I'd liked the museums and the street corners better. He was having fun. But I was not. I was a young mother sitting on a park bench in a playground talking to other women about babies, for God's sake.

I wasn't quite as young as the other mothers. Almost all of them had been working women, but none for so long as I. Their husbands were younger and they had financial difficulties that Martin and I hadn't had for many years. Most of them were college graduates, but all they could talk about was their children and related subjects. Didn't Maggie look lovely today, when she wasn't creaming little Benny with a rubber baseball bat? Rico had such dreadful nightmares last night. Paul still wets his bed. Stephanie, come over here and wipe your hands this minute. Who's your pediatrician? You want to know what mine said? Where're you going to send your kid to nursery school? My friend Helen has a kid there and believe me you wouldn't want a child of yours . . .

I used to listen to them and wonder why these well-educated women talked about nothing else. Long afterward I realized that I had missed the anxiety in their voices, missed a lot of cues, but at the time I wondered, why can't we ever talk about Vietnam? About what's happening in the world, or maybe just about books? I'd heard that some mothers felt they were going nuts with just their kids to listen to, but these mothers drove *me* nuts. It was not only that they bored me, but also that they seemed to be better mothers than I.

Even I could tell that Jon was getting too attached to me. This was odd, in a way, because he ignored me altogether when he was lording it over his sandbox subjects and playing with the kids next door. A lot of his life was involved with the neighborhood and especially with the post-toddlers down the hall, including a couple of little girls who let him order them around as if he were the sultan of the harem.

But one evening when Martin and I were having an argument about some not particularly important thing, Jon heard us yelling and threatened to kill his father.

"I hate you," he told Martin. "I'm going to get a real gun and not an imaginary one and I'm going to kill you."

"Why, son?" asked Martin.

"Because you're not good to my mommy," said Jon.

I had a mixed reaction to that. Naturally I was pleased that he loved me so much, but his intensity frightened me a little. I felt it was not good for Jon to feel that way about his father.

Martin's reaction was also mixed. He was amused, in a way. He understood it was natural for a little boy to dote on his mommy. But it was very soon after that that we sent Jon to nursery school and started talking once again about adopting a baby.

Looking back, I realized that we probably would not have taken action unless someone else had triggered it. With Jon in school I could have gone back to work without feeling guilty. It would perhaps have been the more logical thing to do.

I had hated the anonymity of two years I spent home. The telephone never rang. Not for me. For *us*, perhaps, for a social evening, but not for me. I needed a world with working people who needed me. Without it, I felt I wasn't part of the world at all. I felt like nobody.

Then the telephone did ring. For Martin. It was a lawyer friend, who asked, "Do you know anybody who wants to adopt a baby?" We had done nothing about adoption until then. I am almost sure that if Herb had not called, we would have drifted along as we were. I would probably have gone back to work and shaken off the depression of being nobody.

"Yes," said Martin. "We do."

It seemed there was a pregnant stewardess looking for a home for her unexpected child-to-be.

So we nominated ourselves as parents of someone else's unborn baby, to be picked up sight unseen.

I was mildly cheered by the thought of some novelty in our lives. Adoption was perhaps better than going back to work. I still didn't think it was a great idea. Jonny could have been an only child. There were plenty of only children. Martin felt very strongly that it wasn't fair to a kid, but I didn't particularly agree. My feeling was that mothers like Martin's could have ruined twelve kids.

But now that we had gotten the impetus to adopt, I was ready to go along with it.

Of course, the child had to be a girl. It was enough to confront Jon with a rival sibling without forcing him to compete with a baby brother. For myself, I wanted a girl anyway, but I also had a feeling that I would not be able to love an adopted son as much as I loved Jon. But a little girl, I thought, was a different matter.

My primary concern was to prepare Jon for what I was sure was going to be his little sister. Thinking of my own extreme jealousy when my sister was born, I bent over backward to make sure that Jon would not be jealous.

Cautiously I asked him, "How would you feel about having a baby in the house? A little brother or sister?"

To my immense relief, he said he'd like it.

"Now I'll be like everyone else," he said. "All the other kids have brothers or sisters."

True. His next-door neighbors and most of his classmates had a brother or sister or both.

And then, willing his answer, I asked him, "Do you want a brother or a sister?"

"A sister," he said, without missing a beat.

So far, so good. I let it go for the time being, and came back to it later. I wanted to be sure I had him brainwashed. His fourth birthday was coming up and we started playing a game.

"What do you want for your birthday?" I would ask.

"A fire engine," he'd answer. "And a cart. And a baby."

"A boy baby or a girl baby?"

"A girl baby."

"Why a girl?" I asked once, daringly.

He looked at me as if I should know the answer. (Of course I did. It was because I wanted a girl and he would do anything to please me.)

"Because you already have a boy," he said. And he smiled.

Four-year-old machismo. I was enchanted.

Right about then, I started wearing a pink ribbon in my hair.

But I'd started a little early.

Martin's lawyer friend called and said the adoption had fallen through. The young woman had gone to her parents, who did what I hope I would do under the same circumstances. They told her, "We love you. Please keep the baby. Come home."

To my surprise, I was despondent. It seemed I had been counting on this baby I hadn't really wanted very badly. Something had been taken away from me. I felt all the emotions women talk about after suffering miscarriages.

It was only then that I felt I must have another child and began to get personally involved in adopting one.

I went about getting a baby much the way one goes about getting an apartment. One starts by asking around amongst one's friends. I deliberately avoided the agency route because I felt it would be too difficult and time-consuming. Martin and I were not a dewy-eyed young couple in our twenties. I had been divorced. There were questions of placing babies with families of the same religion, which limited our options and made for delay—and having decided I wanted a new baby, I wanted that baby *now*.

I called everyone I knew, mothers and otherwise. One of the mothers was my friend Rusty, who lived in Washington.

Rusty, after having had two daughters, had adopted a baby boy the year before. He had become as much a part of her as the two girls.

"Help me," I begged.

And she did.

Rusty's husband's secretary—that's the way these things work—happened to know a nurse in a small hospital in Virginia, the same hospital where Rusty and her husband had found their Tony. Rusty promised to make inquiries, starting with the nurse.

"You know, of course," she said, "that if we find you an expectant mother in the right ball park, you'll have to decide beforehand whether you want the child or not. No backing down afterward if it isn't exactly what you ordered."

Absolutely. We understood that.

But my mother was distressed.

"How can you do this?" she asked. "You don't know what you're getting. It could be some . . . some *hippie's* child."

*Hippie* was the worst word my mother knew.

"It'll be all right, mama," I said with all the confidence of a healthy, expectant mother. "Wherever we get the baby, they won't let us have one that's not right for us."

I was still calling people when, about a week later, I got a call from a doctor who introduced himself and said he was affiliated with the hospital in Virginia.

"I understand you're interested in adopting a baby," he said. Indeed I was. I told him a little about ourselves, and he filled me in on procedures. Then he said, "We'll have one in a couple of weeks. There's every reason to believe it'll be a fine and healthy child. And it has a good pedigree."

What an interesting word for a baby, I thought. As if it were a puppy.

"I'll let you know as soon as the baby arrives," he said, and we hung up.

I could scarcely believe it was turning out to be so simple.

I bought a new pink ribbon and a pink layette and started

praying with all the fervor of the desperate teenager I'd once been. "Please, God, let it be a girl. Please, God, let it be a girl."

And perfect. She must be perfect. She must be beautiful. I could not stand it if she were an ugly baby. I could not stand it if she were . . . a *he*. Jon would hate that. I'd virtually promised him a baby sister. Crazy of me.

As the days passed, my confidence ebbed. What would I do if the child was a boy? Keep it, of course, but we'd all three be disappointed. Which would hardly be a good start for a baby.

When the call came, I was overcome with relief.

There's also something rather strange about being told over the phone that you're a mother.

"Congratulations, Mrs. Caine. You have a girl—"

Hooray!

"—a fine, healthy, eight-pound baby girl."

Our daughter had been born that morning. We could drive down to Virginia the next day, if that suited us, and pick up the baby the day after.

Until that moment I had given little thought to the adoption other than to pray for a girl and try to prepare Jonny. I was the one who needed to be prepared, and I wasn't. Belatedly, I glimpsed an unwelcome truth: I was afraid that the baby would come between my son and me. I didn't want another child. I didn't want another child!

The three of us—Martin, Jon, and I—drove down to Washington the next day and spent the night with Rusty.

It was a night of agony for me. The whole household was asleep and I was pacing the living room floor, wallowing in second thoughts, sure that I was making a terrible mistake. What did we know about the baby's father? Nothing. God knows what he was like. The girl had been at Berkeley. Had she used drugs? Had he? Campuses, for God's sake, were hotbeds of casual sex, maybe group sex, and drugging and acid tripping and—and didn't drugs alter gene structure?

What would I do if . . .? If what? What could I do? Even if

the parents were perfect, the child would still not be truly ours. "What am I getting into?" I moaned to myself. "Who needs this? *Who the hell needs this?*"

Now, at last, for the first time, I thought about what this baby was going to mean to us and how she would change the life we led. But it was too late to think of that.

We drove to the hospital early the next morning through the changing scenes of the last day of September. The leaves were turning and some had already fallen. Horses grazed in fields that were still green. White picket fences gleamed in the sun. No doubt birds were singing their heads off. I didn't hear them. I barely registered the beauty of the countryside. I saw the mellow, expectant look on Martin's face and I felt terrible inside.

The arrangement was that the mother would hand the baby over to our lawyer, who would then give her to us. The little girl was only two and a half days old. It was too much to hope that she'd be pretty. But please Lord, let the mother be pretty. In my nervous state I was reduced to the detail of prettiness. I was past worrying about promiscuous junkie dropouts. I cared terribly about looks.

The time had come. I saw our lawyer, a woman, coming toward us with three other people. No, four. The girl was holding a pink bundle in her arms. Flanking her were a man and a woman. The girl's uncle and aunt, I learned later. They were very good-looking people.

The girl, the mother, was lovely. She was tall and slim and fair, with the high-bridged nose I have come to know so well. My daughter's nose.

She looked at me and I gazed back at her. She seemed to hold the baby a little closer. I will never forget the sight of her holding her baby. The last time she was ever going to hold her.

This is a good person with a caring family. This young woman has more strength than I.

I must have looked sorry for her because the look I got from her was, "Don't feel sorry for me. It's okay."

She handed the pink bundle to our lawyer, who handed it to Martin, who handed it to me. The blanket, I noted automatically, was beautifully soft and of good quality. Just as good as the fancy layette I had all ready in the car.

I parted the folds of the blanket. Oh, the darling face! She's too little to be so beautiful, but she is beautiful! And she was dressed in a little pink handmade dress, smocked, so pretty, so much care. This was a message loud and clear. There may be no father of record, but here is no girl off the streets. No, a nice girl. And a beauty.

The baby in the blanket looked like a little black-eyed susan, enormous chocolate brown eyes and lovely, long black eyelashes set off by a creamy skin. She was irresistible.

"Our daughter," Martin said proudly, grinning like a kid. He glowed.

It was instant love for both of us.

In the background, the young mother turned and walked away.

We called our baby doll Elizabeth Ruskin Caine. A feminine, dignified name. Also Eliza, Lizzie, Bessie, Elizababy-browneyes, and eventually Buffy, as she called herself when she first tried out her name. Buffy, world's most adorable little girl.

Lucky Caines. Lucky me. I had everything I wanted. The most wonderful husband in the world, who was now ecstatically happy. A boy for me, a girl for him, and we're all set to live happily ever after.

It was fascinating to me to see that Martin felt so much freer to cuddle Buffy than he had ever felt with Jon. He seemed to feel he had to be an example to his son, but he could relax and be demonstrative with his baby daughter. But when he wasn't lavishing love on her he was spending more time than ever before with Jon and doing more things with him.

I still felt I had a special relationship with Jon. A firstborn child myself, I very much identified with the oldest child. And I think, also, that I shared the common conviction of the time:

males are superior. Perhaps I didn't, but I've since learned that many mothers feel—in spite of themselves and in spite of the women's movement—that biology is destiny, that boys are born with advantages, that they are less vulnerable than girls, that in the world's tradition it is the sons who matter most, and that therefore boys are "better."

And yet our little girl baby was special.

From the beginning, she had a feminine quality that I felt I had never had. From her curly hair to her long, slender fingers, from her extraordinary, flirty eyes to the temperament I saw as placid, she was everything that I was not. I loved what she was. Not with the passion I had felt for Jon, but with a kind of gratitude and something close to envy.

We played and cuddled and cooed. I dressed her up and brushed her copper hair into gleaming ringlets. As she grew into a toddler and then a little girl we used to dance around the house and sing, and we made up songs together. We both liked clothes and hair ribbons. I loved buying pretty little dresses for her and dolling her up in them on Saturday and Sunday afternoons. I read to her from *A Child's Garden of Verses* and played records for her.

Martin had taught me about poetry and music. Now I was teaching Buffy. She loved music. When she was still only four years old she took music lessons from a woman in our building who had been an opera singer. The woman was crazy about Buffy. She taught her how to play the guitar and sing. I remember, vividly, how Buffy looked when I saw her once with her small guitar and the sun glinting on her hair while she was singing. Like a little folk singer, inexpressibly adorable.

We were getting to be a real family. Martin had a little seat for Buffy on the back of his bike and he would often go off with her and Jon, riding his own bike, in the park on Sundays. Sometimes I would go with them, and we would stop for lunch in the zoo cafeteria.

I had found a wonderful new job as publicity manager for a Boston-based publishing company with an office in New York.

It was glamorous and exciting and I enjoyed it tremendously. One of the nicest things about it was that it didn't give me time to be a jaded mother. I was a mother who loved going home to be with my husband and children. Sometimes I felt a pang of guilt at being a part-time mother, but I could talk myself out of that. Why should I feel guilty when everything was so terrific? I would have been the world's most dissatisfied and incompetent mother-wife if I'd been home all the time, and as it was we were sharing the best of both worlds.

I always had Sunday mornings to myself because I made breakfast the rest of the week. Martin and the kids would go to Zabar's, New York's famous Upper West Side delicatessen, and bring back smoked salmon and bagels for me. Almost always, Martin would buy me a flower for my breakfast tray. Every Sunday was like Mother's Day. I read the paper in bed and drank coffee. The kids played around. Martin listened to music. We all smooched and cuddled a lot. Those Sunday late breakfasts were filled with sunshine.

Martin loved being a father. He was the energetic parent, the one who did things with the kids. When Buffy and I were content to snuggle at home he took Jon to Gettysburg, to Monticello, to the Jersey shore. He reveled in sharing his knowledge of history with his son.

Then we all took trips together. To Palm Beach, where the sun "bited" Buffy's face. To Vermont, where there was a rambling farmhouse that Martin dreamed of buying. (He loved the idea of a house in the country, filled with kids.) To Maine, summer after summer, where Martin went camping with Jonny and showed him the trails through the woods and how to choose a campsite and how to pitch a tent.

Then Martin got sick.

And then he died.

With one deathblow, the part-time mother, full of the joys of a satisfying job and doing family things like picnicking and going to the corner for pizza, became a single parent, wracked with anguish and completely unprepared to cope with loss or with the children.

Jon was nine, Buffy was five. Jon was sturdy, self-reliant, and sassy, a bit of a behavior problem at school. Buffy was docile and sweet at nursery school, a little rambunctious at home. I—what was I? Martin had been my love, their parent, our support. In the weeks, months, and years that followed, I told myself again and again that the kids would have been far better off if I had been the one who had died. He was the nurturer, mother and father in one.

I was Widow, subjecting my children to all my sorrows, inadequacies, rages, and fears. I didn't realize until long afterward how bewildered and disturbed my children were by their double loss: the death of their father, and the loss of their mother as a functioning human being.

But we seemed to be recovering. We weathered the storm of my widowhood and the children's loss. Gradually we settled into a pattern as a family of three. My mother helped as best she could.

As time passed I persuaded myself that we had come out whole. I went around telling the world how the wounds had healed. Every once in a while the thought occurred that I had never really been cut out for motherhood. But I had to brush the thought aside because I *was* a mother and I had responsibilities. My children needed love, security, a comfortable, open home, and an education. They were getting all that.

Then came the second great blow. Both Jon and Buffy, in their different ways, were in trouble. I'd been so consumed with guilt over not being there for them emotionally when they most needed me, so busy overcompensating for that great fault by becoming a martyr to the need to support them financially, that I'd neglected their real needs. They needed a parent who could give them the security of guidelines—and enforce them.

I'd set some rules for my children, but I hadn't followed through. When I felt tired and overextended, it was easier just to let things slide. I didn't assign them any chores, so they didn't do any. I didn't set aside a time for them to do their homework, and I didn't check to see that they had done it. I gave them no regular allowance, so they were always panhandling from me and getting pretty much what they wanted. I would often say no to them, and then let them change my no to yes. I had given them no sense that they had any responsibility for themselves or other people.

I had been deluding myself that all was well. I was ruining the lot of us.

And again, I was overstating the case, as mothers will.

What was happening was not all my fault. At the same time, I *was* the only one who had any direct control of events.

What this small family needed, I decided, was a mother free to be herself and fully available to her children, both emotionally and physically. Someone both loving and capable of taking action.

# CHAPTER SIX

# Living without Security

IT was an even more grotesque scene than Jeff had said it was.
I'd been a New Yorker all my adult life and I'd never seen anything like this. Neither the Upper West Side nor the Times
Square area is exactly Middletown, USA, but this was appalling.

Sunday in Central Park with the daddies and the mommies
and the guitar strummers and the junkies. A revelation. Part of
the story of my summer vacation.

Jon and I had an interview appointment up at the Hyde
School the next day, following an early-morning flight to Bath,
Maine. During the last week or two he'd been so indecisive
about going that I'd become very concerned that he might not
show up for the flight. In fact, at one point, he'd abruptly
changed his mind and flatly refused to go.

Come Saturday evening, I didn't know where he was. If he
came in overnight I didn't hear him, didn't see him.

Sunday I took a walk and, elaborately casual, asked his
friends if they happened to have seen him around. He'd been
seen hanging around the Band Shell, and of course I should
have known that.

Well, maybe he would come home.

Then again, flaky as he'd been lately, he might not.

I decided to find him that afternoon and make sure he'd be
on hand for the Monday morning flight, rather than worry all
night about whether or not he'd show up.

Dressed appropriately, I thought, in boots, jeans, and Berg-dorf silk shirt, I sauntered into the park and headed for the Band Shell.

It was a typical late summer's day on the village green: dappled sun shining on very young children with young Sunday fathers; on not-quite-so-young children with oldish fathers trying to look young, wearing gold chains, cowboy boots, and unbuttoned shirts revealing mats of gray hair; on ethnic groups and fake ethnic groups folk dancing; and on every kind of band playing every kind of music—Greek, Israeli, Hispanic, hot rock, country and western, new wave, amateur classical, and mainly loud but pleasantly exuberant in the open air.

Couples made love under the trees. Frisbees swirled threateningly overhead. Sailboats bobbed on the pond. Wherever I looked there were picnickers, roller skaters, skate boarders, bicyclists, T'ai Chi devotees, kite flyers, people standing on their heads, people meditating, people rolling in the grass, and people pushing everything from pretzels and peanuts and nickel bags of marijuana to loose joints, cocaine, acid, and God knows what else.

And they were soliciting *me.* Served me right for getting rigged up like an aging hippie. Maybe if I'd gone with a couple of ancient paper bags and stuck a cigarette to my lower lip I'd have been less conspicuous. Or taken a sack of bread crumbs for the pigeons. As it was, I looked like a mark.

"Hey, lady, two joints for a buck!"

"Want some good stuff, hey, want some?" The pitchman would flash a little envelope and I would avert my eyes.

I was shocked by the openness of the offers. The woods were full of these people, hands outstretched with their wares, teenagers buying with quick cool movements. And uniformed cops were standing all over the place.

Stung into action by this incredibly brazen display of lawlessness and cynicism, I marched right over to the nearest member of New York's finest and jabbed an accusing finger toward an individual who was doing a particularly brisk trade in tiny packets.

"Officer," I announced dramatically, as if I had just discovered America—and in a way, I had—"that man over there is selling drugs!"

"Yeah, well, I can't do anything about him," said the law, fishing out a cigarette.

"What do you mean, you can't? It's illegal, isn't it? These people have to be stopped—"

"Lady, will you listen? I'm not with the Narcotics Squad, y'unnerstand?"

"But he's selling drugs to children, to minor children, to little kids. Why don't you tell him to get out of the park? Threaten him, at least. Scare him. Put the fear of God or the law or something into him. You can't just ignore this."

It seemed that he could. Casting a contemptuous eye at me, he yawned, mumbling something about telling someone from the Narcotics Squad, and walked away.

I stood there frustrated, furious. All I could do was swear and stomp off.

At the Band Shell the drug soliciting was even more open. Everybody was pushing. I practically had to push the pushers out of my way. Was this where my son spent his days and nights? It was shocking beyond belief. Kids were reeling around glassy-eyed, yammering bits of phrases without meaning, leaning against the trees with maniacal smiles on their pitifully young faces. Tangle-haired boys and girls just sitting, looking at nothing. And nice young parents romping all around. It was bizarre.

My inclination was to run home. But I was intent on finding Jon and I stayed and stayed, revolted and fascinated at the same time, seeing more and more of the underlife of the park as the surface became familiar. I couldn't believe how many varieties of hustling were going on, right out there in the open.

An hour went by. Then two. Still no sign of Jon. There seemed no point in hanging about any longer.

I was on the point of leaving when I caught sight of one of Jon's buddies, the son of a neighbor.

"Hi, Ned," I called out to him. "Have you seen Jon? We're going to Maine first thing in the morning . . . Ned? Ned?"

I might as well have been addressing the statue of Columbus.

The boy was stoned out of his mind, swaying on his feet and gazing at things I couldn't see.

I tried once more to make contact.

"Ned, it's Mrs. Caine, Jon's mother. I'd like to find him so we can get ready for our trip . . ."

But Ned was on a trip of his own. He looked at me blindly, out of awful, dead eyes, then he turned and shambled off, going nowhere.

I couldn't let the kid wander around in that condition. But what could I do? I felt a painful pang of sympathy for Ned's father, a young widower raising three children alone. The two younger boys were scarcely more than toddlers. I didn't know the family very well, but I felt I knew them well enough to give Ned's father a call.

Perhaps, as it turned out, I didn't.

I called from the nearest working phone booth, introduced myself, and blurted out, "Mr. Anderson, come and get Ned out of the park before they bring him home to you on a slab."

Silence. I thought the phone had gone dead.

"Mr. Anderson? Did you hear me? I'm in the park near the Band Shell and I just saw Ned, but he can't see anyone—he's so out of it, so stoned. You can't let him stay here alone. Anything can happen to him."

I heard a sigh. "Mrs. Caine, I can't leave his little brothers here alone, either. Besides, I'm working on some blueprints that are due tomorrow. I have to earn a living, you know."

Sure, I knew about having to earn a living.

I'm no good with blueprints, but I could offer to baby-sit, which I did. But nothing I could say made any difference. I hung up feeling defeated, and with the sense that Tom Anderson felt defeated too. Or perhaps he didn't think Ned's problem was serious and that I was just a busybody.

But of course it was serious! Of course he was concerned. He had to be. What *were* parents supposed to do in situations like this? And why did the kids do this? What was so seductive about drugs?

I tried to think what it must be like to be high, floating free and high and happy as I supposed they must think they are, but I was too angry. I couldn't find my own son, couldn't persuade Ned's father to collect his boy, couldn't find answers to all the questions that were troubling me as a human being and a mother.

I left the park in a state of renewed rage at my husband for dying and leaving me to cope alone with his wayward adolescent son. I raged, also, at my own impotence.

But at the same time I was more determined than ever that Jon's life had to be dramatically altered. Scrounging around in my past had given me some clues to my own inadequacies, some reasons for my mistakes. Obviously, in spite of the fact that I had come from an ostensibly stable home and had had a good marriage, I was about as ill prepared for motherhood as anyone could have been. But now I had to start looking ahead. This was no way for any family to live.

Jon stayed out all that night. At five in the morning I heard his key in the door and he came dragging in. With an attitude. Namely, surly and defiant.

With a heroic effort I checked my temper and suggested that he clean himself up in a hurry because we'd have to leave in about half an hour. The plane left—

Yes, yes, he knew.

We made the cab, we made the plane. Both by a hair.

The first part of the trip was silent. Jon was catnapping and I was brooding, as usual, about whether or not I was doing the right thing.

My departure from the company had been a big move and had left me feeling even more insecure than I'd expected. There was money in the bank and I had plenty of free-lance work coming up, but gone were the weekly paychecks and all the various forms of insurance benefits. It was scary. Now we were headed for another of those umpty-thousand-dollar-a-year schools because I didn't know how to bring up my own son. I had one of those emergency cards in my wallet. Mine read: *No accidents or illness allowed in this family!* It was supposed to be mildly funny, but it really wasn't. I couldn't have handled any extra difficulties.

In spite of the financial cushion of the moment I felt we had no psychological net beneath us. If we were to fall somehow, beyond our own ability to come bouncing back, who would help us? There was nobody.

And yet, I thought, we would not be taking this ride if friends had not cared how much we needed help.

Lil had kept calling me. "He needs tough love," she had said. "He needs discipline. You've got to be willing to let go and take your chances that this tough love will straighten him out."

Jon woke up midway through the flight and we immediately started arguing about some sort of paper we were supposed to have written about our life, a small essay that the Hyde School referred to as a vignette. Oh, he'd do it when we got there. It was just a lot of b.s. anyway.

The plane banked over the deep green woods of Maine and he looked down and laughed, suddenly in high good humor.

"You afraid I won't get in?" he asked. "I'll get in. There's a couple of guys give you the interview, y'know? Both at once. I know what they want to hear. I'm just going to talk those guys all over the place. I just know I'm going to get into that school."

I didn't want to ask questions—(What d'you mean, you know what they want to hear?)—or make any sounds suggestive of either approval or disapproval. Silence was hard too; I didn't want him to think I wasn't interested in his observations.

"Well, I hope you'll like the looks of it," I said lamely, after a long moment of unproductive thought.

Jon was suddenly absorbed in scribbling notes onto a grundgy piece of paper. Notes for conning the guys, no doubt, I thought. Or perhaps he was finally doing his version of life with mother.

I myself felt quite virtuous. Between trips out in search of Jon I had written a somewhat expurgated version of my own life, my family relationships, and my hopes for the future. Honesty was what the school interviews had asked for, but they didn't have to know everything.

We landed, took another cab, fell into silence again as we drove through Bath, and pulled up into the driveway of a compound of buildings sprawled on the grass between stands of trees.

We were met by a very young man named Larry. Soon I would be struck by how young all the staff members were.

"You may find the interview a little different from the standard school interview," Larry observed, leading us into a sunlit room. "What we try to do is have a conversation—a really honest conversation—with the parent and the youngster at the same time. The objective is to find out what your objectives are, what opportunities you'll be looking for at Hyde." He showed us into a couple of comfortable seats. "Joe Gauld, the headmaster, will see you later. Paul and David will be with you right away."

He left us looking at each other.

Paul and David. And Jon and Larry and Joe and, no doubt, Lynn, I thought cynically. Very cutesy.

"How different can the interview be?" I asked Jon, who was looking uncommonly alert. "Sounds like the usual. A hard sell on how great the school is, so we can grovel to get in. But two people? A good guy and a bad guy?"

Jon shrugged. "They can pick and choose. But I'll get in if I want to."

I wasn't really looking forward to the next two or three hours. I'd heard from other parents that we'd have an interview the likes of which we'd never had before, but I'd never been given any details. Later I could understand why.

I have no clear memory of what I afterward thought of as a surreal interview.

Two young men sat down with us and one held the floor for much of the first hour and a half. Then the other young man took over.

"Let's talk about your values," they began. Or I think they did. "Who are you? What do you want to be? What are the problems you want to deal with here? What are your strengths, and how can they be reinforced? What are your weaknesses and how can they be curtailed? Do you understand the reason for them? Do you have any idea how to work on them? Why are you going to school? What do you want out of life? What do you feel you're good at? How do you get along with your mother?" (And with me sitting right there beside him!) "What does she do for a living? Does she like it? What does she like about it? Is it fulfilling? Mrs. Caine, what does your son do really well?"

I was jolted, momentarily, out of my bemusement. They didn't call me Lynn, they called me Mrs. Caine. "He's good with his hands," I said. "He builds well. He likes to repair and renovate. He's good at that. He's good at living with nature. He reads intelligently. He's articulate. He writes well. He does wonderful graffiti. Really artistic."

I meant that. His work was truly wonderful. It was all over his walls and doors and furniture at home—as well as on the IRT, BMT, and IND subways.

"Jon, what do you believe in? How do you feel about the holocaust? What would you have done? What is important to you? What do you want to be after you graduate? How do you get along with your sister? How do you like being the only son?

How do you feel about having lost your father? Why have you come here? Why this place? Where do you want to live? What are your dreams?"

Jon answered carefully. "My father loved Maine," he said. "That means a lot to me. My father's spirit is here. I would like to live here. First I'd like to work with a band for a while. Then I'd like to buy a farm. I want to be a father and have a lot of kids and live in the country on a farm. I would like to help people."

"Help them how? You feel you need some help yourself? How often do you get high, Jon? How high do you get? How long does it last? What do you use?"

I stiffened a bit. I hadn't been prepared for this kind of interrogation, which seemed to be based on an assumption of guilt. Sure, Jon's highs were a concern of mine. But Hyde wasn't known as a rehabilitation center and that wasn't what I was looking for. My son needed an education, and the right environment for it.

"Well, getting high, it doesn't really affect me, anyway. I mean, I can do things just as well when I'm high as when I'm straight. So it really doesn't make any difference."

They pounced. They hammered on him. It seems to me there was some sort of semilogical discussion, although God knows I'd never been able to have one with him on the subject of being high. They weren't arguing. They were explaining to him that he was wrong. Eventually he gave an inch or two, and then another.

Then there was more about his hopes and dreams. So he wanted a farm and a family. Did he have any larger dreams? What about doing something for the community? "Don't you live in a community?" they asked. "Don't you feel you have any responsibility to the community? Is there something of particular value that you would like to do?"

"I think I'd like to go into outer space," Jon said thoughtfully. "I'd like to be active in the space program."

There was a moment of silence, filled with massive skepticism.

"What qualifications could you bring to the space program?" asked the second young man, very quietly.

"None yet," I think Jon answered. "I could learn."

"Really. Do you know that nothing you've said has anything to do with being part of the real world? Especially going off into space."

There you are wrong, I thought to myself. He knows about going into space. That's real to him.

"What's wrong with wanting to go into the space program?" Jon asked hotly.

"Nothing at all. Except that you're going to need a lot of preparation."

Then they turned to me.

"Mrs. Caine. Do you think you've overprotected your son?"

"Overprotected!" Jon exclaimed. "I've been on the streets since I was twelve!"

"He's right. I've neglected him," I said. "Yes, he's been on the streets. And you're right. I *have* overprotected him. I've overprotected him from responsibility, from accountability, from honest work. I've never really defined his boundaries. I've overprotected him from everything that matters."

Jon rolled his eyes at the excesses of his mother.

Paul and David busily took notes.

There was more. Much of it is lost to me. But I remember the end of it. Jon and I both do.

The young man said, "Okay, Jon. What have you learned in these past three hours?"

And he said, "What I've learned is that it's not so easy for us city folks to con you country folks."

Back on the plane.

I, feeling dazed, had founder and first headmaster Joseph Gauld's book tucked under my arm, an oversize paperback full of short pieces by students and many longer pieces by Joe himself. Also a good many pictures of Joe on the cover and inside. Joe with students, Joe with family, Joe as a little boy, Joe the charismatic at various adult stages. Much philosophy by Joe. I get the feeling of some kind of ego. But an ego directed at teaching apple-pie honesty and all the clean-living virtues. No lying. No stealing. No smoking. No drinking. No promiscuous sex. All the golden rules. Any infringement of rules, golden or otherwise, would be reported by any student who happened to notice it. Plenty of hard work, mental and physical.

There had been other parents up for interviews. They looked, I thought, somewhat apprehensive. Mostly couples, but not all. I asked the young man Larry if there were many single parents.

"Oh, yes. This is not an unusual circumstance. Usually we're dealing with pretty fractured families, so the single-parent situation is not uncommon."

"I am a widow," I said bravely.

"I know," he said.

There was a lot to think about on the way home, if I could only get it sorted out.

It seemed to me that the school could prove to be some sort of boot camp if Jon did not permit himself to be shaped up. That came after another *if.* Larry and David and Paul and Joe himself had all made it very clear that there were plenty of applicants not only waiting in the wings, but crowding onto the stage, mugging for attention.

"What did you think that interview was all about, Jon?"

He roused himself from a doze.

"They were trying to determine whether or not I'm ready to go to that school," he said, in the oddly pedantic style that cheers me so much when I fear for my children's literacy.

"What about all that no smoking, no drinking, no getting high? And ratting on somebody who does?"

He gave a dismissive shrug. "I can handle that. If I go."

He clamped his eyes shut.

It is very hard to communicate with your teenager at almost any time, but particularly when you are overanxious.

I sank back into thought.

The Hyde curriculum was tough, stressing the values of early rising, cold showers, outdoor sports. Academic standards were high, class hours were long, and plenty of homework was required. Strength through suffering, it seemed to me. "Boot camp" was not too far off the mark. Any infringement of the rules meant not only extra homework, but extra outdoor work. Cutting underbrush, chopping trees, hoisting and toting the results. Joe believed in the virtues of fresh air and physical labor. Chop, dig, lift, haul—keep the young body busy with healthy pursuits and the young body won't have time or inclination to do whatever it is that the young body would otherwise tend to do. Exhaust those frenzied little hormones, that was the idea.

So *if* Jon was accepted, it wasn't going to be easy for him. Or for me. Kids had been known to find Hyde School so tough that they had run away. Some had gone back. Some hadn't. But if a runaway child were to call home for the fare—and from Bath, Maine, it took money to go anyplace—he was to be refused. If he managed to get home, he was to be turned away with just enough money to get back to school on his own steam, there to have one more chance.

Interesting. What else was interesting was that the education process was not to be confined to the youngsters. The parents had to be educated, too, and not simply in the usual parent-teacher meetings of the traditional schools. No, this was active parent participation in school programs designed to get children and grown-ups involved with each other's problems.

Does mother drink at odd hours of the day? Let's talk about it. Father runs around with other women? Let us discuss how this affects family relationships. Is there any abuse in the family history? Is the marriage shaky, or is it sound? Does the father like his job? What does the mother do?. Is the child adopted and, if so, how does he feel about it? What is the child's position in the family hierarchy? Is there jealousy involved?

All these things and more would be dragged out in the open and discussed at various meetings, sometimes between parents and staff and sometimes with the children present. We, the parents, would all have to go to school ourselves, a couple of times a year at the Family Learning Center at Hyde and various additional times throughout the year at parent seminars set up for our convenience in the New York–Connecticut area, where most of the families seemed to hail from, and at these ghastly get-togethers we would write our little confessional vignettes and bare our souls.

I was torn between hoping against hope that, for Jon's sake, all this clean living and togetherness would work, and a deep skepticism about some of the teachings of the school. Or were they devices? Gimmicks? Precepts? Doctrines? . . . No, teachings covered it.

The vignettes and the open discussions disturbed me. Absolute honesty may be useful and possibly even inspiring, but pouring the parental soul down on paper and then critiquing it seemed to me downright distasteful.

And I didn't care for some of the little slogans I'd been hearing. "The apple doesn't fall far from the tree," for God's sake. Was that supposed to mean that the problems of the child could be traced directly to the parents? Was this going to be another parent-blaming, guilt-inducing experience?

Also, "No pain, no gain." Don't expect it to be comfortable, folks. Not for you, Jon. Not for you, Mrs. Caine. You must be willing to work hard. Nobody gets something for nothing. It must *hurt.*

Yes, yes, of course. I was all for the virtues of hard work and just desserts. I just didn't think educators should express themselves like bumper stickers.

One thing was sure: this school was as unlike Greenwood as possible.

I riffled through Joe Gauld's book, mainly a compilation of newspaper columns, glancing at opening paragraphs and chapter headings. *Bet on the Truth . . . When You Need a Brother . . . Living with an Alcoholic . . . Giving Confidence to a Ghetto Kid . . . Slap May Be Just What Child Needs . . . Hard to Hear with Your Mouth Open . . . A True Teacher Is 100% Committed . . . Let's Make Schools Accountable . . . Just Who Are Problem Kids? . . . Character Development Begins at Home . . . A Headmaster Faces Student Power . . . Kids and Pot . . . Let's Break Through Our Sexual Guilt . . .*

Seemed there was nothing he didn't feel qualified to pontificate about.

But he wasn't actually pontificating. He was, I thought, being direct and honest. And making a lot of sense. I did not see anything about bad apples in these pages, or gain through pain. I saw something down-to-earth and decent.

Maybe we were on to something. And maybe the idea of a family learning center wasn't all bad, either.

In fact, I thought, the concept of educating the parents was, in some ways, quite appealing. I have had no training in this line of work, and it is high time I had.

For all my good intentions as a parent, I was still too passive on the one hand and too much of a screamer on the other. Gentle mother, yelling father? I had much to learn. Perhaps participating in a group would help. I wasn't doing too well on my own.

Also, the academic prospectus was excellent and there were severe penalties for smoking pot. Classes were a healthy mix of boys and girls, dormitories separate in the good old-fashioned way. And if my son still wanted a role model, there were plenty of high-principled, muscular young men around.

Of course, we'd tried that role-model stuff at his last boarding school, and it hadn't worked. That place had been too gentlemanly, too behind-the-times. What was needed was a tougher model, a firmer example, preferably an outdoorsy person or group of people who shared Jon's love of the outdoors. As his father had.

Yes, on the whole I felt the school would be good for Jon. If he was accepted. And if he decided to go.

CHAPTER SEVEN

# The Problems of Single Mothers

WE marked time, waiting to hear from Hyde.

For several days my life was a whirl of television appearances in which I was called upon to talk about my workshops and conferences. Fortunately, most of them were local and kept me in the city—a city in the summer doldrums. I felt like a rerun, a familiar act pulled in to fill a programming gap. Ordinarily I would have been actively working to develop the workshops and lecture programs I had started around the country before leaving my job, but I didn't want too many out-of-town trips for a while.

One afternoon I appeared as a panelist on a talk show hosted by Beverly Sills. The subject was single parents.

Ms. Sills's first question was a simple and obvious one that had never before been addressed to me quite so plainly and directly.

"What is the most difficult thing about being a single parent?"

We guests looked around at each other, men and women who for one reason or another were bringing up our children alone.

I thought of nothing and everything. "Just surviving!" leapt to mind, but I felt that might sound flip and glib even though I was deadly serious. There were so many problems of survival for the single-parent family that I couldn't put my finger on any as outstanding. For once, I was silent.

One of the panelists, a young father with two small boys, said wearily, "It's the fatigue. Unremitting fatigue. I'm exhausted all the time. Sometimes I'm so tired I feel like slinging them out of the window."

Little did he know that most mothers, single or not, feel like that at one time or another.

Another panelist, mother of a preteen daughter, said that her sex life was unmanageable. Because of her child she felt uncomfortable about bringing men home, and equally uncomfortable about staying out.

We talked about fatigue and sex for a while and then the program was over. I was home before I had my own thoughts in some sort of order.

My main problem, I thought, was that I'd gotten to the point of such exhaustion, physically and psychologically, that I felt powerless to deal effectively with my life. I didn't know anymore what I owed my children and what I owed myself if we were all to survive intact. With resources—energy, time, money—so limited, how much should I share with them and how much should I save for me?

Like many single parents, I realized, I was overcompensating. I felt sorry for my children because they didn't have a father. So I gave them things that often we couldn't realistically afford. As if *things* could make up for the nurturing they needed from me.

Some women try to fill in the gaps for their children by smothering them with affection. Not me. I hang tough, spend money on them, lie awake brooding about what I should have done and shouldn't have said, then repeat all my old mistakes. Including yelling at the kids when my own errors—and, yes, my resentments and fatigue—make me angry.

For all that I wanted to give my children, I had succeeded mainly in giving them unrealistic expectations of what life had to offer. I had not shown them how to pull their own weight. The world would demand more responsibility of them than I did. At the same time, my obsession with their immediate needs had bred a resentment in me that might be terribly destructive to the relationship between us. What child is strong enough to bear the burden of a resentful parent? A parent whose resentment has generated in her an agonizing core of guilt?

Nurturing and self-nurturing, finding a balance that works, is an enormous problem for most single mothers. So is nurturing while not allowing oneself to be exploited. A child catches on to a parent's sense of guilt. What child doesn't have a talent for exploiting that weakness?

When I thought about it, I realized I hadn't actually given up that much. What I owed to my children and myself was actually pretty simple.

There was no way I could compensate for something irrevocably gone. The best I could do was give my children the love I felt for them, as much structure in their lives as possible, a mother who had pride in them and in herself as a person, who was doing something useful with her life and could at least be a worthy example. I wasn't there yet, but I felt I was on the way.

Another problem for a parent alone, it occurred to me, was the burden of solitary love: one adult loving the children when there should be at least two.

Everybody has moods. The little sweethearts aren't always delightful. Things go wrong throughout the day and the mother who starts the day with a song on her lips may be a swearing bitch by nightfall. How much does this wound the children? How much more vulnerable to rotten moods are kids already hurt and made insecure by the loss of a parent? I really didn't know. But I did know that if someone else had been there to love my children when I was raging and hateful, we would all have been the happier for it.

I also knew it would have been easier if I had been a less volatile woman. But I am what I am: not always consistent, not always serene, not always able to laugh off cares and disappointments, not always able to give or receive.

The truth of it was that I did not like my children all the time. They didn't like me all the time. Sometimes we even loathed each other. At those times they undoubtedly felt unloved, shaken by our mutual hostility. And feeling unloved, even temporarily, is painful and scary.

Usually, when there are such apparent lapses in love, one parent can fill in for another. A parent alone doesn't have that backup for his or her kids, or someone to say, "Cool it. You need a break. I'll take over for a while."

I warmed to my solitary theme, wishing I was back on the TV show.

A very great problem of the single parent, closely related to that of solitary love, is the aloneness. When you are alone there is no feedback. A parent without a partner may discuss matters concerning the children with other family members, but this is not the same as sharing problems equally with an equally concerned spouse. For most people, there is a role in marriage for both man and wife. Subtract one, and you've obviously got half of what you started with. A major component is missing. I still had a sense of needing my other half. We could at least have talked, have figured out things together. Argued, perhaps, but hammered out our problems like two people with the same stake in them.

One person cannot be everything to the child. This was apparent to me, in different ways, with my two very different children.

Buffy, first. Buffy was making it increasingly clear that she hated my out-of-town trips more than ever. My absences frightened her. All children who have experienced the death of a parent early in life live in constant fear of losing the second parent as well. I had tried to keep the longer-distance trips to a minimum, and keep them short, yet even a few were too many at that time in our lives. Patty was always there when I was not. Neighbors were alerted. My mother was on standby. And yet Buffy hated it when I was away.

She would have my schedule and my telephone number and strict instructions to call me any time, anywhere, for whatever reason, even if she just felt like talking.

And she did. One night I'd been battling insomnia and she called very late, just after I'd dropped off to sleep in Corpus Christi, to tell me she was very sad and worried.

I snapped awake panicky, then screamed with rage in reaction.

"You called me at this time of the night to tell me your goddamn hamster is sick!"

"Gerbil, mom, ger—"

"Goddamn gerbil is sick! It's three o'clock in the morning out here! And why aren't you in bed, for Chrissake? What are you doing? Don't you have any consideration? Don't you ever think? For this you have to wake me up?"

So much for the ever-available mother I'd been trying to be.

Yet even as I erupted I knew that Buffy was feeling the kind of loneliness that went beyond my brief absences. She wanted her father and mother.

Well, there wasn't any way she could have them. For all that I tried to give her, I couldn't give her what she wanted most.

Nor could I give it to Jon.

Where Jon was concerned, I was as needy as he. His behavior was well beyond my capacity to control. I prayed that he would be accepted at the Hyde School, that he would go there, and that they would somehow fix him for me. I had been told very firmly that it was not a fix-it school, but I still had high hopes. I was tired of that old simplistic jargon about a male role model. At the same time that was exactly what I wanted Jon to have.

"Male authority figure" sounded more acceptable to me.

I had to make a very honest assessment of what I could and could not give my children. I had a pretty good sense of my limitations. I knew I was not a supermom. I knew I had not yet learned to discipline. Temperamentally, perhaps even intellectually, I could not sit down with my kids every night and supervise their homework. (A) They were not often there at the appointed hour; (B) I had my own work to do; (C) I did not have the patience. I just couldn't be everything to my kids— couldn't give all they obviously needed.

The answer, then, or part of it at least, was to look outside myself. I felt that Jon needed some consistent male authority figure or figures. I wanted to make up for the boy not having a father. (Did the young man on the television show feel a similar need for his motherless children? Did Tom Anderson, whose kid was nodding out in the park?) I hoped that the new school—yet another new school—would supply the influences for Jon that I, as a single, female parent, was unable to supply.

Okay, I wasn't capable of bringing up my boy alone. Therefore I had to give part of the job to somebody else, whether or not it was somebody who had to be paid. If you have the money, use it. If you don't—I had to close my mind to that possibility. There were many women with financial problems far more severe than mine. Dreadful financial problems. And not only financial problems, but terrible complications, such as runaway husbands, or drop-in lovers who abused them and their babies, or congenitally ill or retarded children requiring but never getting special care, or a life pattern of delinquency and despair.

I am heartily thankful that these desperate dilemmas of hundreds of thousands of other mothers are not mine. My problem is one I *think* can be helped by money. Not solved—helped.

Was it a cop-out, to try to buy some structure and authority for my son?

Surely not. A call for help was warranted. It wasn't perhaps the ideal parental technique, but it was better to turn for help to someone or something else than to do nothing. If you haven't sufficient skill yourself, if you don't have enough family or the right kind to help you out, you must find substitutes somewhere. Buffy had made a valiant effort to find her own. Now it was clear that Jon needed some too.

I still wasn't sure what I needed for myself. Peace of mind, I supposed, although that probably wouldn't come until the kids were straight and happy. A vacation from the heavy weight of responsibility and obligations, a release from mental fatigue. Some fun. More music and theater. Time to knit. Exercises at a health club. A more active sex life. Get-togethers with friends. Encounters with people who might prove to be more than casual acquaintances. Season tickets to the Yankee ball games . . .

That was a joke. I hadn't been a baseball fan for years. But going to the ball part represented to me the sort of thing a father did with his children on days off, which made me think in turn of the things we used to do together and the trips we took as a family. This meant something to me other than solitary love, or solitary authority. This was a question of missing out on the pleasures of family life because the family was incomplete.

It is a simple and inescapable fact that when you have become accustomed to a man of your own it is damn hard to find a replacement for him as husband, lover, provider, father, companion, playmate, and fellow watcher of your children growing up. You wonder if the comfort, the laughter, and the fun are permanently gone.

Other people might have managed, and often do manage, to adapt more graciously to being deprived of a beloved life partner, and succeed in fashioning a different way of life in which the discipline and fun are nonetheless present in the right quantities. This person, this mother, was not a highly qualified parent to begin with. I had relied too heavily on my husband to set guidelines and enforce them.

(Although, when Jon started acting up in nursery school, it was I who was called in, not Jon's father. Martin had rather distanced himself from the children's school affairs. School business was mother's work.)

What about any help I could have sought from my own mother, and sometimes had? No, that was not right for me, I thought, nor for her. If I know anything about being a mother, I learned it from her. My father was the heavy. My mothering style is my mother's, up to a point. Like her, I feel helpless without help. I don't know the appropriate things to do. For all my volatility, I am nonconfrontational, as generous as I know how, and I put up with a lot. Then, suddenly, I can't stand it anymore. I turn into my father, and I erupt.

My gentle mother never raised her voice or lifted a hand against us kids. Just that little warning: wait till your father gets home.

I guess I'm still waiting for father to get home—in the shape of a disciplinary male figure or structured school for Jon, or somebody to tell *me* what to do.

What every parent without a partner lacks, at least in the beginning of the unplanned single state, is some kind of group or communal support. The community I missed, wanted, and had been unable to think beyond was a husband. But, as I was beginning to realize, there were other communities out there.

I was also beginning to realize that, for all my wonderfully liberating career, I was in a way quite old-fashioned. I had grown up with the idea that men are supposed to take care of women. I thought I had buried it pretty deeply within me or put it behind me, but when I looked it was still there and scarcely hidden at all. It was perfectly obvious that I was going to have to get rid of this illusion, firmly and finally.

Well, some other time.

Meanwhile, I was overjoyed to hear from Hyde—at last!— that Jon had been accepted and would be welcome in the fall.

My plans to get closer to Buffy were on the shelf again. She had chosen to return to riding camp for the balance of the summer. I might as well, I thought, fill in a few late-summer engagements with my workshop groups.

In fact, I was not only beginning to have a good time with them, I was finding them personally rewarding. I was neither a joiner nor a leader, and it seemed incongruous to me that I should be traveling around the country rallying widows and forming support groups. But I liked doing it, and the response astounded me. Women cared that I knew what they had gone through. They appreciated it when I spoke about our mutual losses and fears. I felt a growing sense of wonder that I had something to say that struck a chord with people, and that seemed to help them. All I was doing was voicing their thoughts along with mine. They accepted me.

Then I realized that they were voicing their own thoughts as much as I was mine. I'd been sharing my experiences of widowhood with them and getting as much in return as I was offering them.

I had already learned that none of my feelings was exclusive to me. Now that I had learned to listen, I could hear what women were telling me about being women, being themselves, being mothers, being people not solely concerned with the sorry condition of widowhood, but concerned with all parts of their lives and with other people.

To me, it was a revelation. I had never realized how isolated I had become. As a woman and as a mother, I was slowly learning to be less alone, less of a New York woman and more of an Everywoman, and beginning to see that the way to be a human being was to include people in my life. I still had enormous difficulty in being completely open and honest with the people closest to me, but I was on my way to joining the world.

Shortly after hearing the good news from Hyde I had occasion to address a single mothers conference in Virginia. For the first time in my experience there were divorced women in the group as well as widows, which opened up areas of discussion that I had not dealt with in my groups before.

In a general discussion of mothers' epidemic sense of inadequacy a woman in her early thirties interjected suddenly, "How can you not feel inadequate when you feel demeaned? I could be making more money on welfare than I'm making now. It's just a matter of pride that I'm not on welfare instead of trying to make my own living. There's a lot of contempt for welfare mothers, but often they're driven to it for their children's sake. Somebody has to earn the money. Somebody has to look after the kids.

"*Money* is the problem. Lack of money is the worst problem. If you're constantly worried about where the rent's going to come from, or whether there'll be enough money to feed the kids properly, you not only can't be the kind of mother you want to be to them, but you're trapped in a cycle of fear and tension. Is this what motherhood's about?"

No, it isn't. But an unfortunate fact of life is that financial need is what drives the vast majority of mothers to work—and then to worry about the consequences of their absence for their children. This is true even of mothers in two-parent households. But the single mothers are obviously hardest hit. Many of them are the sole support of their families. Their numbers are increasing.

The number of female-headed households has skyrocketed within the last quarter of a century from 4.5 million in 1960 to 10 million in 1983, when one in every five mothers in the labor force was supporting her own family. Child-support payments to divorced mothers are negligible. Only 30 percent of all eligible mothers actually receive *any part* of what is due them. Average payment is $1,800 a year; less than $35 a week. But at least there is some hope that delinquent fathers may eventually be persuaded to make some contribution to the upbringing of their children. Young widows and unwed mothers often have only themselves to rely on. They must work.

Job or no job, support or no support, the worst single problem for most single mothers is simply not having enough money.

Exacerbating financial worry is the guilt factor: the enormous guilt felt by nearly all mothers who must leave their child or children in someone else's care. Will he be emotionally deprived? Physically or psychologically abused? Will she transfer her affections to her caretaker? Will something go wrong when I'm not there? And if it does, "Oh, God, it's because I was working. It's all my fault."

What are the other problems of a single, female parent?

Discipline. Exhaustion. Impatience. Frustration. "I miss having someone to help me. I don't always want to make the decisions. I don't always want to be the bad guy."

A look on the bright side: "Some of the time, it's better being single. There's no one to undermine the discipline, no way to be set off as the good parent versus the bad parent. No conflict between adults, and no conflict to lay off on the kids."

But there is the other side, which I know so well myself: loneliness and emptiness. No one with whom to share the good and bad times. The deglamorization of the single mother versus the desirability of the eligible bachelor with children. Erratic or nonexistent social life. Lowered self-esteem because of an inability to provide the best for the children.

"Sometimes I feel bad that I haven't been able to give them more," a woman in one of my workshops said. "Intellectually I know that my kids had it pretty easy, and had the good neighborhoods, summer camps, some trips, the 'right' schools, but I also know I've expended a lot of energy making sure that they had those things, and it's been tiring. I think if things had been a little easier financially I would have had time to be more fun as a mother. This is something I think, not based on anything they've said or any way they've behaved. It's probably just silly. They've turned out just fine anyway."

The quality of mothering. "Sometimes I feel guilty that I was so toughened trying to deal with the world and trying to raise my oldest boy that he isn't as giving to people as I wish he were. He's not openly loving. I hope someday he will be."

Sex. "I may have a midwestern puritanical streak, but I always thought it necessary to be incredibly discreet about sex. I've been *agonizingly* discreet. If I was in a situation where I wanted to be with a person, I worked out a way to do it. Strangely enough, I only managed to upset my mother, not my kids. At forty-four years old I've just had the worst fight of my life with her. I told her I went off for a weekend with a guy to a place not far from where she lives, and she said, 'My God, what if any of my friends had seen you?' "

Fear. Fear that the beautiful thirteen-year-old boy getting out of school at three o'clock in the afternoon would be scooped up by a creep because "his old lady" didn't turn up from the city until a quarter after seven. Fear that the proverbial—and only too real—dirty old man would lure the little girl away from her scheduled ride. Fear of a countless variety of bad influences and accidents. Fear of being too much of a mother.

"He and I were getting too close. His three sisters were off at school and he and I were getting just a little too friendly, I was beginning to think. Nothing incestuous, but we got to taking trips and going sailing together and having a lot of shared occasions and giggling at the same things. Well, if you're a boy, you just don't want your mother for your best friend, and I thought it was time to quit that. I couldn't just quit cold, so the solution seemed to be to let *him* do the quitting by going away to school. Luckily, he wanted a change of school anyway."

And the mother of two little girls: "I pay too much attention to them because there's not another adult in the house. That's the thing I worry about most as a single parent, and it worries me a whole lot. We do get child support. But I feel tremendous pressure to get out and do other things so that the children will not be suffocated in my presence. This is where the big problem is, because I'm very contented, to tell you the truth, to be the three of us just huddled together, just have our close little family thing going, and I *know* this is not good for them. I try to arrange get-togethers with other families and stay out of their school and camp life as much as possible. But I'm very worried about our mutual dependence, and I'm afraid I may be hurting them.

"Another thing that worries me all the time is that I don't know if my kids are ever going to have a relationship with a man, because I don't have any relationships with men. One good thing is that their father and I are on fairly good terms and they see him often. There's not much antagonistic stuff going on, and certainly not in front of them, so at least they're not pawns in a game or anything like that. But they're not seeing a healthy male-female relationship. I feel tremendous pressure on account of that."

Other strains.

"Not being able to give the kids enough time and attention."

"Not listening to them properly because I'm thinking of money, men, and my job."

"Trying to reconcile my career agenda with bringing up the children."

"Guilt about the divorce. Not having daddy live with them."

"Getting used to the idea that my youngest son decided to live with his father. Ricky having to make the choice that if he wants to have his daddy, he had to give up his mommy."

"Trying not to let on to the kids what a shit I think their father is."

"Blaming myself for having married an alcoholic. I should have chosen a better husband and father. My choice was my mistake."

Ultimately, I think it was my friend Diane who said it all, or most of it, for most of us. She had no horror stories to tell; no severe financial woes; just a story familiar to millions of women.

Diane is the divorced mother of two sons. She was an advertising executive before marriage and was able to return to her field when she had to. The divorce was amicable but, Diane feels, necessary. Yet it left its burden of guilt.

"Those boys had a right to have a mommy and a daddy, resident together. But I had no choice. It was them or me and it was a very selfish choice. I had to do it to save my life.

"The father didn't raise the boys. I did. We had a property settlement and alimony and he was good about honoring that agreement, but it was not enough to live on.

"I had tremendous guilt about getting divorced. It was the one thing I was never going to do because I had seen what it had done to me as a kid, and I was never going to do that to my children. And then I did.

"I knew certain things: I knew I could never be in two places at one time and I knew I couldn't hold two thoughts at one time, so what I learned how to do was to juggle and organize and prioritize to a superb degree. And I was very lucky because my skill was a portable one, and well paid if you were good at it. So I was able to hold onto the house, which was crucial to me, because I was determined not to move the boys out of their home and out of the schools they were going to. However I had to do it, I was going to maintain as much of their world as I could so that there could be something they could focus on—the same house, the same school, and the same people they were used to.

"More than many people, I was lucky because I could work out of the house, because I wasn't in a dead-end beat-em-up job, and because I did have job satisfaction. I knew that my number-one role was breadwinner. I never lost sight of that. But I usually did have enough energy left over to be a mother. I could put my business world on hold when an emergency came up, when something needed to be handled, without going to pieces or yelling and screaming.

"But I did feel guilt and I still feel guilt that I wasn't always there when they needed me, that I didn't always have the right answers. I guess what I am really saying is that I wanted to be the perfect mother, not even knowing what that is. But I had this fantasy about the woman who does all this, and I guess I feel guilty because I failed to live up to that fantasy. I was often just too tired and strung out.

"Another reason for feeling guilty is called 'getting sick.' You have to be alive and fully functioning 365 days a year. This sense was reinforced by the terror I saw in my kids' eyes whenever I did get sick. I couldn't let anything happen to me. It scared them too much. And it kept me from getting them to their appointments, which threw them off base. So I'd get myself off to the doctor the minute I felt anything could possibly be wrong with me, so I could stall it off. They just got too frightened when they couldn't depend on me.

"But the major guilt comes from having been divorced. And I know that it takes two parents to raise children. I know that it takes two adults to handle the problems, even the logistics. In a way I turned the older boy into a surrogate father for his brother Barry, and I'm sorry for that. But once in a while I had to. There's a five-and-a-half-year difference between them, and Sandy's always been levelheaded.

"One evening, for instance, we were watching television. It was early, but we were in our pajamas and ready for bed. And Barry, to be helpful—he was about four and a half—brought in a bowl of popcorn from the kitchen, and he tripped on the step and landed on the bowl. It was a beautiful wedding present that had spikes coming out of the glass—not narrow ones, but chunky ones—and he got one right between the eyes.

"I looked over and I could see the blood shooting artesian-like out of his head and he was quietly sobbing. So I pressed my thumb on him to stop the blood and I said, very calmly, 'Sandy, go into your room and get your clothes, get Barry's clothes and get my clothes.' Which he did.

"But as he did it I hated it that I couldn't turn and say to his father, 'Help me.' I guess perhaps I have very rigid rules, but in my family as I was growing up nobody helped anybody else. I was amazed that I had any presence of mind, but after Sandy got his clothes on I showed him how to hold his thumb on Barry. And since I had to drive, he had to hold Barry all the way. And I think that was an awful lot to ask of a ten-year-old boy.

"Years later, when Sandy was in his teens, it suddenly seemed very important to him to let me know what I had done wrong as a mother. I knew it was a set-the-record-straight session, and I knew I couldn't pull any parental power trips and try to shut him off. I knew I had to listen to him for however long it went on. I think it went on for about twelve hours. It was a laundry list of all my failings, but the bottom line was that I had deprived him of childhood. Unlike the other kids, whoever they were, he hadn't had a mother or a father. No mother? Well, he had a mother who did nothing but make him grow up too fast because someone had to look out for the younger boy and he was it.

"He talked wistfully about aprons and pies. I looked at him in total disbelief and I said, 'You wanted one of those?' And he said yes. I said, 'Where did you hear about them? I am amazed, because I thought that, warts and all, you were fairly happy with me.' And he said, 'Well, if you had just put on an apron once in a while and baked more pies, things would have been a whole lot better.'

"In his view, I had shut out his childhood.

"What about his father? Did he blame him at all? You know very well that the absent parent is the one who is vested with all the marvelous clothing. You see, there were two different sets of rules. I was the one who was going to be held accountable, and anything he got from his father was manna from heaven."

# CHAPTER EIGHT

# Mommy Always Liked You Best!

IT was no real surprise to me that my hopes of spending more time with my daughter had been thwarted by my daughter herself. I had thought that we could take some trips together, she and I and perhaps all three of us, but Buffy preferred to spend her vacation with the horses at her riding camp.

She didn't like Jon's being home. He had settled down to being only half wild and was actually doing some visible studying. This pleased me, but Buffy was angry when he was in the house, in his own room. If Jon was going to be in the city, she was not, and anyway, she'd rather be at Longacres.

Fine. Summer camp is good for a kid. New York isn't, particularly. I was happy to have her out of doors in the country, if that was what she wanted.

Before she left she made me promise to come up and see her ride in the weekend contests. I'm terrified of horses and they make me sneeze, but she was absolutely adamant, and of course I wanted to visit her. She rode beautifully, masterfully, and I was thrilled and proud to watch her.

In fact, it was more rewarding to visit her than to have her around. Except for an occasional clash that brought them together, she and Jon had seemed to be living on separate planes but on the brink of some devastating encounter. Until some sort of understanding was reached between them, it might be

119

better to have them apart. Belatedly, it came to me that she was actually violently jealous of him, and that when we were all together she resented both of us.

What was this, classic sibling rivalry? I hated such jargon. Women used it all the time in discussing their children, but when I was growing up I didn't have siblings, I had a brother and a sister. It was only when I reached adulthood that I found the term in psychology books, and since then I've been hearing it throughout my children's school years and in virtually every discussion group I attend. I suppose "sibling rivalry" is as useful a description as any, but I find it a rather slick label for a situation that can be anything from very simple to extremely complex.

" 'Sibling' is not a family term,' said a mother in one group, voicing my sentiments exactly. "Sure, there's rivalry and competition, and it can get ugly. But I don't see any need to get psychological about it. You wind up relating to your kids as if they're mentally ill or something. To me, it's not too good an idea to approach my kids as if I were a psychiatrist. I really believe in keeping our relationships human."

I warmed to such talk. I remembered when Jon was a little boy and school counselors had suggested that sibling rivalry was a good thing, not only to be expected but inevitable. Desirable. Healthy. I was not finding it so. Many other mothers, I discovered, found it extremely difficult to cope with, and blamed themselves for their kids apparently hating each other.

Recalling my own childhood, I, of course, realized that I had felt jealous, envious, replaced. As the firstborn, I had been an only child, only grandchild, and only niece for three years until the competition had come along. Neither my brother nor my sister could ever catch up with my years of glorious supremacy. They could, however, dethrone me. They could crowd into my space and grab my toys and hog all the attention, and the grown-ups would think they were indescribably adorable. Not only my singularity but my babyhood was gone forever. Certainly I resented my sister and, to a lesser degree, my brother.

But Jon didn't feel replaced. At no time had he seemed to regard Buffy as a threat to his position. I could not honestly believe this was a result of my pre-Buffy brainwashing.

I checked out the possibility with a number of friends. According to the parents I talked with, preconditioning cuts very little ice at all. In the beginning it seems to have effect, but when number-two child starts crawling around and making off with blocks and teddies—that's when the volcano erupts.

"We spend a lot of time trying to prepare the first child for the new baby," said one experienced mother, "and we forget all about the developmental stages. Usually the older child does think, in the beginning, that the new baby is kind of interesting and cute. There is some resentment toward the baby, but if there is any anger it is generally directed toward the mother because of the little one getting so much attention. Early on, there generally is an acceptance. The rejection comes later. The absolute apex of sibling rivalry is when the baby starts to emerge as a personality. Smiles! Crawls! Action! Intrusion! He knocks down castles and breaks up games and gets into the older kid's space and *that's* when you have trouble."

That hadn't exactly happened with Jon and Buffy. But I had to consider: was Jon acting up belatedly because he hadn't really wanted a rival?

Nonsense. He had no rival. Acting up because he had lost his father, maybe; because his mother wasn't much of a disciplinarian, probably; because he was a teenager, certainly; but not because his sister had toppled him from his role as king of the castle. She hadn't. He was firstborn son, never to be replaced. Buffy was the one who was jealous.

She had moments of passionate rage when she said, "When is it going to be my turn? When do I get to come first?"

I tried to say that there was no first, no second, that I loved my children equally, but she brushed my protestations aside. Her outbursts surprised me, because I still thought of her as a basically docile child.

She was supposed to be docile. She was a girl. A very feminine, pretty girl, with a great head of hair that would curl or hang straight or tie into braids or whatever she wanted to do with it. She was more than pretty. She was beautiful, getting tall and lithe, her skin as creamy and pure as it had been when she was a baby, a stunning setting for her huge dark eyes. She was entirely unlike me—all that a girl should be.

I wondered how much of my gender preference—more jargon, it occurred to me, but as valid as any current cliché—I had been conveying to her. I had not, until recently, particularly liked women. I had gone from your basic tomboy to femme fatale, I rather liked to think, and quite proudly considered myself to be a man's woman. The truth was, I thought, that I didn't—or hadn't—liked myself very much, and deep down inside I still felt that the boy child was superior just because he was a boy.

Thinking of this, I chuckled uneasily at the tale of the little girl whose parents had so desperately wanted their first child to be a son that they couldn't manage to hide their preference from their baby daughter. In small ways and wistful words they conveyed their feelings to this perceptive child. Soon she was wearing a dinky little baseball cap and playing halfheartedly with the truck and mechanical toys daddy brought home. One wonderful day another bundle in blue appeared in the house. A son, at last. And Robin said, "Oh, good! Now I don't have to be a boy anymore."

Another mother observed, "Position in the family counts. A parent who was the older child tends to identify with the older child. This preference shows, just as much as gender preference shows. Rivalry between kids has a lot to do with this sense of preference. All you can do is try your best not to show favoritism—and, by God, that's hard!" And she told the story of the little boy whose older brother, the firstborn, was the obvious family favorite, adored and pampered by all. One day the little one asked, "What do you want to be when you grow up, Billy?" Without missing a beat, he answered, "I want to be Paul."

Cute. And poignant. And, naturally, guilt-inducing.

Many of the mothers I talked to were far more critical of their daughters than of their sons. "She's driving me crazy," was a common complaint. "I could kill her. . . . I can't wait until school starts. . . . My son never made me feel like this. . . . Why is my son so much easier to get along with? . . . My son never said these terrible things to me. . . ."

I didn't feel quite the same way, because at that point it was my son who was driving me crazy. How my daughter looked and how she behaved was important to me, and even though we had our differences and an occasional eruption, she was easy to get along with. Perhaps I was looking to her to be the little feminine, curly-haired charmer I'd never been. And yet—and yet—I felt more comfortable with my son. I felt that Buffy wasn't like me. I felt that Jon was. His personality was like mine, or what I felt was mine. In his more clearly defined moments he was funny and energetic, which I thought Buffy was not.

I could identify with him more clearly because of this. And Buffy, presumably, knew it. For the time being I shied away from considering the implications and stayed tuned into what others had to say about sibling rivalry, and how it might perhaps be avoided by treating all children alike.

But they are not, of course, alike.

"Each kid is unique. How can you treat them equally? There are temperamental differences, physiological and emotional differences. Go with it the way it is. If you have a docile child and a spirited child, you can't treat them the same and you can't make them the same. The fact that personalities are different is not the parents' fault. You can't take the blame on yourself."

Not unless you set the stage for competition by trying too hard to make things equal.

"What every kid wants is to be the most dearly beloved one. The trick is to make each kid feel that way. And you don't do this by trying to treat them all equally. It's not possible to cut each piece of the pie equally every time. There's no such thing as being fair. Trying to make everything equal leads to subterfuge and to pitting one against the other. You give one a treat, the other has to have one, and you can't keep things absolutely even. They'll just start keeping score and getting into fights, and you're the one who loses."

I heard about score keeping in its most basic form from Mary and Jake, whose two girls, three years apart, have been classic sibling rivals throughout their lives, beginning with the biting of the younger by the older and continuing with the usual fights over territory, toys, and parental attention.

"Then," said Mary, "as soon as the kids could count, score keeping began. Which meant, for Jake and me, two piles of presents carefully counted out on Christmas Eve to make sure they were even. And still continuing, to this day. One for Katy, one for Ginny, one for Katy, one for Ginny—carefully balanced and measured. Yet the twenty-two-year-old, upon observing the gift of a rhinestone thrift-shop bracelet to her sister still remarked, '*She* always gets the jewelry.' This despite her grandfather's small diamond on her finger, a gift to her just three months earlier."

I thought this was very amusing until I found out about the score keeping that was going on in my own family. But that revelation came to me only in the new school year that started in the fall.

Meanwhile, I was hearing a great many stories of rivalry and competition between brothers and sisters, not all of them amusing. It became clear to me that even in apparently ideal families there may be children who are—for a time, at least—completely incompatible, and there's not much that any mother can do about it except try not to feel it is her fault. On the other hand, there are a lot of families in which parents play their children against each other, which inevitably leads to rivalry.

I hoped that I was not guilty of such parental game playing and felt that I was not, although I was uneasily aware that my daughter had reason to believe I favored Jon. Other than the sore point of favoritism, little I heard applied directly to me. But that was not surprising. Individual experiences, personalities, and perceptions are sharply different. I could understand that it is possible to love each child differently, yet love each just as much. I could understand the relationship between parental preference and sibling rivalry; understand, too, that there was often a favorite child—and that it wasn't always the same favorite. That was the good thing about it. Sometimes one child is favored, sometimes the other.

Parents are not consistent. It takes an emotional genius to be consistent. In my early years as a mother, I had been advised that the absolute of mothering absolutes was consistency, and I knew that I could never succeed in this. I am consistent only in my inconsistency. Now it was becoming apparent to me that consistency was more of an ideal than an actuality, and it wasn't necessarily a fine idea at all times. I could be consistently awful, I supposed, but I wasn't sure that was better than being fairly nice maybe half the time.

I reviewed my family. What we have here, I reminded myself, is a single female parent apparently resistant to training, one miracle boy who lacks—here we go again—a male role model, and a younger girl who was adopted into a nice family that splintered and left her without a father. She has been doubly deprived.

I have to face it: she has reason to resent Jon. He does not return the sentiment, because she barely exists for him. Or so he says. It is not unusual in an older brother–younger sister relationship for the boy to ignore the girl. Jon may not feel secure about many things in his life, but he has always been serenely aware of being number-one son, unsurpable. Buffy has no doubt been fully aware of his favored position. My gender preference had probably been no secret from her, any more than had been the temperamental kinship between my boy and me.

She does not need this constant reminder that she is adopted.

It seared my heart to think that she might feel she was the less loved because of being the adopted one, that her rage at Jon was not only because he was the crown prince, but because she felt like a second-class citizen in our family. Ours was too small a family to accommodate such feelings. In this very tight family situation we had no room for free-and-easy give-and-take. We didn't have enough targets to disperse the blows. There was no healthy rough-and-tumble. Well, some rough, but not much tumble. More would have been better.

Interestingly, Buffy in her own way had come to a similar conclusion in trying to create her own larger family. And then felt disappointed not only because it was an artificial family, a little girl's fabrication, but because I, her mother—"real" or otherwise—was not its core. It was a touching effort, which had moved me even while making me feel guilty for not being there for my baby.

Would we really have been better off if there had been more of us? My friend Harriet, a battle-scarred veteran mother of six grown children, gave me a fresh perspective on large families. Happily, all her kids are fine.

It is true, she said, that the large family tends to take the heat off individuals. "But it's not the number that counts. It's the general atmosphere you create in the family. There's *always* some kind of rivalry. It is a simple fact of life that one kid is going to be madder than hell when another comes along to grab attention away from him. And it's true that after a while, when there are a lot of kids in a basically stable and loving family, they're not going to care so much about the competition. Relationships kind of shift around. Today's rivalry is tomorrow's 'Let's all tell mom how much we hate her.' But the intensity of sibling rivalry has nothing to do with number."

In her own healthy, rough-and-tumble family, Harriet's oldest daughter accepted the second-born Simon fairly placidly. But when the third child, another daughter, was born, Nancy made serious attempts to kill her, nearly drowning her on one occasion and nearly strangling her on another. Two years later, Simon almost succeeded in gouging his little brother's eyes out before going on a rampage and almost wrecking the house. In the following years he made many attempts to mutilate Benjy, in which endeavors he was usually thwarted by his four squabbling sisters.

The intensity of sibling rivalry—the *hatred*—can be very fierce indeed. Mothers sometimes joke about it, but it is no joke. I worried when I saw the hostility between my children. It hadn't been evident when they were younger, when we were a happy family of four and adolescence was years away. I knew that they had been undergoing the normal changes of growing children. But I also knew that, in those years when my main concern had been for myself, I had been divisive, setting them against each other without realizing the harm I might be causing. I'd made them incompatible.

But not permanently. Surely not. All youngsters pass through stages. Innumerable ones. They play together like little cherubs, they claw each other to pieces, they bore each other, they hate each other, and then one day they start acting like civilized human beings. They get over this childish rivalry. Or do they?

Uneasily, I recalled another of Harriet's observations.

"They never get over it," she had said emphatically. "Sibling rivalry *never* abates. Brothers or sisters at eighty or ninety years old are still arguing about who should or should not have gotten the family silver. Sibling rivalry is a lifelong proposition. Mommy always liked you best! You always got everything! I never got anything! Believe me, it goes on and on. Accommodations are made, peace sometimes breaks out, people learn to get along. But underneath it all, the siblings are seething."

Mine certainly seemed to be.

Sibling rivalry, it seemed to me, could be dirtier, deeper and longer-lasting than I could have imagined possible.

But please! Not in my family!

Jon was being predictably changeable about going off to Hyde. One day he was gung-ho, the next day he was sullen, the day after that he didn't come home, and the day after *that* he accused me of trying to get him out of my life by sending him away.

At worst he was impossible to live with: hostile, abusive, accusatory, and completely unconscious of the fact that he might have some obligations around the house. There were times when we openly resented each other's presence, and he equally openly vented his rage over my consigning him to Hyde. For a period of several days he flatly refused to go.

I gave him options. Somehow I found the strength to take something of a stand.

"You cannot live with me anymore if you are going to keep on this way," I said. "I will pay for your room and board somewhere else. But I am not going to educate you anymore, because you do not deserve it. You are not taking advantage of your opportunities. Find an alternative school for yourself and figure out a way to pay for it. That's one option. The other option is Hyde."

He vanished for a while and then came back. Again he alternated between sullenness and enthusiasm, with a variety of interim moods.

None of his attitudes surprised me, and I felt I bore them all quite well.

On his gung-ho days some of the old closeness came back, and we laughed a lot. He actually seemed pleased when I came back from Longacres on Sunday evening and told him about the trophy Buffy had won.

Harmony vanished the moment she came back from camp, about a week before Jon was due to leave for Maine.

"I thought you'd be gone," she said icily. And that was the beginning of hell week.

It is hard to describe just what she did to provoke him, but she did plenty when she couldn't succeed in avoiding him. She needled him. She moved his things around. She made jeering remarks about his girl friends. An odd combination of the extremely meticulous and tenacious—as a highly self-disciplined rider—and the very messy, she took books out of the bookcases. She tore things up. She scattered them around. Not necessarily his things, but anything that happened to irritate her at the moment. He kept complaining to me that she was spoiled, and that I was letting her get away with murder. One way and another, Buffy managed to drive Jon into a frenzy. Next: "Mom, he hit me!" And he hit hard.

In all fairness, Jon could be provocative too and he had a hair-trigger temper. Buffy was in a rage, with a deep-rooted anger and aggression that expressed itself in general destruction. His hot temper and her subterranean rage, blended with natural competitiveness and seasoned with a variety of more complicated factors, added up to some almost gory scenes. This was not child's play. The hostility was intense and almost frightening.

Abruptly, Jon decided that the thing he wanted most in life was to get out into the fresh country air. A friend picked him up in a rattletrap car to drive him to school in Maine. Jon threw in his books, his ghastly collection of clothes and—with more care—the new stereo I had given him for his room at Hyde.

There was peace in the house and a welcome silence from Maine.

Buffy brightened up and moved herself and her things into his room. There was no point in objecting, because Jon would not be coming home for weekends and his large, sunny room would have been unused. The room was next to mine and Buffy, unlike Jon, thought it a prime location.

"Now it's my turn," Buffy said happily.

She hated the graffiti on the walls and ceiling. Next thing I knew, she had inveigled Zigrid to come over and paint the room for her. It looked good in powder blue.

I was sensing a gradual change in Buffy. She was growing up, and there was a new feistiness and restlessness about her that was unfamiliar—and disquieting. We spent quite a lot of time together, eating out often at local restaurants because she thought it was fun and she seemed to like me better out of the house, and yet I did not feel that we were close.

Somehow we were not on the same wavelength. It was as if she was living beside me instead of with me.

Whatever the nature of the anger Buffy felt inside, it began spilling out and engulfing me. Again, and far more intensely than before, she began talking about going back to her real mother. At first, she asked if I would help to find her mother and go with her to the first meeting. I said I would. Then she stopped asking me and declared that she would go alone.

She made no move to go, but I could feel her continuing rage. I had heard that the rage against the biological mother was often transferred to the adoptive mother, and I guessed that this was what was happening. But Buffy found more things wrong with me than I would ever have imagined.

Whenever Buffy talked about me in my hearing, which was often, she referred to me not as "my mother" or "mom" but as "she." I felt like a creature. Then my daughter, having seen the annual television revival of the *Wizard of Oz*, began addressing me and talking about me as the wicked witch of the West Side.

What was so wicked about me?

I favored Jon. I was always giving him things. I always gave Jon more things than I gave Buffy.

What things? Just give me one example.

The stereo. That's one example.

But what about the $600 saddle and the riding boots I've just given you?

That's different. They were for my birthday. Everybody gets

a birthday present. Anyway, you could have given them to me while I was at riding camp.

Then she gave me a rundown on all the wonderful things I had given Jon and the few paltry things I had given her. He always got more valuable gifts. She'd get a doll. She never liked dolls. He'd get a bike. There was about a hundred dollars difference, or even more. He'd gotten that stereo, a huge stereo. He got to pick it out and everything. Why couldn't she get a stereo? And I'd said to her, she told me, "When you're older, you'll get a stereo."

A familiar message was coming through. Buffy was keeping score. Two for him and one for her. His was expensive, hers was not. Hers was a required gift, as in a birthday present; his was a bonus, undeserved. Add them all up and they spelled "unfair wicked witch."

No sooner had I reconciled myself to being the wicked witch than I discovered that Buffy was keeping a "hate book" dedicated to me. I saw her writing in it. She told me what it was, then hid it. My daughter was keeping track of my shortcomings, which were obviously many. I was never able to locate this volume, though I must admit I did try, but every once in a while I found scribbled hate notes lying around the house. Sometimes she quoted from the book: "You love him more than me. He gets more stuff than I do." "You say you want to spend more time with me and then you never do. You lied to me."

And then there were the imploring little missives: "I try not to ask for much in life, but when I do I try not to make it some major thing. Please would you let me have Janie sleep over since I stayed home yesterday and today. . . ." Little Janie was heavily into drugs and I did not want to have her staying over. "Please, oh, pretty please."

*No.*

"You bitch, you witch, you miserable mean mother."

She seemed to be developing allergies. After a particularly severe session of wheezing I took her to a specialist, who tested her relentlessly and told us she had asthma. Buffy was triumphant on the way home. "*You* gave it to me," she said. "You smoke too much. You gave me asthma."

Shortly after that I gave up smoking, but Buffy's asthma slowly got worse and worse, in a sporadic, unpredictable kind of way. Buffy told me it was psychosomatic, a big word she had recently picked up and liked a lot, and that it was my fault whether I smoked or not.

She attended school and did her homework with reasonable diligence, if no great interest. Knowing that she still disliked my absences, I tried to take her on short trips whenever I could, but I soon stopped that. The main reason was that she walked out in the middle of a lecture I was giving across the river in New Jersey, and though I made a joke of it to the audience, it bothered me.

"If my own child walks out on me, what can I expect from the rest of you?" I asked, playing for the laugh I knew I'd get. It came, but I was in no hurry to repeat the experience.

Why had she done that?

She was bored. She'd heard all that stuff before.

Of course she knew that it had hurt me.

And she continued to use her mythical search for her biological mother as a weapon against me.

I figured that I had it coming to me, both her laundry list of my shortcomings and her threats about leaving me. It was perfectly evident that I was not the nurturing fairy godmother of her dreams. But I was astonished by how much she seemed to blame me. Two or three years before, she had forgiven me everything. Now I was the worst person in the world. My docile child was galloping into adolescence with a vengeance, and I'd scarcely even realized what was happening. She was no longer the child I'd thought she was. Perhaps she never had been.

That thought struck me one day when I was sorting through some pictures of her at riding camp. The contrast between the sheer power of the beautifully muscled horse and the light, sure touch of the delicate little girl astride the great beast—here was the image of the essential Buffy. She was graceful, competent, in control. Within that slight body was a really strong young person, capable of expressing herself and getting what she wanted without having to resort to giving me cunning little signals through hate notes or threats of going to search for her real mother. Certainly she would use her whole arsenal of teenage guile to prick my conscience and fan the ever-ready sparks of guilt, but when she wanted something concrete—as I realized upon thinking back over the past few years—she went right out and got it. I was amazed that I hadn't seen before how determined and direct she could be.

The horses, for instance. She loved animals, she had wanted to ride, and she had been looking for something to distinguish her. She had found that something and gone for it. She hadn't hinted, hadn't left half-hidden notes for me to find; she hadn't hesitated to tell me what she wanted, and she'd gotten it. And there was no trace of fear in her when she was riding or grooming these enormous, frightening creatures.

Her support system. She had gathered around her an informal family of kids, and she had taken it upon herself to go out and find substitute mothers when I had seemed insufficient. To be sure, her network hadn't worked out in the end, but she made the effort. For a time, her effort had served her well. I couldn't help admiring such initiative. Since then, she had shown herself to be enormously gregarious and always had a huge gang of friends to whom she dispensed popcorn, comfort, and advice. This was a self-effacing child?

Then there was her reign as the queen of Chess City; my daughter, the gambler. The one who stayed out late and came home with her pockets full of winnings. This was a docile kid? This precociously street-smart child? I was amazed that I could have pigeon-holed my little girl that way.

More recently was the episode of her taking over from Jon.

"When do I get to come first?" she had demanded. And then she had declared triumphantly, "Now it's my turn." No submissive little angel of a child would have said this, would have persuaded one of her retired surrogate mothers to repaint her brother's room for her. Now that I thought of it, there was some kind of raw power here that I rather envied. But what she had been saying was, Look, *I'm* here now, and you are here for me, and I want what's mine. And she'd had no problem about expressing this in action.

Another case in point was her insistence upon dragging me out of the house when she wanted to talk about something she felt was important. Sensitive to the demands of my working life, she understood the value of getting me away from my home office, the pressure, and the constantly ringing phone. "C'mon, let's go out and talk." This was pretty smart for a little girl.

The more I thought about it, the more I questioned how I'd labeled her. She was nothing like the image of peaches-and-cream docility I had assigned to her. She was an active, energetic young woman.

I realized that, up to a point, children tend to play the roles expected of them. I'd let Jon be Jon, and he was Jon, with all his eccentricities. But I'd been trying to force Buffy into the role of a Lynn-child who had never been. Perhaps trying to fit the pattern I was laying on her, she had shown a surface docility, but I had read her wrong and missed the cues she'd given me about the child she really was. I was the product of male supremacy, told by my father that it was a man's world, but that a smart woman could get anything she wanted by being demure and acting dumb. I expected Buffy to be what I had been expected to be. And she wasn't. She was a demanding, gutsy kid, wanting what was rightfully hers.

In all likelihood, the anxieties and concerns I had attributed to her were the ones I had grown up with and assumed she must share because she, too, had been born female. What I hadn't taken into account was what had happened to women since I was a child, and what had happened to the world. Women had demonstrated their strength, and it was no longer a man's world. Buffy had apparently realized long before I had that it was neither necessary nor helpful to be submissive and ingratiating in order to succeed in life—especially if her mother was going to play favorites.

And I had shown favoritism. I'd been insensitive not to have been aware of it before. Now I could no longer deny to myself that I had been partial to Jon, not so much in the matter of presents—there, I felt, she was truly wrong—as in appreciating him more as a person. I did have a special feeling for him because he was that valued being, a son; because he was the first-born, as I had been; because I had felt that, in some ways, Jon and I were so much alike. So now I faced this, and Buffy's accusations of my partiality added to my store of guilt.

But now it was beginning to look as though Buffy was the one who was most like me. I had been expected to be the pliant little girl, and I wasn't. I had rebelled. Buffy was doing very much the same thing, more openly, for the  most part, and more successfully.

I could see now, too, that the question of Buffy's adoption in the context of my favoritism was a phony issue. Like other adoptive mothers, I felt my daughter was as much a part of me as if she had been born to me. Her hurts about adoption gave me just one more thing to feel guilty about and gave her a powerful weapon for getting at me. Other than that, it seldom assumed any importance in our lives and had no significant bearing upon her relationship with her brother.

I asked her outright, once, why she was so jealous of her brother and he not of her, expecting her to say that he had nothing to be jealous about. I was wrong again.

She laughed scornfully. "Of course he's jealous. He just doesn't want to admit it. Do you think he likes me having you all to myself and taking his place in the house? You bet he doesn't. Why do you think he keeps picking on everything I do and telling you all the time that I'm getting away with murder? Because he wants you to blame everything on me."

Maybe she was right. Maybe it was a two-way street. And I agreed with her that Jon would never admit it. In that sense, as in perhaps others, Buffy was the more open of the two.

I had been incredibly wrong about her. She was a little tiger, an energetic, spirited kid who was evidently going to treat me to all the awfulness of her adolescence—and I had a feeling that might be awful indeed.

By this time I had talked to enough mothers to realize that I had not been singled out by fate to suffer the scorn of my daughter. Or my son either, for that matter. We all knew that our plight was virtually universal and were sure we had to have been doing something wrong.

What puzzled me was that the fathers, by their own account and by that of their wives, seemed not to share either the guilt or the blame. Somehow they seemed insulated by the distance they managed to achieve from most of their children's problems. They did not feel hated or inadequate or responsible for them. *That* was for women to feel.

And we do.

I have seldom met a guilty father. A few, yes. Very few. And I have met a number of women who do not flagellate themselves—at least, not visibly—because things are going so well for them that they would be crazy if they thought they had anything to feel remorseful about. Oh, an occasional rap on the knuckles perhaps, or the rare harsh word, but that is nothing. The rest of us could probably spend hours making lists just like Buffy's, spelling out what we shouldn't have done and what we shouldn't have said and what we should try to do and say to make things better.

Very few men do this. Perhaps our guilt is a condition of womankind, a weakness of the sex, the natural softness of the nurturer.

I cudgeled my conscience and made my mental lists.

But this was silly. There were experts out there telling mothers how to mother and dealing with women's inadequacies in great detail. Nearly all their advice, it seemed to me, was child-directed, which was all right as far as it went. But didn't mother ever get a break? Was it not human to make mistakes? Were those paper experts human? How was a mother to choose which expert to rely on, when they very often contradicted each other and even themselves?

That's the tough part. The contradictions. Also the blanket advice from millions of different women in millions of different situations.

Still, I thought I could use some new perspectives. I would check out an expert or two. After I was sure that Jon was safely tucked into his new school.

# CHAPTER NINE

# Boot Camp

FROM the moment the meeting began, I knew I had made an appalling mistake. I had suspected it when the letters and the phone calls and the follow-up memos had started to pour in, but now I was convinced.

I was attending my first Hyde parent seminar, a regional and—heaven help me!—monthly event held in a Huguenot church in Westchester for parents in the New York–New Jersey–Connecticut area. First, the school had sent me a notice advising me of the seminar schedule and commanding my attendance. Next, a Westchester mother, an enthusiastic volunteer and seminar leader of the New York group, had bombarded me with phone calls and assorted bits of printed materials she called "literature." Then, the school filled in the gaps with a series of what I thought were insultingly unnecessary reminders.

Now I was there, anonymous in a group of parental zealots, listening to Mitzi, the Westchester mother, holding forth interminably about herself, her parents, and her "golden children." I was amazed that nobody interrupted her, not even the regional coordinator, who was another hard-sell enthusiast. Under other circumstances I would probably have made some cutting comment, but I was the new kid on the block and I hesitated to do anything that might be considered inappropriate.

On and on she droned.

A fine-featured, somehow familiar-looking woman sitting on my left was fidgeting and looking at her watch, but neither she nor anyone else made any attempt to wrest control from the relentless Mitzi. How Mitzi felt anyone could be interested in her self-centered monologue was beyond me. My irritation turned into resentment, then into outrage. I was going to explode.

But I didn't. I neither vented steam nor let out a peep of protest. By that time I thought it was best not to. It was characteristic of me to let my anger build up until I could no longer contain it, then blow up, go out of control, and say a lot of things I later regretted. I could feel this beginning to happen, and I felt I must not permit it. I had done enough to Jon already, and I didn't want to do or say anything at this meaningless meeting to discredit him.

So I sat in silent fury, vowing never to attend another such farce.

It took an hour for Mitzi to relieve herself, and by then it was almost time to go home. I couldn't believe that anything had been accomplished.

In the few remaining minutes I mingled halfheartedly with the other parents, many of whom I had met briefly before Mitzi had assumed center stage.

They were not my type. Although this was supposedly the New York group, most of the parents were suburban people and not Manhattanites. I felt uncomfortable; clearly I was still a New Yorker at heart. If this was a sampling of Hyde parents, I knew I would be totally unable to identify with any of them. Especially with the zealous mothers. Mostly they were stay-at-home women with husbands who "took care of them." Or so I thought.

I hated them. Was jealous of them. Felt superior to them. Most of all, I felt contempt for them—for their uncool gung-ho attitude, for their proselytizing, for their parroting of the Hyde School party line and for the Hyde School clichés they spouted: the apple doesn't fall far from the tree; no pain, no gain; feelings aren't facts; to try is to lie. Really, it was revolting, especially since I couldn't understand some of their little slogans. To try is to lie? What garbage.

What do these women know, anyway? I asked myself. They're just a bunch of housewives living off someone else's paychecks. They've never been out on the barricades, the sole wage earner with no support system. All they have to worry about is their children.

I was horrified by the whole thing and furious with Jon. If it hadn't been for him I wouldn't be going through this humiliating experience. No way was I going to subject myself to it again. Bad enough to go through it among people with whom I had something in common, but a roomful of Mitzi lookalikes—albeit silent ones—was unthinkable.

Just before leaving I sounded out the woman who had been sitting on my left and learned that she was just as appalled as I, and just as unassertive in such situations. Neither was she one of the protected stay-at-home mothers I resented. On the contrary, she was a woman who knew the world very well indeed, a wonderful actress and a sensitive, sophisticated person. At last, a mother with whom I could identify.

And for weeks and months to come, she was the only Hyde parent I could stand.

Because I did go back to the group. Regularly, once a month, I gritted my teeth, got on the train to Westchester, and resigned myself to torment.

Going to the seminars was part of my contract with Jon and the school. After the first shock, I was determined to do everything the Hyde leaders told me to do. Reluctantly, halfheartedly, resistantly, however I did it, *I must do it.* I had taken the action of getting my son into Hyde, knowing very well that active parent participation was required, and it was up to me to follow up on what I'd started. I would now start being the good mother I was convinced I had not been.

Also, in a curious way, I felt that Jon was hostage to the school. All the kids were hostage to the school. I had to play along, or else there might be consequences for Jon. I couldn't imagine what, but I was anxious.

My group continued to seem like a bunch of cheerleaders to me. I was glad to observe that Mitzi didn't always dominate, but disappointed that everybody but my actress friend seemed to share the dreadful enthusiasm of the recently converted and an evangelical fervor to stand up and spill their guts about their feelings and their fears. I was not interested in their family problems or their fund raisers or other get-together programs. I wasn't about to expose my maternal inadequacy to these over-familiar, intrusive, unsophisticated, insensitive yahoos.

For all my recent contact with other mothers in the real world, I was not yet a willing participant in the human race. It took a long time for me to realize that what I mainly felt was self-pity in that company of people. I envied those boring housewives with their husbands and station wagons and their own little kaffeeklatsch support system. I was on the outside looking in, hoping that Jon was less uncomfortable than I. Hoping also that he was learning something, because I certainly was not.

My chance came at my introduction to the Family Learning Center up in Maine, and I blew it. That visit was a disaster. The saving grace was that I saw Jon and he was looking good, if not particularly thrilled with life. The shave and haircut, though not as drastic as I might have liked, had improved his appearance, if not his general mood. He didn't care much for the school, but he didn't hate it either. Not yet.

I felt as though we were sort of partners in crime, guilty accomplices doing penance in our respective ways. I was not looking forward to a good time.

If there was one thing I had learned at the seminars, it was that the meetings at the center were going to be *tough*. We had to be completely honest and open about our family problems, ourselves, our vices, our fears, and our feelings, and if we were not we would be figuratively stripped in public.

"Right," Jon agreed. "If you come across phony in any way, they'll getcha. You're gonna get nailed."

I felt offended in advance. My original concept of what a family learning center would and should be like was that of a milieu in which concerned parents such as I could learn to understand our children's needs and how to meet them. It was a school for parents. I had been prepared for civilized discussion, lecture notes, and homework, perhaps even group sessions comparing our children's behavior. But this was beginning to sound like sadomasochistic group therapy, and I rebelled at the idea.

I had arrived carefully dressed in my little black and brown Cacherel suit, wearing a determinedly supercilious look on my face and brandishing a notebook to convey the message that I was there not as a participant, but as an observer. Thus armed, I was ready to take them on—"them" being the Joe Gauld gang. What I was going to do was control the situation by concealing my sense of inadequacy and my fear. My *dread*. To get out of this with my ego intact, I had to be in control.

The controlling began the first night up in the women's dorm, where gradually a gathering of strangers began to warm up to each other. They were from all over the country, as unlike each other as they were unlike me.

There was one common denominator: all the mothers feared the group meetings conducted by Joe Gauld. All feared being stripped of their defenses. Truth time was painful. Joe was known to be brutally honest, sometimes cruel in his efforts to get to the truth.

I took over, cosseted the women. After all, wasn't I the most sophisticated of the lot? There was strength in numbers, I reminded them, dipping into my small supply of emergency tranquilizers to proffer chemical comfort to the more anxious ones.

"We must organize," I advised. "Defend one another. If he goes too far, the rest of us must disagree, protest."

Sounded good. There were murmurs of assent. This was to be a weekend of torment, and we might as well hang in there together.

I marched into the old mansion, the main school building in which the meetings were to be held, ready to do battle. Mothers and fathers I had met and talked to the day before greeted me with warm smiles. I took my place among them at the huge, rectangular mahogany table and waited for my turn to "get nailed." Nestled in my notebook was a little something I had written about myself in compliance with instructions, which I was prepared to read when asked. Other than that, I did not intend to dredge up hidden guilts and fears for public scrutiny.

The meeting opened with remarks by Joe Gauld and Larry Pray—who I considered a wise-assed young provincial—explaining why we were there and what we were trying to do. They talked about values, about the importance of writing vignettes and reading them for all to hear, about coming out with something true about ourselves. Each vignette, they said earnestly, should be an honest conversation with oneself. *Honest.* If it did not ring true, it must be done over and over until it did.

Now let us start with a self-introduction and a statement by each parent.

Joe methodically worked his way around the great table, parent by parent, pointing what seemed to me to be an accusatory finger at each one in turn and asking questions calculated to strip them of their facades and expose their deepest, most secret concerns. Unerringly, he hit home. They fell like bowling pins. The truth! One after the other, they blurted out their pain.

One mother put up a valiant struggle to conceal her fear that her son was a homosexual. Joe skillfully drew the issue out into the open. "Why hide it?" he demanded. "Are you ashamed? Of who? Yourself? Your son? Why should you be hurting? Do you think you have control over his life, what he is and what he does?"

Another mother, a wealthy stay-at-home, expressed her dissatisfaction at having no career, and that her father had brought her brothers into his successful business but never dreamed of making a place for her. This, even after the women's movement had swept the country! Joe expressed sympathy for the women's movement and, implicitly, for her. His comments to her were reasoned and understanding.

I was amazed. The woman could have bought herself a career if that was what she really wanted. I felt that Joe was buttering her up because she was rich. The more I heard the angrier I got, and I muttered, audibly, "He's giving lip service to her and he massacred the poor lady who's worrying about her son's homosexuality. What does he think he's doing, picking on the most vulnerable?"

Joe turned to me instantly, as if he had been waiting to pounce.

"What is going on with you, Mrs. Caine? From the moment you arrived, you've been uncooperative. You think you know more than anyone else. You don't. You may know the publishing business, but here you are nothing but a rookie. A rookie in education. And you're making no effort to learn. You've only showed up for a few of the activities. I don't know why you bothered coming up in the first place. You are an interloper. You are spoiling the spirit of the group."

He paused, lowered his eyebrows at me, and said, "So why don't you just leave? Get out!"

Silence in the room. I had never been spoken to like that before in my life, and I was shocked and insulted. At the same time, I was almost relieved to get straight talk from the man instead of what I saw as his manipulative, intimidating questions. Abusive straight talk, to a mother who was paying good money to send her son to his school.

I waited for my dorm buddies to protest. We'll show that demogogic son of a bitch that he can't abuse us just because he's got our kids hostage, I thought.

And I waited. And I looked around for my support system. And I had none.

Every single mother and father was looking inward, not at me. Never mind that I had made friends with many of them the previous day. They were all immersed in their own concerns, in their own needs. Not one of them gave a damn about the way Joe Gauld was talking to me. So much for my support system.

I had to save face. And I was angry, not at the parents, but at this man, who I found so offensive. I had come up for help, not for abuse and judgment. I'll fix him, I thought. I leave when I want to leave, not when Joe Gauld tells me to.

"No, I don't want to leave yet," I said. "I'd like to stay. Perhaps," I added ever so sweetly, "I do have something to learn."

Next case.

God, was I bored. And annoyed with what I considered manipulation of parental fear. I sat for exactly ten minutes. Then I gathered my notebook and handbag and left.

Jon was hanging about outside with a group of other youngsters, trying to look as though he hadn't been waiting for me.

The minute he saw me he asked, "Did you get nailed?"

"Did I ever!"

"I knew you would," said Jon. And drifted off with his friends.

I sat down beneath the trees and thought. Angry as I was at Gauld, and disappointed by the anxious mothers who had failed to protest my crucifixion, I knew I'd got what I deserved. I *was* an interloper. I was an uncooperative interloper, unable to understand what was going on or what they were attempting to do and making no effort to find out. Unwilling to find out. The other parents were cooperating even though they were in pain. And the school had a fine reputation, even though it was unorthodox. Or, perhaps, because it was unorthodox.

Why should I not be able to share my thoughts and fears, if other people could? I wasn't even trying.

Just like my kid. I knew he wasn't doing well. His grades were terrible and his attitude was arrogant, uncooperative. The staff had told me that. Yet they did not seem to think his case was terminal.

Maybe I'd better examine my own attitudes.

What, indeed, was I doing here?

I had come because they made me come. I'd no choice but to cooperate. It was part of the process of helping Jon. Obviously, I wasn't helping. But maybe I had it wrong. The staff insisted that the parents were asked to come not for the children, but for themselves. To learn about themselves. And that this could not be done without writing those damn vignettes and airing all the rest of your dirty linen in public.

And some of these parents have been coming back time after time, and will do so until their kids graduate. They can take it. They are willing to share each other's concerns.

I had a lot to think about.

I liked the school's values: honesty, openness, accountability for oneself, boundaries that could not be crossed with impunity, respect for excellence. Good, old-fashioned stretching oneself, mentally and physically. I liked the stress on the importance of exercise and outdoor, physical hard work. The enthusiasm of the young staff, even if they were a bit priggish. They believed that everybody had something to offer.

These values were my values, or had been. I had gotten into a far too insular world, so immersed in the business of promotion and publishing and status that I had begun to lose sight of other worlds. Apparently, my meetings with so many other women in workshops throughout the country—groups in which I had never been put on the spot—hadn't taught me as much as I'd thought.

The group finally broke up and parents, looking more relieved than pained, started coming out of the mansion. I got up from my shady spot as I saw Joe Gauld coming down the steps, and I stopped him as he walked past me. I looked him in the eye, reached out my hand, and said, "You really gave me a good kick in the ass. Maybe I deserved it. Let's be friends."

He flashed an enormous, toothy, wonderful smile, took my hand and shook it firmly, but at the same time very gently.

I liked the combination of gentleness, firmness, and warmth.

Something valuable probably is going on here, I said to myself. Something I seem to have been missing.

No overnight miracle transformed me. Years of being mired in guilt and feelings of inadequacy had given me a habit of trying to protect myself lest anyone find out what a rotten, ineffectual mother I believed I was. For the remainder of that weekend and for many Hyde encounters to follow, I periodically muttered in the cloakrooms, put others down, made wisecracks, and did anything I could to keep the focus off myself.

But I was focusing on myself. Trying to figure out what to do and how to be to make myself better for my children.

Wrong, said the group leaders and converted parents.

"Sometimes to focus on yourself means you are only looking inside. And what was the last positive thing you found there? Sometimes you have to say, Will you stop thinking about yourself all the time and start thinking about what you can do for these kids or the example you are setting for them? Some people are so busy doing external things, they never think about their own hearts. Other people focus on themselves so much that they neglect what they might be giving to their families and their friends and their coworkers."

So what's the middle line?

"Action! We're talking about taking the kind of action that

makes you change. That is what you can give to the kids. Accountability. You're accountable for your actions. They are for theirs. By the time they're in junior high, you no longer have complete control. You have to relinquish it. They are responsible for their own lives."

But they are incapable.

"They are not incapable. They have to have guidelines. They have to have structure. They have to recognize their accountability. They have to know when you are serious. We say, 'There's no smoking here.' They say, 'Sure, sure,' because they've heard that before at other schools. And we know that on the first night half the kids will be out somewhere in the woods smoking. But by the end of school that is no longer true. They find out that we are serious. The standards mean something. And once they find that out, they can start to have some self-esteem."

It had never struck me that Jon lacked self-esteem, but perhaps that was the missing ingredient. Or one way of defining it. Though there was no measurable improvement in him, I thought something might be going on. Larry Pray, who I discovered to be the leading figure of the Learning Center, had told me of his first direct encounter with my son. It had come soon after Jon's arrival at Hyde.

"He was pulling an attitude. He wasn't going to do this, he wasn't going to do that. And I explained, 'This is a school, and that is not your best. That's unacceptable.' He seemed sort of taken aback, as if he hadn't run up against that for a while!"

Which indeed he had not. Nor had he ever been taken aback when I had yelled at him about his flaws.

He was still smoking pot, but apparently not often. Once, according to his own account, he had been turned in by a fellow student. The next time he turned himself in because he figured he was going to get caught. He'd been ordered out of bed at the crack of dawn and sent on a work crew of similiar offenders to chop wood and rake leaves. I asked him about his studies. He shrugged. I waited for elucidation. None came. So he wasn't studying, and he was sulky.

Still, I felt mildly encouraged. He was showing some evidence of progress, making some kind of effort. It would be unrealistic of me, at this early stage, to expect much more.

By my second required visit to the Family Learning Center several months later I had reconciled myself to the Westchester seminars and was struggling to understand what it was that I was supposed to be learning.

Despite years of therapy and extensive reading of books on every aspect of psychology, I found it difficult to grasp the favorite Hyde cliché: feelings aren't facts.

Feelings are feelings, I kept hearing. They have nothing to do with facts. Feelings are the way you feel and you don't have to stuff them down or try to control them.

And finally I caught on.

You are not responsible for your feelings. You are responsible for your reactions to them. It is essential for parents and children to understand that anger, jealousy, and hatred are simply feelings. It is okay to feel like murdering somebody. The feeling is not the fact. There are times when tired, frustrated mothers and jealous siblings do feel murderous. And then they feel guilty. They are afraid they are going to translate that feeling into action. Everyone feels this way. It is a human feeling, and it is okay to be human.

The trick is to translate that feeling into positive action. Today, for example, I allow myself to feel the discomfort, identify it—resentment, rage, fear, guilt—and ask myself what action I can take. Sometimes simple identification is enough, and the feeling passes. Sometimes the issue must be tackled head-on and decisions made.

But it took a while for that realization to dawn.

One of the things that the school was trying to teach was that introspection without action was worthless, and that simply to try or claim to be trying was little better. The point of self-understanding was to impel you to take the actions that make you change. That, they said, was accountability; that was something that could be given to the kids.

They taught this in terms of a Chinese proverb I heard more times than I could count: "I hear, I forget. I see, I remember. I *do*, I *understand*."

"I do, I do, and I understand," they repeated. "You've got to do. You can't just talk. You can't just try. You've got to do to really understand things."

And again: "Growing up requires facing problems. Kids have to know this. So do the parents. We want to get dilemmas and problems right smack into the open. What is the truth, as best we can find it, about who you are? What do you see, how do you see it, what is your dream? Have you cashed it in, or not? How are you going to enact it? How healthy is your marriage? What is hurting you the most? What are your strengths? How can you use them?"

Then more commands: "You must understand the dynamics of the family. Family therapy is important. You have to be challenged. You have to do what's hard. You must work at what you're doing here. Work, work, work!"

To those of us who ventured to wonder why it was necessary for the school to be quite so hard on the parents, the answer was, "Just as you, the parents, are expecting your children to skate out on thin ice and try some new turns and see what's going to happen, so you too must do that. You can't just sit there safely on the sidelines on some kind of throne and assume it's all up to your child to do the work."

And then Joe or Larry or Ed or one of the others would add, "When there's a problem in the family, there are usually two responses. One is extreme and almost absurd guilt. The parent, more often than not the mother, says, 'It's all my fault.' But you can't assume that everything is your fault and mire yourself in guilt. And the other response is detachment. You see

what's happening and you assume it's all your child's fault. Or
society is to blame. So someone else has to bail you out. But
neither attitude is constructive.

"A more appropriate response is to get at some basic truths
and wrench them out. Here, that is a process that begins with
the vignettes and goes on with revealing your strengths and
weaknesses to yourselves, each other, and your kids. They
don't know what's going on with you. They only see the surface. You've got to open up."

The process of opening up was awful, sometimes unbear-
able. I heard things that I'd never dreamed of hearing in public, wrenched out of parents in agony—parents who had
brought their children to Hyde to cut them loose from the
family problems affecting their home lives. A husband was
drinking himself into oblivion and abusing the entire family. A
wife was a drug addict, another a suicide. A teenage daughter
lied about where she was going, stole from her mother's purse,
and had twice been caught shoplifting. Another had just had
her second abortion. A boy threatened his parents with bodily
harm when they refused his demands for money and smoked
pot in the bedroom he never cleaned up. A child had threatened to kill himself if his parents did not meet certain conditions. One borrowed cars for joyrides. Others beat up on their
brothers or sisters or neighbors, ran away from home and came
back stoned, were destroying their families, sabotaging their
education and their future. . . . But more often than not, the
problems were with the parents themselves, tormented men
and women who feared that their rocky marriages or personal
inadequacies were threatening their children.

The guilt and the pain and the misery were palpable.

Nothing that was happening to me or mine was nearly as
bad as some of the stories I heard. I felt better on that score,
yet at the same time relieved that many parents had no such
family delinquencies to report. I also felt comfort in the begin-
nings of involvement with other people. Contrary to my ex-

pectations, I was finding friends among people who came from Ohio, West Virginia, Indiana, Arizona, New Hampshire, and Westchester. No matter what our backgrounds, we all had similar doubts about ourselves and concerns for our children. I met on common ground with people completely unlike myself and found that much of what Jon and I had been going through could be seen as the normal problems of growing up in an increasingly hazardous and chaotic world.

The meetings were extraordinary experiences. Few were as passionately emotional or searing as the ones led by Joe, but not one was easy.

In the early stages, parents felt apprehensive and alienated. We sat in seminars feeling like strangers. Then all at once someone would say something with which others could identify, and we became an instant support group.

Or we would be in the most boring meeting in the world, going nowhere, and then a parent would say something so true to the mark that we were all galvanized and the whole tone changed completely.

Or our minds would be on idle and we'd sit there looking smug, thinking, That's got nothing to do with me, when suddenly *kaboom!* It *did* have something to do with us. And the camouflage of smugness was blasted away.

I remember one parent saying, "People here know me more truly than anywhere else. Here I am not a boss or a member of the board or a deacon at my church, with all those cover-ups. Here I can just be a human being."

And another said, "I hate this, but I have to do it. I get in my car and I drive to the school and get sicker and sicker the nearer I get to it. Why do I do it? Because I figure I might not like these people, I might not agree with them, I might want to fight with them to the death, but there is a sincerity here that I can't find anywhere else."

I was impressed by these statements. More than I wanted to be.

I saw things that made me change my own tune. I'd been defensive about turning my kid over to what I had seen as a rehab school. That's not what this was. No cures were offered for addicts, alcoholics, or incorrigibles of any sort. Many of the students were not there to be "shaped up," as some of us put it, but to benefit from the school's exemplary academic and disciplinary standards, as well as its outdoor facilities. Their parents had selected Hyde precisely because of its educational innovations. The school, in turn, accepted only those students who seemed likely to respond to its framework.

What was offered was a form of tough love, for parents and children alike. It was an experiment in living and in education, we were told. There were no magical, hard-and-fast "expert" solutions. This wasn't for everybody, they said. It could be hard; they knew that. But that's the way it was.

This is it, folks. Take it or leave it. You do your job, the kids do theirs, we do ours.

If you couldn't take it, you dropped out. Some children, some parents, ran away.

I could understand that.

The process of airing dirty linen in public was an agony to me. But what I minded most was what I still thought of as the *sadomasochistic group therapy*. The pain of it was excruciating. I was stripped beyond my defenses, stripped to the raw.

Near the end of my second visit to the Family Learning Center, Jon and I had a fight. He'd been busted twice again, his head was shaved as punishment, and he looked like a convict. He was encountering the consequences of his behavior, and he was hurting.

That night I went back to my motel room, preferring the privacy of it to the women's dormitory at the school, and licked my latest wounds. I'd had a hard time in the soul-baring sessions of the weekend and I was sad about my earlier encounter with Jon.

At midnight he came hammering on the door. I was fully

aware that his hot temper was a reflection of mine, but I didn't like it anyway. Now he was furiously angry and threatening to kick the door down.

"Will you please leave me alone," I yelled, "and get the hell out of here?"

"No! Let me in!"

"Then stop that noise first."

I let him in. His rage was almost frightening.

"What's the matter with you?" I demanded. "I've had a foul day. I don't need this goddamn agony I go through every time I come here. Why don't you just leave me alone, *please?*"

He stared at me for a minute and burst into tears. My big, tough kid with the convict's head was crying.

"What about my pain?" he asked. "You're so concerned about your own. What about mine?"

He had never said anything like that before.

"Well, if we are both in pain," I said, "I guess we need each other."

For the first time in ages, we gave each other an enormous hug.

I left the next day, as did the other parents, worried that Jon might run away.

He did not.

And I knew he was so resistant to authority that he would have run away if he hadn't needed to stay.

It was at last apparent to me that my son's exasperating acting out was a scream for help, for order in his life. He knew, perhaps better than I, that he needed this experience, an amalgam of academic training and rigorous discipline. Not to mention having his mother put through the wringer on a regular basis. "Where were the grown-ups?" he'd been pleading. "Why don't they shape up and do something? I'm only a kid. Help!"

I was proud of him for hanging in there and showed it in my frequent letters.

To his enormous credit, he went on hanging in there.

I felt that he was, for a change, profiting by positive peer pressure as well as firm adult authority. Perhaps the school was doing my job for me, but I was enormously glad for both his sake and mine. And I too was learning something. The experience of group exchange and idea participation was a revelation, albeit an unwanted one. I was finding comfort in the company and conversation of parents who had problems similar to mine, and worse.

I learned it was okay to air dirty linen in public—far better than keeping it moldering in the closet. I learned that it was too hard to try to do everything yourself, that it's not only legitimate but necessary to get help.

It was the sharing that I liked the most, the sharing of ideas and problems and solutions. After my initial stubborn resistance, I found it a relief to talk openly and listen to other people without feeling singled out for criticism or attack. We were all trying to find a better way.

As time went by I became increasingly involved with the parents and the activities demanded of us. I balked, I complained, I bitched, I complied, I kept track of my son's progress as he went from one work crew to another and gradually buckled down to occasional spurts of work, and I tried to show how proud I was of him.

I learned more and more about the depth and scope of parental guilt, fear, and feelings of inadequacy. There were many sensitive and caring fathers, but it seemed to me that the mothers flagellated themselves the most. My oldest son is in a juvenile correctional facility. What did I do wrong? My little one locks herself up in her room. What did I do wrong?

We talked, and we assuaged each other's guilts, and sometimes we found solutions, or at least a course of action. It struck me that Jon and I were both benefiting by the support of a community we wouldn't have been caught dead with perhaps a year before. What had happened?

We had been ready for change, and we had gotten lucky. Obviously, what we were experiencing was not a universal panacea. It might not, ultimately, prove to be the best answer for us. But meanwhile it was serving a valuable purpose. And the way it had come about was enlightening to me.

Another mother who had herself been troubled had reached out a hand to help, had shown us a possible way. Through her we had found a kind of extended family.

# CHAPTER TEN

# Just Another Struggling Human Being

WITH Jon away at school, Buffy's rage receded. As soon as she was sure he was not about to come back and reclaim his newly painted room, she made the most of her opportunity to be number-one kid. We were actually beginning to enjoy being mother and daugher together. I heard a lot more about myself as a wicked witch, but on the whole we got along and she seemed happy.

For years I had been consulting experts for various kinds of counsel. Now I had time to assess the advice that had been given to me as a mother and try to track down the wellsprings of the mother guilt and mother blame that pervade our culture. I would read those child development books to which I had given such short shrift as a young mother; I would interview psychologists, therapists, guidance counselors, educators; I would set out on a voyage of discovery, to find out where mothers like myself go wrong.

The first thing I gleaned from a brisk reading of the stack of instructive volumes available to mothers is that, for decades, telling mother what to do has been a national industry. Scarcely had mother been honored in 1908 with a special day of her own than her image of tender perfection began to waver under a shower of presumably well-meant criticism and instruction. With the passing of the years the shower became a deluge. Innumerable child-rearing experts, mostly male, appeared among us with new sets of rules, many of them no doubt sorely needed, but just as many ill advised, contradictory, and riddled with implicit accusations.

You think not? Read them. See how in their condescending tomes our mentors reveal a breathtaking bias toward the child and an almost total lack of interest in the mother.

"In the twentieth century," writes Dr. Arlene Skolnick, research psychologist at the University of California's Institute of Human Development, in the February 1978 issue of *Psychology Today*, "this traditional American obsession with children has generated new kinds of child-rearing experts—psychologists and psychiatrists, clothed in the authority of modern science, who issue prescriptions for child-rearing. Most child-care advice assumes that if the parents administer the proper prescriptions, the child will develop as planned. It places exaggerated faith not only in the perfectibility of the children and their parents, but in the infallibility of the child-rearing technique as well. But increasing evidence suggests that parents simply do not have that much control over their children's development; too many other factors are influencing it."

What we read and what we are told implies parental omnipotence, the possibility of parental perfection. It implies the possibility of total parental control. It implies that if we, the perfect ones, follow instructions, we will produce perfect children. Unfortunately, this is not quite the way it works.

Perhaps it was when disillusionment over our lack of perfection set in that various authors and other individual malcontents with big voices on the public stage began to tear the medals from mom and blame her for her children's woes. I don't know if there is a connection between the how-to books that lay motherhood on women like an onerous task—implying she is to blame for all hitches in her child's development—and the amateur mother haters who make mother look like a villain or a fool, but it seems to me that the soreheads may well have taken their cue from the earnest experts. It's quite possible that popularization and misinterpretation of Freudian psychology unleashed the antimother forces that lurk in the hearts of sons and daughters.

But it almost doesn't matter why other people blame us. The real questions are: Why do we let them? Why do we blame ourselves?

I asked myself these questions as I continued searching for the roots of mother blaming and mothers' feelings of inadequacy. I was sure, and still am, that our self-blame has much to do with our having resented our own mother for many things, particularly for her imperfections, vowing not to be like her as a parent, and then making the same mistakes. Many women of my mother's generation, including my mother, were very young and completely unprepared for the responsibilities of raising children. Motherhood is obviously a role that a girl cannot adequately rehearse or get right the first time.

Blaming our mothers for their shortcomings, and perhaps for those we feel we have inherited from them, we also blame ourselves as mothers. We, at least, should be perfect. Our primary task is motherhood, women's normal and natural task, so we really ought to be perfect at it.

And somehow we are not. We don't live up to our expectations, and we excoriate ourselves. So does society.

Wracked with guilt, aware of our inadequacies, we look for help. And it struck me that, again and again while seeking guidance, I had repeatedly been bulldozed, sidetracked, condescended to, exploited, and sneered at, particularly when looking for help with my children and their needs.

Not always, of course, and not always in the flesh. Books and articles begin the process of confusing mothers. Much of what I had read about child development and mothering methods, not to mention mothers' recommended conversational style with their children, made me feel that I was on some other wavelength. Could I possibly have dealt with Jon and Buffy in that way? I couldn't believe it. Yet I knew that what some of these people were saying was probably very sensible, particularly the much-loved Dr. Spock, and that I was no doubt to blame because I couldn't manage to fit their patterns.

I am simply not a good study. Therefore I cannot claim to have a case against any "expert," however an expert may be defined. Essentially I feel that child development professionals don't speak my language and I don't understand theirs. I had probably just not found the right ones for my needs.

But, often, what I read and what I was told reinforced my fears of what I was and what I was doing to my children.

Which made me wonder: Is this reinforcement of my negative feelings, or is it in fact the material that initiated them?

I didn't know then and I still don't know, but during that period and since then I have heard and read things that have astounded me. Mom gets it, and keeps getting it.

Mother was at fault for her child's schizophrenia.

We now know that researchers have found substances in the blood and urine of schizophrenic patients that are not present in the systems of normal people, and that certain chemicals are capable of producing symptoms of schizophrenia in normal people.

And yet for years, analysts, in trying to identify environmental factors as the causes of schizophrenia, attempted to pinpoint an individual as the scapegoat: mother. Again, not all experts were thus at fault, but not a few talked about the types of mothers who created schizophrenia in their children.

How could one avoid causing schizophrenia in one's child? Well, er.

Of course they didn't know.

Today the emphasis is on biochemical origins for the disease, and biochemical treatments for it, with some peripheral interest in the uses of psychotherapy as an adjunct to such treatment. Meanwhile, however, generations of mothers have had to live with the accusation that they had created schizophrenia in their children.

Mother was also at fault for her child's autism.

The common characteristic of autistic children is that they cannot respond to other human beings. They seem to be locked inside themselves, isolated from love and warmth. A common response has been that the condition is caused by parental coldness or neglect. Mother, a rejecting mother, was long the prime target of the critics.

"Over the years we have seen parents driven to desperation by analytically oriented psychiatrists who told them *they* were responsible for this child's illness," observes Dr. Louise Bates Ames, associate director of the Gesell Institute of Human Development in New Haven, Connecticut. "We tried to reassure them that autism was probably a physiological problem similar to retardation . . . but often we were a lone voice in the wilderness."

Many scientists still resist the idea—and, for all I know, quite rightly—that autism is either a birth defect or a form of genetic disease. Meanwhile, mothers suffer.

Jacqueline Susann, according to her husband, Irving Mansfield, was one such suffering mother. "Why did I do this to you?" she would cry. Her son was handsome, well built, sweet smiling—but somewhere else. It was shattering to both parents.

"Why did I let it happen?"

She didn't let it happen. It happened.

Jackie, according to Mansfield, carried an enormous burden of guilt over Guy. "She felt," he said, "that his problems were somehow her fault. She shouldn't have let nurses spend so much time with him. She should have been with him herself every moment. Maybe a nurse or a sitter had dropped him on his head or let him fall. She tortured herself with these thoughts, and when she slipped into a mood of self-blame, I could find no way to comfort her."

To add to the torment of the parents was the fact that not all the doctors agreed on the cause or definition of autism.

"Was he damaged before birth, during birth, afterward?" Mansfield asks. "Was he a perfectly normal baby during his first years, as he seemed to us and the doctors who took care of him? Or was it hopeless from the beginning?"

No answers were forthcoming. Yet the mother carried the burden of guilt, wondering endlessly what had gone wrong.

To me, the quintessential mother-blaming story is told by columnist Mary Kay Blakely. When Blakely was seventeen her brother was taken by her parents to the University of Chicago to be studied and treated for a mental illness then little understood. Initial procedures concentrated on rummaging through the mother's past to find the roots of the boy's problem.

"The doctors probed deeply for signs of 'overmothering' or 'dominance' or 'aggression' or 'neglect.' It was a luckless search, though, because under thorough examination, my mother proved to be uncommonly competent."

However, a relentless quest for "rejection" turned up something that had occurred when the boy was three. A pediatrician had bound the child's head in an attempt to flatten his ears.

"His tiny ears stuck out at what my mother thought was an adorable angle, but the doctor soon convinced her that they wouldn't be so adorable when he was a young man. They would mar his attractiveness and possibly threaten his sex life."

As the bindings were applied, the mother winced in sympathy and reached out a hand of comfort.

Wrong move.

"The pediatrician, a disciplined, authoritative man, disapproved of the soft-touch approach. He warned her of the dangers of coddling, especially of coddling boy babies. There were plenty of stories, back then, about how many young men's lives were wrecked by homosexuality because their mothers kissed them too much. Between his ears and his mother, the doctor believed that my brother had a very narrow chance of leading a normal life."

Blakely's mother was awake all that night, listening to the cries of her child and willing herself not to rush in and cradle him in her comforting arms.

Perhaps that was when he might have felt rejected, she told the probing doctors. He could not have known how she had longed to come to him, that she had held back because of her pediatrician's stern warnings.

Aha, now perhaps the investigators were onto something! Was it not possible, they suggested, that she had *indeed* been rejecting him because, deep down, she herself thought he was homely?

No, it was not possible. Anyone, *anyone*, could see that the boy was beautiful.

The relentless pursuit of something to pin on mother went on and on. "Until they finally asked the question I'll never forget: 'Well, why, then, did you follow the doctor's orders? Why didn't you trust your own instincts?'

"The brilliant doctors at the University of Chicago obviously thought the neighborhood baby doctor was an unenlightened soothsayer. Studies now prove, they said with authority, that too little nurturing does far more damage than too much. They supplied my mother with their facts, twenty years after she needed them.

"A vow formed in my mind that night, which, through the years, has evolved into this theory: 'Don't ever accept an expert's opinion if it violates your own, because the experts can change their minds. Ultimately, you stand alone, and your own instincts are the only safe ground to stand upon. Only your own explanations will be defensible in court some day.'"

Blakely concludes: "When I am hauled up for trial, I intend to take the doctors and pediatricians and principals and teachers and peer groups along with me—not as witnesses, but as codefendants. I am convinced that no mother should plead guilty alone. She is but one stamp on a life, and probably the one that hoped for it, and loved it, the most."

I dwell on this tale because to me it speaks volumes.

Experts of various stripes are here today and gone tomorrow, leaving their contradictions strewn in our paths. But their blame is always with us.

It is easy to find blame and blamers without looking. When it comes to telling mother what a bad job she's doing, everybody's an expert. Thumb sucking, bed wetting, shoplifting, rage, and violence are generally laid at the maternal door by the professional experts. Childish tantrums, bad manners, disobedience, loathing for spinach, reluctance to go to bed, an excessive attachment to the television set, poor marks, and acting spoiled or downtrodden are blame fodder for mothers-in-law, grandparents, aunts, and childless friends. Screaming in public, tipping cans off supermarket shelves, running into the street against the DON'T WALK sign, being obstreperous on the crosstown bus, and punching out the little girl next door elicit mother blaming and insulting advice from cashiers, clerks, bus drivers, neighbors, crossing guards, and passing bag persons.

A year passes, and where are we? The child is a year older and is, as we say, "acting out" in different ways. The child-guidance experts upon whom we have been relying have changed their minds about the goals and techniques they have set for mothers and children. The only consistency to be found is with relatives, neighbors, schoolteachers—and, often, other mothers. Their accusatory message seems not to have changed with the changing times. Perhaps there is some sense of security in this.

My friend Wendy says, "The world is an irrational and insecure place. It causes us to look for ways to assign guilt. If you can point fingers at guilt, you are finding a way to impose order. Everybody is very quick to assign guilt to other mothers. If we were less judgmental of other mothers, we could be more forgiving of ourselves."

She is, I feel, right. But even forgiving others, it is hard to forgive ourselves if others do not forgive us. And it is not easy to understand others if their function is to offer guidance and they give us stones.

I have had many encounters with experts in my time. I think the first (apart from the sterility doctors) was the nursery school director who interviewed me when I was looking for a kindergarten for Jonny. *She* interviewed *me*. And I acted like a kid. The interchange was a sort of personality test. And I cheated.

As I knew from the sandbox set of which I was an unwilling part at that time, nursery school fever was at a pitch and the competition for the one Martin and I had selected was feverish. It was important to us that Jonny be accepted because the school had a fine reputation and was only a few blocks from our home. Furthermore, it was permissive, and we liked the idea that Jonny's ingenuity and eagerness to learn would be given free rein.

School being mother's business more than father's, I made the appointment for Jonny and me. We were both to be evaluated by the school's director, fortunately not in the same room at the same time. He would not be considered until I had passed muster.

Although Jon was already showing signs of becoming a little bit of a behavior problem, I wasn't worried that he would flunk his interview. Bright and beguiling as he was, he was bound to appeal to educators who encouraged flexibility and self-expression. I, however, was not necessarily of the right material, and I felt that my job was to convince the director that I was an acceptable parent.

I asked friends and neighbors, a couple of whom were teachers, what to expect. They briefed me on the appropriate child-development books to bone up on, the questions to anticipate, and the answers that would probably be welcomed. I did my homework well and approached the interview with brittle confidence.

Toilet training? "Oh, yes, he's toilet trained. No, I didn't do it. He trained himself when he was ready." The fact was that his nanny had toilet-trained him at fourteen months, but I knew that I couldn't tell the woman interviewing me that. *A nanny?*

I also didn't tell her that I picked Jonny up and took him to the potty every night before I went to bed. Just in case.

Breast feeding? A friend had told me that this woman set great store by breast feeding. I was tempted to lie, but I didn't have the guts.

"I wanted to," I said sadly, "but I couldn't."

Sibling rivalry? Here we were on interesting ground. The woman knew from our application form that Jonny was an only child. *I* knew from my informants that sibling rivalry was a big thing with her, a good thing. Just why it was good I didn't know. I hadn't found my own case of sibling rivalry to be particularly pleasant or productive. But if that was what was wanted, okay. Perhaps they figured that into every youngster's life a little grief must fall and that juvenile friction fitted the bill.

"We are adopting a baby," I said demurely. "I expect there will be a certain amount of sibling rivalry."

The director smiled understandingly.

I had scored another point.

It did not occur to me until after Jonny was accepted that an interview is a two-way street. In my anxiety to get my child into what I thought was the right school, I neglected to make sure that it was right for him.

My doubts began almost immediately. Jon was tall for his age at that time and had excellent manual dexterity. In his play school the year before he had shown himself to be glib and precocious, probably because he spent a lot of time with adults and adolescents. And he already knew how to read and write. I assumed he would be put in the advanced class, for which he was old enough in any event.

No, he wasn't, said the director. He was two weeks too young to be eligible for the advanced class. He would be placed in intermediate. Girls, she told me, mature faster than boys, and it would be good for him to be the oldest boy in his group.

But that would be no challenge for him, I observed.

We do not believe in competition, I was told. Each child was unique, and could best find his or her own strengths in a noncompetitive atmosphere.

I wasn't sure that my unique child would thrive under those conditions. He needed something to measure himself against. And if he failed in one category he would succeed in another, thus finding his own strengths anyway. He would be bored silly in the baby class.

But into the baby class he went, standing out as the oldest and tallest. I didn't care for this, but felt that the educators must know better than I.

Even as he began his schooldays, I belatedly observed something that should have struck me sooner. There were finger paintings on the classroom walls. Selected finger paintings. Those that were considered the best. The minute you select children's finger paintings to pin on the walls, I told myself, you have competition. There are some contradictions here.

There were also some problems for Jonny. He was bored silly. Being with the "little kids" was beneath his dignity and he was not interested in the activities offered.

During the year he became a full-time behavior problem, aggressive and manipulative with his little classmates and pushy and demanding at home.

When Jonny had been disruptive in class just once too often the director suggested that we seek help for him. She gave me the name of a psychologist with imposing European credentials. When I called to make an appointment for Jonny and myself, Dr. Tatti said he wanted to talk to Martin and me before seeing the child.

Martin was supposed to meet me at the doctor's office. He

was late. I assured the psychologist that he would be along soon. Something must have come up at the office. Ordinarily he was the most punctual of men.

"Very well, let us begin then," said the doctor. "I understand your little boy is in trouble." He paused and gave me a piercing look. At least, I felt pierced. He said, "I find the problem usually has its genesis in the mother."

"Oh?" What could a mother say?

"Tell me, please, about his sexual habits."

I couldn't believe my ears. Sexual habits? At four?

"I don't think he has any," I said feebly.

An impatient shake of the head, and a *tch tch* sound.

"Please, does he masturbate?"

"Well, I guess he does play with himself. Just to find out where all the parts are and what they do."

A frown. "What does he call his penis?"

I felt like saying that he called it Sigmund, but Dr. Tatti intimidated me. "I think he calls it his penis," I said. And added defensively, "That's what I call it."

The questions kept coming. Martin did not show up to help me out. When the forty-five-minute hour was up the man said, "I can see you and your son next Tuesday afternoon at three."

This was one of the few times I trusted my own judgment.

"Thank you, I'll call you," I said. I had no intention of seeing Tatti again, never mind letting him see Jon.

I asked Martin that night what had happened to him and he said he'd forgotten about it. I told him it didn't matter; it would have been a waste of his time to rush uptown to see that man. Still, something had to be done.

Next stop: my pediatrician, Virginia Pomeranz.

"How much time does his father spend with him?" she asked.

Woman talk. Women know. Some, anyway.

Martin and I agreed that the boy needed more time with his

father. That was when Martin started doing a great many things with Jonny, including taking him on small camping trips in Maine, and our son's disruptive behavior improved considerably.

Yet I continued to be cowed by people I regarded as experts, perhaps because I had and still have enormous respect for expertise and learning.

One year, the kids and I went away for the summer, sharing a house on the Maine coast with another family. Martin came up Thursdays for long weekends, as did his friend Matthew, who happened to be a child therapist. For the rest of the time Vanessa (Matthew's wife) and I, her two children, and my two were together in a beautiful, rambling summer house on a wild and wonderful bluff overlooking the sea.

Matthew and his schoolteacher wife were bringing their children up by the book, and those kids were dramatically different from the little Caines. It took only a couple of weekends for Martin and me to realize how intently our housemates observed their children and discussed their every move with solemn psychoanalytic interpretations. They were so controlling that they had the two little girls go to bed in their underpants so that they wouldn't play with themselves, which somehow made me doubt the parents' wisdom.

Martin and I were even a little amused when they started analyzing Jonny's behavior too—Buffy being exempt because she was still lurching around happily in her playpen—and none too subtly suggesting that Jon should go to bed earlier, that he should learn to share, that he must be taught to obey, that I was deficient in my mothering style.

But they were intelligent, amusing people, and the kids were having fun together—that is, when Jonny wasn't "overexcited," "aggressive," "selfish," or whatever Matthew labeled him at any particular time. No doubt about it: Jon's galloping ego and exuberance often got beyond me. It was obvious that I was not in full control.

Matthew took a vacation week in July and Jon chose that time to be more than usually sassy. Vanessa tried to be diplomatic, but Matthew voiced his disapproval more and more openly. One morning, as Matt sat reading on the deck, Jon and I had an exchange of words that climaxed in a dazzling display of freshness and disobedience by my son.

I knew Matt was taking it all in and I had had enough of his criticism. I had to show that I knew something about being a good mother, that there were limits of misbehavior beyond which I would not permit my child to stray.

"You can't talk to me like that," I said crisply. "Come here this minute and apologize."

Jon made a face and turned away from me. I went after him, furious that he was acting this way in front of Matthew, with some idea of catching him and spanking him. He ran, laughing. And he ran right through a closed glass door.

Glass and blood were all over the place. Blood poured down his face, over his eyes, down his neck, his arms, his legs, his entire body. "I can't see!" he screamed. I held him close, his blood all over me.

Suddenly everyone was in motion. Matthew running for the car. The housekeeper bringing ice. Vanessa calling the state troopers to ask for an escort to the state hospital in Augusta.

A frantic call to Martin's office. Tires squealing, siren wailing, mother in the waiting room shivering with fear.

Blood all over his face and in his eyes. Great shards of bloody glass on the porch floor, scattered there by his hurtling body. What had I done? Was he blind? Would he be scarred all over his face and body and even his mind? Would he hate me, be afraid of me?

Then inexpressible relief. His eyes were undamaged, main arteries intact, nothing vital had been injured. Wounds were clean and the doctor was suturing the cuts.

Over a hundred stitches later, Jonny looked at me through his bandages and smiled with pride. He had more stitches than any other kid in Maine. I had made his summer.

*I* was the one who was scarred for life.

Later, back at the house, I went to my room, shut the door, and collapsed on my bed. I had done the brave mother bit and kept myself together. Jon was in the hospital and okay, Martin was on his way to Maine, and now it was safe for me to let go. Crying is hard for me, but this time I cried.

Muffled consultations outside the door. Sounds of Matthew getting irritated. Intimations that Matthew is about to give me the benefit of some of his training. Requests for me to come downstairs and talk about it. More sobs from me. Matthew's voice hardens, as much as Matthew's voice ever hardens.

"Stop crying, Lynn! This is *his* castration anxiety, not yours."

Oh, Matthew. Instead of being your caring self, you comfort me with jargon.

Later yet, still in my bedroom at the house on the bluff, I reviewed the scene of the morning. Was it my fault that Jon had gone through that door?

Well, yes. I had been so concerned with what Matthew thought about me and my mothering style that I had nearly killed my child. And I couldn't blame Matthew for that.

Still, I did, a little. His criticism had impelled me to do a damn fool thing that I would not otherwise have done. Matt was a child therapist, practicing on his friend Lynn. It was hard to believe that his attitude was not in some measure responsible for mine.

In time, I became increasingly disenchanted with certified experts. Not all, but many of them. Particularly educators.

When Buffy was seven I got fed up with permissive education and decided to take her out of the school she had been attending and put her in a more structured situation. The school of my choice required that I have her tested for scholastic aptitude and social adjustment, so I set up a test appointment for her.

I almost changed my mind when I realized how upset she

was at the prospect of leaving her schoolmates, of yet another upheaval in her young life, but I truly believed she would benefit by the change, so I went ahead with my plans.

Buffy did not. She had a plan of her own.

As she told me later, she had devised an ingenious way of remaining at her school. If she failed her I.Q. examination, she reasoned, no other school would want her.

And so she gave answers she knew to be wrong. Mainly in arithmetic, at which she excelled. Four plus four equals nine, three times four equals twenty, five twelves are forty-eight, and so on and so on.

The psychologist who tested her concluded that she was intellectually and socially immature. Buffy not only knew all the wrong answers, but refused to "relate" to her. Advice: the child needs help.

Well, perhaps she did, but not of the kind I thought was being suggested. Truth to tell, I was really impressed that little Buffy had been smart enough to think of cheating on her test in order to remain in a school where she felt liked and understood. This time I was not intimidated by the expert. Buffy stayed where she was and worked just a little harder.

I was rather surprised that the psychologist hadn't caught on to Buffy's tricks and thought them worthy of discussion, but ultimately I was glad that she hadn't.

Not long afterward I heard a couple of other "the child needs help" stories that made me very glad some mothers consult professionals and then rely upon their own instincts.

When my friend Karen's boy was seven, he suddenly became disruptive in school. "He wasn't fully involved," Karen said, "he wasn't following directions, he was inattentive and he talked a lot. I was called in by the school and his teacher recommended that I take Tommy to a therapist.

"I was dead against it. Even though he had become an acute behavior problem, I didn't want him to go to a therapist. For one thing, it would brand him, particularly to himself. For another, I felt I could work on and work out with him. He's a very intelligent little boy, and he was bored. I also had the strong sense that there was a personality conflict between him and his teacher.

"So I decided that I would work things out with him, then if the problems persisted I could take some other action. I made it clear to him that his behavior in school was unacceptable and that an adjustment would have to be made. Since then he's calmed down. I don't know how much effect I had on him, but I feel he was just going through a stage. I'm glad I didn't take him to a therapist."

Alice's little girl was hyperactive, acting up and being aggressive in class. School authorities advised that the child be taken to a psychiatrist. Alice did so, and after a cursory examination and discussion, this expert prescribed Ritalin, a mood-altering drug used with increasing frequency in special schools or classes of pathologically hyperactive children.

Alice said, "No way. I will not give my child drugs. I start her on drugs now, what is she going to be on when she's a teenager?"

Within a year, and without drugs, Alice's child—like many of her age group—came out of her hyperactive phase and found other ways to disturb her teachers and her mother.

Greenwood. Where the staff and parents weren't even supposed to speak to each other. What sort of farce of expertise was this? How can a child's education, if that is what it was, be so separated from the rest of his life that teachers and parents do not even meet? Hyde was hell, but at least Jon and I were going through something together, we both knew what we were going through, and we shared the school's objectives.

Still in my investigative mood, I talked to several therapists. One said she believed that motherhood was a full-time career. Women shouldn't have children, she said, if they were not willing to stay home with them, at least in the early years. Say, until the youngest child was five or six.

I don't think many of us have that choice anymore, I observed.

But if you are looking for causes of mother guilt and mother blame, you have one right there.

Another suggested that my daughter's asthma was psychosomatic and that I was the cause. Buffy thought so too. I didn't.

A third unwittingly made me aware that it was not ultimately helpful, to me at least, to work on problems on a one-to-one basis. Whatever such a method might do for my own self-understanding, it did not help me deal with people and things outside myself. I needed to get outside myself.

Many of the authority figures whose work I read and with whom I spoke in the early part of my quest seemed dogmatic, unrealistic, detached, gimmicky, and either openly or implicitly critical of parents, especially mothers. They also, from time to time and from person to person, demonstrated an inconsistency that is said to be characteristic of bad mothers—indeed, of nearly all mothers and other human beings. Mothers are supposed to be, are urged to be, consistent. But those who advise us—are they consistent? Even the tried and true, or partly true, child development experts whose names have become familiar to us throughout the years cannot be consistently relied upon. There is much that is good in them, and more than a few mothers have found guidance suitable for themselves and for their children. But even experts change their minds.

Oh, sorry, they say, that's something I thought seven years ago. I don't think that today.

Well, thanks a lot. Too bad I bought your first printing, not your third. You've learned something? Swell. Meanwhile my kid's eleven and he's still not toilet trained.

Disillusionment with the experts was setting in, and disillusionment also with my own ability to assess them. Could this be yet another flaw in me? Were they onto something I simply didn't understand?

Then I read something that cheered me enormously.

Psychologist Arlene Skolnick, of the University of California at Berkeley, wrote in the February 1978 issue of *Psychology Today*:

Popular and professional knowledge does not seem to have made parenting easier. On the contrary, the insights and guidelines provided by the experts seem to have made parents more anxious. Since modern child-rearing literature asserts that parents can do irreparable harm to their children's social and emotional development, modern parents must examine their words and actions for a significance that parents in the past had never imagined. Besides, psychological experts disagree among themselves. Not only have they been divided into competing schools, but they also have repeatedly shifted their emphasis from one developmental goal to another, from one technique to another.

Yes, that's what I thought! But what does a mother do?

Recently I asked several dozen young mothers out in grass-roots country away from New York where they sought advice when they needed it. Some looked surprised, thought a while, then came up with Mom or Dr. Spock.

Other answers were: "mother, father, physician, church"; "husband, pediatrician, mother, sister, and close friends"; "mother, sisters, grandma, God." Several said, "friends who have good children," or, "I look around for a good product—healthy, stable kids—and then I ask their mother." One young woman said, "I ask my mother, sister, grandmother, mother-in-law, pediatrician, and my friends, check the books, then do what I wanted to anyway."

She's the one, I feel, who's on the right track: do your homework. Take action—shop around to find the help you need. Get referrals. Interview the recommended specialists. Evaluate. Then trust your own judgment. For yourself, for your own child, it's generally the best there is.

Of course, one still wonders what to make of all those highly qualified experts who confidently proffer so much help and often turn out to have feet slightly tinged with clay.

Quite coincidentally, I found a quotation I like in the book *If You Meet the Buddha on the Road, Kill Him!* by psychotherapist Sheldon B. Kopp: "The most important things that each man must learn, no man can teach him. Once he accepts his disappointment, he will be able to stop depending on the therapist [for therapist, read expert, educator, authority, or what you will], the guru who turns out to be just another struggling human being."

And, particularly if he is a mother blamer, a rather old-fashioned one too, it seems to me.

Just another struggling human being.

# CHAPTER ELEVEN

# Magical Mother Eyes

STRUGGLING along in my own way, I pursued my quest for helpful experts. Belatedly, it had occurred to me to check around among my own friends and acquaintances in the mental health field, people who inevitably use some of the jargon of their trade, but nevertheless make sense.

"What is this thing called guilt?" I asked.

"Painful feelings having to do with falling short of your standards or social standards that you have made your own," says analyst Edith Gould. "Often, a screen for other, less acceptable, emotions, impulses and fantasies."

Oh.

"I am going to tell you an interesting story," said Leah Schaefer, once a jazz singer and now a psychologist. "One Christmas, Thomas and I—Thomas is the man I live with—decided to visit his mother in Florida. I'm crazy about trains, so we made plans to go by rail. A train ride to Fort Lauderdale takes about twenty-four to twenty-five hours. My daughter, then fourteen, decided that she didn't want to go with us. There were school parties and she really wanted to stay home. I realized there was no reason why she couldn't, but I told her I would like her girl friend to stay with her because we were going to be gone for about five or six days and I didn't like the idea of her being alone.

"But she really wanted to stay alone. It made her feel very grown-up. And indeed she was an extremely responsible person. She'd been baby-sitting for other kids since she was ten, so why couldn't she baby-sit for herself? Anyway, ours is a very safe building. We always doublelock our doors, the doormen know and like us, we have many nice neighbors, and the ones across the hall are very near and dear. In short, she'd be as safe alone as she would if I had been in the house. I can't exactly thwart a burglar myself.

"So we left home at four o'clock in the afternoon and got on the train.

"In the middle of the night I woke up. 'What have you done?' I asked myself. 'Are you crazy, letting a fourteen-year-old child stay in a New York apartment alone? Do you realize what might happen? Do you realize she could be run over by a car in the street? My God, how could I have done such a thing? And there's no telephone on the train, no way to make a phone call to her.'

"I got up, went looking for the conductor, and I said, 'When do we make a stop where I can use a telephone?' 'At noontime,' he said, 'we make a stop in Jacksonville. We stop there for half an hour.' And he gave me the number of the car that stopped exactly in front of the telephone booth so that I could be the first person to use the phone.

"I went back to bed knowing that I had to sweat this out until noon.

"Then I got to thinking, and I said to myself, 'What do you think you could do if you were in the city? She could have an accident while you were there. She could have an accident going to school. What makes you think, because you are her mother and you wish her well, that she is never going to have an accident because you are in the city? What makes you think that your open eyes are so magical that as long as you are paying attention and you are looking, you can ward off any bad luck that might happen to her?'

"And I realized how narcissistic it was, this idea that as long as I am in the city nothing bad would happen to her—that when I leave the city and I'm no longer looking at her, all kinds of things will go wrong. It was such *grandiosity*. I said to myself, 'What is the matter with you? You really *are* crazy.'

"That calmed me down a little, and then I went back to sleep. Next day at noon on the dot I made my phone call to Katie. She was enjoying herself and everything was just wonderful. She had of course taken all the precautions I would have taken and which she knew very well how to take. It was such a revelation to me—the grandiosity of the assumption that if I'm watching with my magical mother eyes, no harm will come to her."

What a fascinating concept, I thought. Most, maybe all, mothers have those magical mother eyes. But of course the assumption of such mystical power and control is grandiose.

Yet this was the first time it had been pointed out to me that the guilt, fear, and self-blame of the mother may be rooted in grandiosity. This is more than thinking that if you are not a perfect mother you are a failure. It means that you feel you can influence events that are totally beyond your control, and that if your influence fails, you feel yourself a failure as a mother.

At least, I think that's what it means.

But this was surely an acquired feeling. It made me want to get back to basics, to the feelings of young mothers, particularly first-timers, whose self-doubts and fears seem to arrive along with the baby. I recalled a line I had read by psychologist Ellen Frank of the Western Psychiatric Institute in Pittsburgh: "A new mother thinks she will always love her little infant. Then the baby cries for three hours and she hates its guts."

And, afterward, her own.

Spurred by this thought, I called again on Dr. Virginia Pomeranz, the New York pediatrician who knows my kids almost as well as I do and is regarded by many New Yorkers as the patron saint of mothers.

It is part of the human condition to feel guilt or remorse when we, as parents, direct unworthy emotions toward vulnerable little human beings, and to feel painfully responsible when something happens that we think we should have been able to prevent. But most of us don't realize that these feelings are universal. And we don't understand that our expectations are based on the twin myths that mothers ought to know instinctively how to nurture and otherwise meet the needs of their children, and that babies—unless born defective in some way—are bound to be lovable and rewarding to mothers who are not themselves defective.

"I think there's a big identity crisis here," says Dr. Pomeranz. "Most women I deal with feel competent in their work, for which they have received training. Or they've been to college and learned certain academic skills. But when it comes to motherhood, they suddenly take on a new role for which they've had no education or training at all."

What happens is that the young mother looks at the little helpless infant who is her first baby and is either its instant slave or else doesn't quite know what to make of it. Some mothers, during the first few days or months of motherhood, would like to call the whole thing off. It isn't what they expected at all. The idea, and certainly the ideal, of motherhood is almost a falsehood, Dr. Pomeranz says.

"Most women want to feel there is a natural bonding between mother and child," she observes. "They've looked forward to having a child. They enjoy going through pregnancy and natural childbirth, and the whole daddy bit in the delivery room. They feel they have to love this little creature. He or she is *theirs*. But when the parents get the child to the privacy of their own home, without all the delivery people and relatives and visitors hanging around, they very often look at the baby and say, 'This isn't what I expected. I expected a blond, curly-haired, chubby-cheeked, pink and creamy baby, and I got this long, scrawny, dark-haired, mottled-looking kid, and it really isn't what I had in mind at all.' "

Even the personality isn't what they ordered. It is usually just a matter of getting to know the baby, says Dr. Pomeranz, but many young mothers are less than thrilled with what fate and their genes have handed them. Blown away is their vision of the beautiful, smiling, clean, sweet-smelling, smooth-skinned baby who eats nicely and coos and gurgles and chuckles and sleeps the night through. Instead there is the reality of an unappreciative, egocentric creature, afflicted with diaper rash and possibly colic; noisy, messy, inconsiderate, completely unaware and uncaring of its parents' cares and needs. Never mind that mother or father is exhausted or has a splitting headache. The little elemental being comes first. "This can go on for years," Dr. Pomeranz says. "It's me me me me *me*. And a lot of people get pretty disillusioned."

And frustrated and anguished and quite often afraid.

A child who snuggles and can be easily comforted when it cries makes a mother feel warm and tender toward it. Mother feels like a success, and that's a wonderful feeling. You have an amiable baby and you feel a bond with it. On the other hand, if you have a child who cries a lot and there seems to be nothing you can do to make it stop, you get furious with the brat.

What you say to yourself and the child, according to Dr. Pomeranz—and I know this to be true—is, "How dare you not respond to all my efforts? I feed you, rock you, burp you, love you, change you, this-and-that you, and you don't respond, you miserable little rat!"

And very often there comes a time when you get a surge of hatred for the baby and you want to throttle it or throw it out of the window. But you don't.

I know this doesn't come as news to a lot of mothers, but what may be news is that *most mothers feel murderous at one time or another in their lives* and they feel almost as guilty as if they had actually done the dreadful deed.

But feelings aren't facts, as I had learned at Hyde.

And just as many mothers are scared that they will accidentally do something that will result in the death of the helpless little creature in their care. The baby will roll off the changing table or drown in its tiny tub while the mother answers the phone. Or choke on food or swallow something sharp or, as it becomes more active, crawl out of a window that shouldn't have been left open, run into the street and get hit by a truck, or get stolen by a stranger when its mother's back is turned.

For many mothers, the infancy period is the hardest time of their lives. For others, of course, the terrible teens are the worst. But young, first-time mothers characteristically are terrified of making mistakes.

"This is the bottom line," says Dr. Pomeranz. "I say to mothers, 'You think you don't know what you're doing and you're scared to death you're going to kill this baby. You're just like everybody else.' And when I say this, the mother usually heaves a great sigh of relief because I understand how she feels and because she's not an abnormal person. A woman may have gone to law school for two or three years or become an executive secretary or even studied medicine, and all of a sudden she is stuck with a library of child-care books, all of them conflicting, and presented with this baby, and by God she doesn't know a thing about it!

"A lot of mothers confess that they go through the infancy period because they have to, but they really don't enjoy it. The usual question is, of course, 'What did I do wrong?' Now, that's maternal guilt talking! There always has to be a culprit, and it's usually mom. What did I do wrong that my kid got an earache? Did I take him out too much or am I not taking him out enough? What did I do wrong that my child fell and his tooth cut his lip? What did I do wrong that he doesn't eat? What did I do wrong that he eats too much? 'What did I do wrong' is always the opening gambit. It's ridiculous. Fathers never come in and say, 'What did I do wrong that my kid got sick?' It's the mothers who always have this guilt. I don't know where they get it from, but they sure do have it."

"How do you teach them to get over this?" I ask, because I know that Virginia works as closely with the mothers as with the children.

"I lose no opportunity to tell a mother that she is a good mother, a competent mother, she knows her child, she calls me when it's appropriate. She never lets her child get very sick. Nobody needs to tell her when her child is not well. She knows it right away. And I do this at every conceivable opportunity, to let her know that she understands her child better than anybody and to give her the confidence to trust her instincts. She knows that when a child is running a temperature of 101 at night the child is not deathly sick. And she knows not to wait until that temperature climbs to 104 before calling me. I have to reinforce that all the time. I try to make each mother understand that she's doing a good job.

"Most mothers are so quick to say when they've done wrong, and so reluctant to say when they've done right. I want them to realize how often they are right. And I tell them that children are remarkably resilient. They certainly can tolerate the normal amount of mistakes that a normal parent is going to make. No one is perfect. I say to them, 'If the kid turns out well, you're not going to take all the credit, are you? Well, don't take all the blame if he doesn't, given all the other influences that come into a child's life at a very tender age. If you are being told you're doing a good job, then you will do a good job. But don't take anyone's advice if it goes against the grain. Take it only if you feel comfortable with it.' "

Even your pediatrician's advice?

"*Especially* your pediatrician's. This is terribly important. If you feel your pediatrician is unsympathetic—when you call and feel embarrassed that you might be asking a silly question, or the doctor makes you feel it's a silly question—then that's not the doctor for you. You have to have a pediatrician who will say, 'Mrs. So-and-so, nobody knows your child as well as you do, so if he's not feeling right why don't you bring him in today and let me see what's wrong with him?' Which is what I say.

"Now I can't always do something. The child may be

teething, the child may be coming down with a viral sore throat, which I can't do much about, but at least I can prepare you for what's in store. The chances are, you are right when you think there is something wrong with the baby, and if you don't call when you feel like it, the child might get terribly sick. *Trust* your feelings. You know when the baby isn't right. You know when you're not comfortable with your pediatrician. *You have to listen to your instincts.*"

I'm beginning to.

A mother may not realize it, but a mother knows.

"Why do so many mothers feel guilty over the slightest little thing?" I asked Dr. Ronee Herrmann, a psychiatrist.

"I think women are trained to feel guilty," she replies. "They are trained in this culture to believe they are responsible for other people's happiness. So that when anybody is unhappy, there is an automatic button pushed that the woman should fix it. I think not just as a mother, but in any situation.

"And as a mother of a child going through various stages: I don't know if you're aware how little is known about human development. Only within recent years have there been serious attempts to find out how people develop. There's no such thing as an expert. Just people who set themselves up as experts. They're all talking about their own theories, and they don't know any more than you or I do who is right or who is wrong. That is premise number one, and that is very guilt releasing!"

"No experts?" I ask, shocked, thinking of all the child-development books I had recently read.

"None," says Ronee firmly. "There are many theories, but we really do not know why or how people develop as they do. All the so-called experts are talking from their own bias: what they think or feel, because of what they've observed. But that's all it is, a matter of bias. The process of development is not established. There are many undefined factors. Why should some apparently stable children of apparently stable parents turn out well and others not? There are so many kids I've seen over and over again who are able to turn outward and success- fully use the adults in their environment to maintain their equilibrium. And then there are certain kids who can't— through shyness, introversion, who knows what.

"But of course the bottom line is that women are taught they are responsible for making everybody happy, so if there's anything wrong, they are supposed to fix it. That's the tape we have. So if anything is wrong, we get anxious. The way I see it, there are things you should feel guilty about. Obviously if your behavior is obnoxious, you should feel guilty about it. But I believe that 95 percent of mothers do the best they can—the best they're capable of doing at the time—so whatever hap- pened to make them feel guilty happened because they could not help themselves at that particular moment. And each of us can change. At no matter what age, people can change."

"How does a mother overcome her guilt?" I ask. "How does she let go of it?"

"How can't she let go? You have to wonder why somebody would want to hang onto guilt. Why do they need it? Because I really don't think it's appropriate for people who try their best. Right from the first session, I do not let my patients use the words *right* and *wrong*. I don't think there are such things. Those words are to be banished from their vocabulary forever. We do what we feel we should at a particular time in terms of our world view, our values, and our priorities."

And the rotten mood we happen to be in at the time, I thought.

"But I agree with you," Ronee was saying, "that most moth- ers feel guilty, inadequate, and fearful that they will damage their children. And when they tell me that, I say, 'Good morn- ing, Jesus Christ.' Because you've got to think you are a god to believe that you have that much power."

So. Another suggestion that we guilt-ridden mothers are suffering from—or possibly enjoying—delusions of grandeur. Grandiosity, divinity—what really is the difference?

"About those so-called experts," Dr. Herrmann added, "it is most important that mothers understand what they are about and how to evaluate them. You must realize that what they are telling you is *their* world view. There's no reason, if you don't agree with them, for you not to believe that your own world view is just as valid. That's what I tell people all the time. *Use your head.* You can come up with as good ideas as anybody else.

"I used to be a child psychiatrist and mothers would come to me and say that they felt this or that physical problem was wrong with their kid and that they had tried to tell the doctor and nobody had believed them. But 85 percent of the time, the mothers were right. Mothers are right more often than they realize. No one knows your child as well as you do.

"Yes, you make mistakes. But you have to forgive yourself if you make a mistake, because you are human."

"You have to consider the nature and purpose of guilt," said Dr. Willard Gaylin, a New York psychiatrist and psychoanalyst. "Guilt, like shame and pride, is a positive emotion. It is crucial to the kind of species we are. Just as fear and anxiety are guides to individual survival, driving us to the kind of behavior that presumably protects us as individuals, so do guilt and shame and pride drive us toward group survival.

"That is important, because people tend to be much too individualistic in our society, tend much too much to think of the individual as if he actually existed in isolation, even though we know that simply is not true. Networks of human beings are necessary not just for our comfort or pleasure, but for our survival as human creatures. That cannot be underlined too much."

I thought fleetingly of the network I had found at Hyde and of my own isolation before finding it. I knew that wasn't exactly what Gaylin meant, but it suited my personal—maybe overindividualistic—view of human survival.

"We are a colonial animal," said Dr. Gaylin, "and if you deprive human beings of contact with others, we deteriorate into something that isn't quite human. So guilt and shame, though painful emotions, are excruciatingly important for directing us to do that which may be good for the community on which we are ultimately dependent and restraining us from harming it."

He paused. "Guilt," he said, "is the guardian of our goodness."

To be without it, and without shame, is to be without conscience.

But guilt, like virtually everything with the power for good, can also be a misused or negative emotion.

"Emotions must be appropriate. If you feel guilt inappropriately, it is as much a problem as it is to feel anxiety inappropriately or pleasure inappropriately. If you feel guilty when you have done wrong according to a set of internalized standards, that's a normal reaction, and even though it's painful, it's good for you to feel that guilt. If you feel guilty when indeed you have been a good, decent person according to your internalized standards, then there is an overelaborated sense of guilt, and that is self-destructive.

"Now, why is it that in personal relationships guilt seems to be strongest between parent and child? I suspect that this is because of adaptation. A community is necessary for the survival of the species, and certainly the most critical 'community' is the community of mother and child. I suspect that, built into our biology, is a profound sensitivity to the child and, with that, all the giving emotions—that is, the unselfish emotions—including enormous amounts of guilt. It is the mother, and the father to some extent, who is the ultimate supporting mechanism of the child. So when the mother loses her temper, or is angry, or is self-centered, which she has every right to be because she is a human being, her guilt will be the stablilizing mechanism."

I felt somewhat at a loss. Is mother guilt, then, an instinctual protective device?

No. Not in the human animal. The emotion of guilt goes beyond instinct.

"The human being is an essentially instinct-free animal," said Dr. Gaylin. "A bird, for example, doesn't have to feel guilty. When a bird feeds its young, it's not out of a sense of love. It doesn't feel love. Its action is an instinctive response to that open mouth. It has no choice.

"But we humans have freedom or autonomy to a certain extent and are therefore free to make choices and decisions. The emotions are guides to the decisions. Fear tells us there's big danger coming: run like hell. Anger tell us that we are being confronted with a threat to some kind of survival: attack it, and get rid of it. Guilt tells us that our behavior is wrong and we are damaging the group structure: stop doing that, and behave yourself.

"Guilty-feeling mothers have to be reminded of the nature of guilt. When you look at your child and see it's a mess—or so you think—you say to yourself, 'What did I do wrong?' But why should you assume that you are responsible? The problem is that we feel the emotion of guilt when things go wrong. But we have to realize that it's the nature of human beings to do both wrong and right and to struggle their way to a kind of creative existence. Every mother is going to see her kid do wrong, self-destructive, damaging, foolish things. And if you are going to rush in there with your guilt every time, you are interfering with the process of learning. You must remember that we are not instinctual. We learn by doing.

"And the learning process means making the wrong decisions as well as the right. If your child hasn't gotten into reasonably serious trouble by the time he leaves your house, you haven't been a good parent. It means he's been playing it too close to the vest. A child should have to stretch himself to the limit, and in order to do that, he's going to have to fall on his face. He's going to have to make mistakes, he's going to have to be foolish, he's going to have to be stupid. The only way you can protect against that is to raise a tight, inhibited child who will always play it safe and never fulfill more than a small percentage of his potential.

"There's a wonderful little story told of Bernard Baruch. He was asked, 'To what do you attribute your success?' He replied, 'To making the correct decisions.' 'How do you know what the correct decisions are?' 'From experience.' 'How do you get the experience?' 'By making wrong decisions.'

"So you don't want your child to avoid the learning experiences and the mistakes."

I ask about experts. So far as I can see, it depends on where they're coming from. Or, as I am beginning to learn, what their bias is. Many, maybe even most, are blameful.

"Your kid grows up and isn't an absolutely perfect darling? It must be your fault. The kid takes dope, or didn't get into Harvard. Somehow or other it was your fault. You were either too strict or too lenient. Send the same mother with a problem kid to three or four child psychiatrists and, depending on their persuasion, they will direct the mother to be more indulgent, more strict, more this or more that, according to their bias."

Then there's the mother bias.

"There's something else that mothers might recognize, and that is that there is a thing called chance in our lives, and there is a thing that's called complexity. The whole business of 'What did I do wrong?' stems from grandiosity, from a failure to recognize that there are many other influences involved, including chance. It's as if you think you control everything. Rather than expressing humility, 'What did I do wrong?' implies a kind of foolish feeling of omnipotence. You *don't* control everything. Yet what you're saying is that the product is faulty, and because it is your product the fault must be yours.

So think: what do you really mean when you ask yourself or someone else, 'What did I do wrong?'

I mean I think that whatever goes wrong is all my fault.

Good morning, Jesus Christ.

I talked some more with my friend Leah.

"One of the main drawbacks of the professional advisers," she said, "is that they give you general ideas about what to do as a mother. And general ideas don't deal with the uniqueness of your personality and your children's personalities. Another problem is that they reinforce the mother's feeling that there ought to be an instant bonding between the mother and the child.

"The real miracle is when you get a parent of a certain kind of temperament and a child with the same kind of temperament, as if they were born to be together. The chemistry is just right. I think every once in a while you run across that. My daughter is like that. She's a blessing.

"Recently I was riding in my elevator with a woman who has eight children. She asked after my Katie. 'She's heaven,' I said. 'I'm really, really happy with her.' The woman replied, 'I have one like that.'

"Out of eight kids, she knew she had one, and they were perfectly suited to each other. It was like a match. It's such an accident. You don't know who is going to be born to whom. You can put your hand in a herring barrel sometimes and make a better match. So it's a chancy thing to start with. And then it's a matter of the parent respecting the kid, no matter what the match, and allowing it to grow in its own way. With guidance, of course. I think that's the whole key. What happens is that so many women feel guilty because they don't recognize these phenomena of life. A woman just can't seem to look at her child and say, 'Her personality and mine just don't match. We're going to have a tough time and that's too bad, but that's how it's going to be. There's nothing wrong with her and there's nothing wrong with me.' Women don't recognize that being a mother is not such a natural, instinctive process. It is a very learned process—motherhood after you give birth.

"Also there's the element of disappointment mothers sometimes feel when they don't think the child has measured up to their expectations. And when the mother finds herself disappointed in the child, she feels very, very guilty. 'What kind of a mother am I if I feel this way?' she asks herself. 'If you are a real mother you just love your children. You automatically love them, you automatically sacrifice for them.' But there's nothing automatic about it.

"A theory I have—and I think it's not generally believed—is that love is not something that we owe each other. I believe that love is a glorious by-product you get if you are lucky. When you have a child you have an obligation to raise this child in the best way possible. You have to give this child whatever is possible to give him, and you should give it with the understanding that you are raising him to live in this society, raising him to survive as best he can in this world. That is your obligation: to teach your child the rules of society and how to grow in it, to provide the best education and all the tools you can so that he can not only make a living, but will know how to live, how to learn, how to respect and get along with other people.

"This much you owe your children. What your children owe you is not a hell of a lot, except to do what you ask of them and learn the things you teach them. If they happen to love you in the process, I think you are lucky. If you happen to love them in the process, I think you are lucky. I think it is all a by-product. You do not *owe* love to each other.

"If the child is not what the mother expects, or doesn't function well, the mother thinks, 'It's all my fault. I do not love the way I am supposed to love.'

"Yet the truth is that there may not be love between parents and children. It is not a given. It is not inevitable. And even if there is love, you are not obliged to love them every single minute of their entire lives no matter what they do. I think this is the worst kind of burden to put on yourself and on them. Our obligation is not to love our children, but to rear them to be functioning human beings capable of making healthy relationships with others."

We talked a bit about my own fear that I might have damaged Buffy by not being there for her when perhaps she needed me most, and how of course I feel guilty about it even though I have begun to realize that guilt is unproductive and possibly, well, grandiose.

"If you can clarify what you are feeling guilty about," says Leah, "you may be able to figure out that you couldn't, at the time, have done anything in a different way. It's not just a question of always doing our best, but of doing the best we're capable of at any particular time. What happens when you think you've failed is that your child tunes into the fact that you are guilty, and uses it.

"I am presently seeing two women whose daughters hate them. The mothers feel terribly guilty about their failings. They try to put themselves out in every way possible—and feel completely victimized. I've given both of them the same advice. I told them what they had to do was to establish limits, decide how much they will take from their daughters. I told them, 'You don't have to take anything from them anymore. If they don't treat you nicely, you don't have to treat them nicely. Tell them that they can only live in your house if they do.

"The trouble is that, in their guilt, these women didn't establish any boundaries. That's the worst thing you can do to children, not give them any boundaries, because that makes them feel crazy. What they do is to keep pushing you and pushing you and pushing you. And the kids hate you for allowing them to push you, because that makes them feel guilty too. They feel really guilty for treating their mothers that way, but they can't help themselves and they hate their mothers for letting them do it.

"In truth, both these daughters want their mothers to say, 'Goddammit, you straighten up and act like a *mensch* or get the hell out of here. How dare you treat my house like a garbage can? How dare you bring people here that I don't want here?'

"Both mothers have changed. They started doing what I suggested. They had been afraid. They thought, 'If I do anything like that, something bad might happen to them.' I said, 'Something could have happened to them all along. Don't be so narcissistic. If something happens out there it's not going to be your fault. You can only take care of your half of it, and you are going to feel a lot better and your child is going to feel a lot better if you show a little gumption.'

"Another of my patients had trouble establishing relationships with both her kids because her ex-husband was so competitive. No matter what kind of rules she laid down, he would tell the kids, 'You can come and live with me any time.' So they were always threatening her with, 'If you don't like it, we'll go to dad's house,' and he was always encouraging them.

"I told her she should have told the kids, 'You don't like my rules, go to your father's house and stay there until you decide you would like to live with me and my rules, because that is the way it is going to be.' She should have established guidelines much more clearly and firmly.

"In truth they preferred being with her, rather than with the father, even though they had many more material things with him. But the mother felt too guilty to set any limits. She felt guilty because she had divorced their father, she felt guilty because she liked the son better than the more obstreperous daughter, she felt too guilty about everything to be firm. She felt the way to win the children back was to be nice. She was sacrificing for them, and look how they treated her. They treated her like shit. What they were saying in effect was, 'Why are you letting us get away with all this crap?'

"They didn't really want her to let them get away with it. By her doing it, they had no way in the world of knowing that she loved them. Which, in spite of everything, she did.

"The message is: if you love me even if I shit on you, then

what is your love worth? That's what they're saying to her. I can treat you like a piece of shit, and you say, 'Oh, dear, I still love you. No matter what you do, I still love you. I know you're acting badly, but I still love you.'

"I say to her, 'Why would you still love them when they're acting so bad and mean? What you should say is, *No, I don't love you* when you act just terrible to me. Why don't you treat me nicely, the way I like to be treated, the way *you* expect to be treated, like a decent human being? Love has nothing to do with it,' I told her to tell them. 'It has to do with how we treat each other. You treat me abominably and I'm not going to stand for it. Decent treatment has nothing to do with love. Tell them the truth. If you don't like them or love them when they treat you so badly, say so. Tell them they can get out, if that's the way they're going to be. Give them limits. You'll feel better with each other.'

"And any time people are so self-sacrificing, they are making a deal. They are saying, 'I am wonderful to you. When are you going to be wonderful to me?' But they never include *you* in the deal. They never said, 'Sign the contract.' They didn't say, 'What are you going to do for me?' Maybe either or both of those kids, if asked, would have said, 'Don't be so self-sacrificing for me. I don't want it.'

"I know that many women and quite a few men are too self-sacrificing for their children. Well, for some people it's not natural to be self-sacrificing. Also I believe that when parents sacrifice in some kind of compulsive way, their kids are going to pay for it. These parents may say, 'Look what I did for you! I gave up this and I gave up that, and look how you are to me.' The truth is that they were striking a bargain, and they never told the kid that he was part of the bargain. They didn't say, 'I'm going to sacrifice for you for sixteen or eighteen years of your life and then I expect you to take care of me and be nice to me and let me reap the rewards of your diplomas and your successes.' Sometimes mothers know they are doing this and sometimes they don't. But they don't tell the children, 'I'm making a bargain with you.'

"If you're going to make deals with your kids, you'd better tell them what the deal is about and you'd better find out if they want to be engaged in this contract, because you may be sacrificing a lot for their education and your kid may not be a scholar. Why should they be grateful for something they may not want in the first place?

"You have to make constant renegotiations. You can't assume that they can read your mind any more than you can read theirs. As the kids get older they need new terms, and you have to renegotiate. But you can't take for granted that they're going to be the way you want them to be. All you can do is expose them to your values. You can't make them into anything they're not.

"I think the mothers of this generation and the past generation have it very tough, and probably the next couple of generations will too, because everything is changing very quickly. All the old rules have changed, but there aren't any new ones. Today we have so many choices, and we don't know how to make them. We have a hard time finding a place for ourselves, and that gives us one more thing to feel inadequate about.

"But we are capable of changing, too. The harmful things that we have learned to think and do, we can relearn. Nothing is unlearnable. The new things we need to learn, we can. We will."

In my crash course among the experts I was picking up several common themes.

Narcissism and grandiosity blaze in the magical mother eyes.

Self-indulgence and feelings of omnipotence are expressed in the question, "What did I do wrong?"

Women do not instinctively or automatically know how to take on the role of motherhood. Mothering is learned.

It is a given that, at times, mothers do not like their children.

It is not a given that mothers and children should necessarily love each other.

Nearly all mothers are afraid that, through ignorance or rage, they will do something to damage their children.

There aren't any experts in child development, only people talking from their own bias or their own world view.

Most mothers do the best they are capable of doing at the time.

You have every right and reason to trust your feelings. No one knows your child as well as you do.

Self-sacrifice is a one-way deal.

Guilt, when not overelaborated or used as a screen for less acceptable emotions, is a positive and necessary emotion, "the guardian of our goodness."

Threading through all these themes is one not always directly expressed but always implicit: the patterns of traditional roles are changing. Women no longer feel it is their destiny to marry. They can if they like, but they are no longer stigmatized if they choose not to. They can be single. They can have careers. They can have babies. They can even have a happy marriage and a couple of kids and a designer home and an executive position and freedom from mother guilt. They can have everything.

They can have everything, that is, if they are extraordinary women who know how to handle it all.

To date, there are very few such women. We haven't got it all figured out yet, and it is hard. Even though we are so much freer than we used to be—maybe *because* we are so much freer—we still feel guilty. We're trying to find a new place in our own families and in the working world, perhaps even in the human family. We are unlearning, relearning; and that's painful.

The children are having a hard time too. Their role is also changing.

Where are the children? In a kind of limbo. The distinction between adulthood and childhood has become increasingly and, I think, dangerously blurred. The lure and availability of drugs for all; the various marvels of our electronic age and all the messages they deliver; the changes in sexual attitudes and expressions of sexuality—all these have made parents uncertain of their authority and robbed many children of their youth.

I fear for the children. They are being assaulted in all the terrifying ways of which society is capable.

But mostly not by their mothers.

How mothers deal with society's conflicting signals in these changing times is a question not only for us, but for the people to whom we turn for help. And they, it seems to me, are beginning to face life as it is rather than the paper experts say it should be, because many of them are themselves involved as parents in a drug-oriented, video-arcade, computerized, and violent world.

The magnitude of all the changes is greater than guilt-ridden parents, acting alone, can possibly hope to cope with.

So stick *that* in your magical mother eye.

# CHAPTER TWELVE

# You Didn't Get God's Message?

MY daughter, Buffy, was not born to me. Nor did I choose her out of a gaggle of tiny applicants because she was the one I could not resist. We came to be mother and daughter by happenstance. That has been my good luck and happiness, and I hope it will prove to be hers.

Adopting her was a matter of monumental importance to me, and I believe the birth mother who relinquished her did so in conflict and pain. For her own reasons she felt she had to, and I trust she still thinks that her choice was right. Yet she must many times have wondered how her baby, my Buffy, is today.

It is, of course, easy enough for her to find out. She knows who I am, and in any event I am not exactly reticent about life with Mother Caine. Still, I wonder how much she knows, how much she wonders, how much she cares.

Buffy certainly wonders. As soon as she was old enough to understand, Martin and I told her she was adopted and tried to explain the meaning of adoption. We kept at it, without hammering too hard, and I think she caught on pretty quickly to the basic idea.

But there are parents, even today, who try to avoid telling their adopted children the truth. Their rationale usually is that it would hurt the child to be told that his "real" parents don't want him. This is a legitimate concern. Some children take their babyhood rejection deeply to heart and suffer terribly, even if the adoptive parents use great tact and care in telling them the truth.

But the nature of the child's reaction is, I feel, the nature of the child himself. One who reacts violently to the realization that he has been given away has it in his temperament to respond inappropriately to other situations as well. If he had grown up with his biological parents, chances are he would have found something else to rage about. Not telling an adopted child the truth isn't going to make life easier for him. And a lie is hard for parents to live with for a lifetime.

I think perhaps the main reason parents do not tell their adopted kids the facts of their birth is that they themselves fear the child's reaction, a fear that may easily be unfounded. There were parents at Hyde, I remember, who had never told their seventeen-year-old—or anyone else—that he was an adopted child. Larry Pray, who didn't know the background but had an uncanny sense for these things, suddenly asked the boy if he was adopted. The mother nearly had a fit. The kid said, "Hey, take it easy, Mom. It's okay. I sorta knew it, anyway."

And, sometimes, parents unable to have children of their own feel defective and inadequate for that reason, and shield the adopted child from knowledge that they do not want to face themselves.

Just as times are changing for young mothers who may or may not be able to have everything, and for children who no longer experience the special joys of being young, so are they for adopted children. Kids of Buffy's generation, and some a little older or a little younger, don't understand why they were given away. Unmarried mothers often keep their kids these days. *Illegitimacy* has become a quaint, old-fashioned word. For a time, even the word *marriage* almost went out of style, but it seems to be making something of a comeback.

Marriage or no marriage, today's young women seem increasingly reluctant to put an unplanned child up for adoption.

Not only that: more and more single women are deciding that they *don't* want a husband, but they *do* want children. For most, it is easy to conceive, and after that it's bye-bye bed partner. Others, in increasing numbers, prefer artificial insemination. How all these young mothers explain the absence of a father to their children, and how the kids answer questions about their daddies, is something that I suppose is decided by the individual, and not without difficulty. But the central fact is that children today are not being given away as if they were some awkward complication in life. Mostly they are wanted, they are sought after, they are kept. It is almost impossible, these days, for a would-be adoptive couple to find a healthy, normal, baby or toddler who needs a home.

Today's kids understand the world of today. For better or for worse, what they see when they look around is a mass of unmarried mothers who would fight to the death to keep their children.

So why didn't the adopted kids' mothers want to keep them?

Buffy wanted to know. She was about eight or nine when she started asking me about her biological mother, and I tried to tell her what I could.

What was she like?

Well, she was tall, and she was lovely. Her hair was blond, without your coppery highlights, and her eyes were dark, with long eyelashes just like yours. I only saw her that one time, when we came to get you, but I thought she seemed responsible and intelligent and nice. I liked her.

But why didn't she want to keep me?

I thought there was deep hurt in her voice when she asked me that, which she did repeatedly.

I don't know, baby. Maybe she did want to, but she felt she couldn't. My guess is that she wanted to do what was best for you and for herself. She was a college student, only ten years older than you are now, and she didn't have a husband. Either she didn't want to marry or there was some reason she couldn't marry the man. How was she going to take care of you? She was faced with a hard decision. I think she made the right choice, and that took a lot of courage. It must have been very hard for her.

Again and again she asked me, and again and again I told her, "I'm sure she wanted to keep you. I'm sure she would have, if she possibly could. But she was young, it was hard for her, and she felt she couldn't."

As time went by I began to get the feeling that Buffy wasn't really buying this. I felt it was true, but it didn't work. Came a day when she asked me one more time and I said to myself, I don't know whether or not Buffy's so-called natural mother wanted to keep her, or how much she had agonized over giving her up. What the hell, who was I trying to protect?

I said, "I don't know why, babe. I have no idea why. But I can tell you one thing—I'm sure glad she didn't."

For a while we dropped the question, except for Buff's occasional wonderings about what her biological mother was *really like* as distinct from the way she looked, and what her grandparents were like, which I could not even try to answer. She never asked about the father, as if she assumed he had very little to do with her existence. She may be right. The moments of conception are very brief, compared with the nine months of gestation and the elemental closeness of a woman with her child. A father may be nothing more than a shadow in the night, but a mother's womb is the child's warm, protective world for the first months of its life.

Then came *Roots.*

Ever since Alex Haley's book came out, teachers have been giving kids genealogical charts to fill out. Buffy came home one day when she was eleven and said, "I have this thing to fill out. I don't know what to do. I don't know what my roots are."

Well, of course she didn't. She seemed really troubled. The project, I felt, made her feel that she belonged nowhere.

"Yes, it is a problem," I agreed. "Tell you what—you can use my roots."

"Yeah, okay," she said, and she seemed satisfied.

She filled the chart out and it went back three generations and it seemed nice and substantial to me. Maternal line: New Yorkers from way back. Paternal line: my father had walked across Russia to seek his fortune in the United States. Good stuff. Good roots.

Good grade.

Adopted children have many doubts and questions. Adoptive parents have them too, although theirs are less loaded with anxiety than the children's. They are the active parties in the transaction, and it is a transaction. They are aware, or they are made aware, of the possible problem areas. But there's no way babies or infants can be expected to understand their circumstances and be prepared to cope with them. It is when they grow up and start to think and wonder and fantasize that their adoptive parents must give them extra love and strength.

Yet the adoptive parents themselves have problems that, so far as I can see, are seldom addressed—certainly not in the popular media, which is where most of us learn whatever it is we learn after leaving school. There are things we only find out by experiencing them and talking to each other.

What we have a tendency to do is scrutinize our adopted kids and ask ourselves, Would he be different if he had been adopted by someone else? Would she, if she had grown up with her biological parents? Would a child born to me be doing what this kid is doing now? Is it possible that in the great cosmic scheme of things I was never meant to have children?

Phyllis, a friend of mine who was unable to have her own children and adopted a boy and a girl, tells me that when her daughter was a little baby she got out of her crib and smeared the walls with feces. "All over the dresser," says Phyllis. "All over everything. Disgusting! I was in a fury. How *dare* she do this? And all these years later I remember thinking that if she were mine she wouldn't have done that, she wouldn't have done this kind of thing at all. My kids, my very own, would never do this type of thing."

Lots of kids do it. Revolting though it is, it's not abnormal. But Phyllis saw the child's act as an aberration. Not surprisingly, perhaps, because when her husband's grandmother, a little old lady from Russia, heard that Phyllis and Alec were adopting children, she said, "You didn't get God's message?"

Then there was the business of the candy, Phyllis says.

"When she got older, she always used to steal candy from stores and I used to make her replace it. I was so angry at what I considered to be such devious behavior on her part! *My* kid would never be like that. I remember telling her these stories about how I broke a teacup when I was little, and it bothered me for almost two weeks before I told my mother. That's how honest I was. I saw myself as a person of virtue. No kid of mine would ever lie, be devious.

"I should tell you," Phyllis added, "that before I decided to adopt I really went about psyching myself up. I read every kind of book I could find that claimed that genetics was minimal, that the important thing was environment, that by creating that right environment I was going to make my kid the greatest. That was a philosophy that was handed down to me: that our children had to get better and better. Or maybe it was just the feeling of deficiency of the adoptive mother. I didn't know how to handle her. I felt that if she had been more my own we would have had vibes tuned in. I would have been able to see myself in her and there would be more understanding."

I might have thought that once too, but not since talking to Leah Schaefer. It has become increasingly obvious that a great many "natural" parents and kids are mismatched, or at least not particularly compatible.

However good the match, the adopted child—more often

the girl than the boy—comes to a time when she wants to trace and meet the mother who saw fit to abandon her. My Buffy, from quite an early age, had talked about it without great anxiety or interest. But after the *Roots* project, it seemed to me, she talked about it more often and with more intensity. Her hurt came closer to the surface.

She had two reasons for talking about it. One was the perfectly normal curiosity expressed in, "Tell me again what she looks like. Where did I get my eyes? What color was her hair?" and, more recently, "I want to know my family's medical history." She has asked me to go with her to find her mother, and I've said I would.

Her second reason is to punish me. When angry, she has threatened to leave home and find the fairy princess mother who didn't really mean to lose her to the wicked witch. Kids who are not adopted have exactly the same fantasy. I did, when I was a kid. I fantasized a lot about being adopted, dreaming that someday my real mother would come along and rescue me from my awful fate. It is a frequent pattern of wishful thinking for kids who really think they deserve an easier life. What better way is there to reject a parent, particularly a mother, than to say, "Yuck, you're so awful, you're not really mine"?

The adopted kid, of course, has a stronger case than the everyday fantasizer and often uses it to painful effect. The normal disciplinary discussions between mother and child tend to produce such lines as, "Why should I listen to you? You're not my mother anyway." Immature mothers, or angry ones carried away by the stormy heat of the moment, reply in kind, "And you're not my child. Go back to your *real* mother, if that's what you want. I don't need you."

Frightening as they are, these are usually passing storms. If the relationship is essentially warm and sound, and if other elements in the child's life are supportive, the hurtful things said on both sides tend to be erased by time and happier exchanges.

But what does a mother do when a child seems hopelessly unreconciled to his or her adoption?

I don't know the answer. I wish I did. Therapy, sure. But when? What kind? With whom? For mother, or for child, or both? And what about father?

A woman named Ruth told me the following story.

"I have two adopted kids. My daughter was five days old when I adopted her, and I got my son when he was two days old. One kid, the boy, never questioned, never mentioned, never talked about the fact that he was adopted, that he had any concerns about it. Today, at twenty-one, he's beginning therapy because he hasn't been able to cope with life. I could not get through to him. He shut me out completely. He is very bright, he is gorgeous, he has everything going for him. And yet he regards himself as a turd. He has no sense of self-worth whatsoever. But it's only recently that he's put this into words.

"My daughter, on the other hand, was very explicit about it. When she was in about the seventh or the eighth grade she came and told me that she was nothing but a piece of garbage because nobody wanted her. Her mother didn't want her or she would not have given her away.

"I was appalled at the idea of her thinking she was garbage and tried to explain how much we valued her. At about this time my father-in-law passed away and an incredible number of people came to his funeral. The minister looked over this gathering of friends and said something like, 'I want you to see all these people here today. This has to be a reflection on this man, a demonstration that people, many people, really loved him.'

"I thought of my own relatives and friends and how we felt about each other. Afterward I spent time talking to my daughter.

" 'It doesn't matter who you are related to,' I told her. 'Bloodlines are really so totally unimportant. I'm not friendly with my brother or my sister. I have friends who are as dear to me as anyone I've ever loved. That's the important thing—the relationships that you develop. Not the relationships you are born with. They're just accidents of life. Nobody gives anyone away, because nobody owns anyone. You are free to make your own choices about who you want to love. It's not even written anywhere that you have to love me, or I have to love you. But I do.'

"Since that crisis she has become a very strong, very self-confident person.

"We had watched a program on adoption once, and there was a segment in it about a girl who had gone back to her natural mother and wrecked the woman's life because of her intrusion in it. This made a tremendous impact on my kid. She went to a therapist, but she soon stopped seeing him because he was convinced that every adopted kid inevitably has certain problems, and that all the problems adopted children may turn out to have are based on adoption. There are many therapists like that. They like to cram everything into a niche.

"But my daughter doesn't. She has come to terms with things in her own way. She has said to me, 'I can go and see my mother any time I want to. I know that you would be honest with me and help me find her. The only reason I would want to know anything about her at all is to get medical information. But outside of that—I don't want to wreck her life and I don't want her to wreck mine.'

"So she seems to me very wholesome, very hale and hearty, with a good sense of who she is. Never wanted to have anything to do with drugs. She's an outdoor girl, energetic, really wonderful. Somehow she's worked her way through.

"But the boy, on the other hand . . . there are times when he won't even say good-morning. He's morose and brooding. His interests are short-lived, ephemeral, last maybe a week, a week and a half. Just recently he said, 'I have no motivation. I can't stand to live.'

"I felt so bad about him when I saw he was in trouble. I did everything I could. I sat down with him and tried to help him with his homework, asked his teachers to try to make sure he was keeping up his end of responsibility. This kid's nonaccomplishment was particularly difficult for me because I am a teacher and I thought I must be able to help him. I'd go to his room and I'd say, 'Brad, it helps to talk,' but he'd clam up. I just got a stone wall. I felt so inadequate, so totally incompetent. I felt that somehow I had failed him, and I was making myself physically ill because of it.

"As it turned out, things went from bad to worse. He got into drugs. He didn't function. For four years he was usually in a horizontal position. When he was home he would lock himself in his room. He was a total stranger in this house. And now, at last, he's looking for outside help because he doesn't know how to live.

"So here's the difference between these two kids: one has been able to work through things and actively engage in the struggle for life; and the other has been weak, has gone with anything that made him feel like he belonged, always a follower, always in with crowds, always looking to be one of the gang, always looking for pleasure. A real hedonist. Escape after escape after escape. And then he couldn't stand to live at all. So different. The two of them, so completely different.

"It's so easy, when things go wrong, to blame everything on the fact that the kids are adopted. But I think the professionals muddy the waters by doing this. Who needs to be adopted to have problems? My brother, my sister, and myself are all natural children, but both of them have had a terrible need for crutches. They've had one serious problem after another, without having the rationale of being adopted.

"I really feel at this point that the input adoptive parents have is minimal. We provide a loving environment, or think we do, but there are so many forces involved over which we have no control. With my German background I believe in order, in strict structure, but I don't know any more if this is right. . . . What is the key? Is it nature, nurture, genes, temperament, something I'm doing wrong? Sometimes I wonder, even though I love both kids and Susan is turning out just fine, if nature hasn't been telling me something, that I was never intended to have children."

*God's message strikes again.*

I ask myself, do all adopted children undergo such torment and, in doing so, envelop their parents in their pain? And is it true, as so many psychiatrists seem to think, that every adopted kid is bound to have problems simply because he is adopted?

Jeremy is seventeen, an only child adopted as an infant. By coincidence, both parents had siblings very much older than themselves, so in effect they had grown up as only children. To give Jeremy the benefit of the extended family they felt he needed, they did what many parents of young children do— shared a summer house with a group of other young people and their several kids.

Unlike my experience, it turned out to be a happy arrangement. Jerry struck up a lasting friendship with the two little Moffett girls, five and three when he first met them. He had always known that he was adopted, says his mother, although it was never drummed into him. He grew up accepting it. At one point in his school life, one-third of his classmates were either adoptees or stepchildren. He, therefore, felt it was a natural condition, and he wasn't particularly interested in questioning it.

But the little Moffett girls were fascinated.

"Maybe girls have a stronger sense of family and a greater need to know," says Jerry's mother, Laura, "but they just couldn't give up on it. How could the mother give him away? they kept asking. Where is she? What's she like? How could she do it? I really got quite worried that they were going to upset him. But he didn't seem to be fazed at all."

Not that he wasn't interested or never talked about it.

"He used to have these fantasies," says Laura. "His idea of 'that real mother of mine' was sort of like the old woman who lived in a shoe and had so many children she didn't know what to do. I think he really liked being out of that crowd. Then he'd have the real mother pick him up and take him to nice places. She'd be very elegant on these occasions. Once she took him to the White House, where they were personal guests of the president, and another time she took him to Disneyland. Then he tired of her and took up with some imaginary playmates for a while, I think perhaps some siblings from the shoe. He dropped them all when he got more involved in school and summer activities, and he really doesn't seem to be particularly interested in finding out about his biological parents. For years he didn't even seem to realize that there was a father involved, and when he found out he still didn't think it was interesting. He has a lot of things he loves to do, and a lot of friends. He just thinks of himself as Jeremy Ashton, and so what if he spent the first six weeks of his life with someone else?"

The Ashtons know a lot about the family background and medical history, but not who the mother is. Both Laura and her husband periodically suggest to their boy that if there's anything he wants to know, he has only to ask. He says, "I know," and goes out to play soccer.

Laura suggests that one reason he doesn't ask questions is that he feels he may hurt her by showing interest in another mother. He is, she thinks, very sensitive to other people's feelings. Once, having passed the fantasizing stage, he said something about "that real mother of mine" and abruptly stopped. Afterward he made a big point of showing extra affection toward his mother. "He really thought he might have hurt me," Laura says. "Is he perfect? Good God, no! He's only wonderful."

And she's always thought so. "He was six weeks old when we first saw him. It was a case of incredible love at first sight. We thought he was the most beautiful, gorgeous thing we'd ever seen. Actually, his pictures show him as kind of funny-looking. I think we have a much more successful, much happier parent-child relationship than I ever had with my own family or John with his. We belong together. I can't imagine loving or feeling closer to a child if he'd been born to us. He couldn't be more ours."

I think I may have stumbled onto something almost ideal. Obviously Laura is not subject to the dread disease of mother guilt.

She laughs. "Mother, thy name is guilt! Why should I yell at this kid? But I do. I have a very quick temper, and I tend to yell. And then of course I try to explain why. But he never seems to care. I worry sometimes that he holds too much inside. But I really believe he just doesn't let things get to him."

Genetics? Environment? Unfathomable factor? Who knows?

The adoptive parents I have talked to are about evenly divided between those who adopted through agencies and those who, like myself, adopted privately. Several of those who had made the choice to adopt through agencies said they had done so because they had felt more comfortable working through the formalities rather than going the riskier route I had chosen. They had all known of cases in which the adoptive parents had lost their children to biological parents who had changed their minds and enlisted the law to help them, and two or three had friends whose adoptive children had been sent back to an abusive family.

From my reading of the news, I believe it is less common these days for children to be taken from decent adoptive families and returned to unfit mothers, but what is getting increasingly common is the search of the adopted child for the birth mother.

I do believe in Buffy's right to search, but I have certain fears as well, and so my feelings are mixed. On the positive side, I feel she has a right to know whatever she wants to know about her origins. The majority of adoptees who search are not looking for an alternative set of parents, but trying to fill gaping holes in their backgrounds. There is great yearning and emotional curiosity involved, and I feel this must be satisfied where it exists. The search is more than a quest for roots; it is a search for the answer to the question, "Who am I?" It is a search for the self.

Yet many adoptive parents feel threatened and even betrayed by the child's desire to search. I sometimes think I'd like to meet Buffy's birth mother so that we can talk about "our child." And I sometimes think it might be comforting to Buffy to have some sense of another relative with whom she could correspond or even visit. Yet I have my doubts and fears that what will actually happen will be far from the idyll I like to imagine.

Buffy may very well be rejected a second time. I hate the thought that she might be hurt by a meeting that her birth mother may be extremely anxious to avoid, or may even fear.

Then there is the possibility—remote, but real—that there could be a joyful reunion, that her birth mother might welcome her with open arms and lavish her not only with long-lost love, but offer her a life-style complete with swimming pool, a stable, and a generous allowance.

Ashamed of that fantasy, I banish it. But it does come sneaking back in one form or another. Maybe, by now, the other mother is the better mother.

Or maybe in the life she has built for herself, she doesn't want the intrusion of a child she gave away when she was a different person.

An informal survey conducted several years ago in two widely separated areas of the United States reached more than 500 women who had given up their children at birth and were willing to discuss the possibility of reunion. Of the 212 women subsequently interviewed, more than 90 percent said they dreaded the idea of confronting the past. Each had given up her child for what had seemed good and sufficient reason at the time. Many felt that they could not explain the sudden appearance of a child to their husband, children, relatives, friends, or convent sisters. Others could not endure the prospect of either lying to the unexpected visitor or explaining to the child that he or she was the result of an affair with a married man or of incest or of rape.

Few of the women interviewed regarded themselves as the real mother of the child they had given up. According to the interviewer, a typical response was, "I'm just a woman who gave birth. I'm not a mother. I contributed the months of pregnancy and the hours of delivery. The woman who raised my child contributed her whole life. She's the real mother—not me."

These are the women who fear the opening up of sealed records, which have kept their identities safe and their lives private. They feel they have legitimate reasons for maintaining their privacy, often as much for the child's sake as for their own. Years pass and get closed off. The decision to give up the child was nearly always a necessary one, nearly always a painful one. But then, after all the years have passed, what can be left but shapeless yearning and curiosity? Surely not a sense of something that was meant to be.

"I don't know this child," one woman said. "You can't love someone you don't know. I gave her a set of genes that's responsible in part for how she looks, but if I saw her on the street she wouldn't be my child. She'd be a stranger with a familiar face."

In recent years a reverse search has begun: that of the birth mother for the child she gave up years ago. As the sealed adoption records are being opened and the secrecy surrounding adoption lifts year by year and from state to state, more and more biological parents are looking for their offspring. This makes adoptive parents very uneasy; much more so than when their adoptive children choose to search. "It bothers me that mothers can always change their minds," one adoptive mother said. "The reason that people adopt is for the security of knowing the child is yours. You don't want to be just a baby-sitter."

Typically, searching mothers say that they just want to make sure that the child is alive, well, and in a good home. But lately, more and more mothers are demanding visitation rights. Some have seized them. One woman tracked down and tele-phoned her surrendered child, then fourteen, without warning at the home of her adoptive parents. A reunion was permitted by the understanding adoptive parents, and many visits have taken place since. A kind of friendship has developed between the natural mother and her daughter. Says the natural mother, who gave up the child when she herself was still in her teens, "It's given me peace of mind to know that she's alive and well and healthy. It has also allowed me to grow up in a lot of ways. Part of me was frozen at age eighteen."

Yet the child, now almost eighteen herself, is not altogether enamored of the situation. The initial phone call upset her, sending her into a prolonged crying spell, which she still re-members with resentment. The contact, she feels, should not have been made directly with her and without warning. She also is distressed when her birth mother refers to her as "my daughter." Her mother, she says, is the woman who raised and mothered her and gave her love, and she doesn't want another.

Has her adoptive mother felt resentful or threatened? She has been more than necessarily accommodating and discreetly noncommittal when questioned by outsiders. Yet the daughter seems to sense a hurt in her and feels protective of the woman who has nurtured her for all these years. Meanwhile, the kid is trying hard to work out her relationship with the birth mother, who appears to have changed her mind. One thing the girl is sure of is that she doesn't want two mothers.

Another biological mother who sought and found the child she had given up for adoption expresses her tremendous relief and peace of mind at having located her and finding that she was not dead. Dead? Why dead? The woman had as much as given her up for dead, so why should she care now? Sorry. My bias shows.

"We can't have the years back," this woman has said, "but I can know my daughter and begin to have a relationship with her rather than continue to have a black hole in my heart."

I suggest that the adoptive mother—who has loved the child through his growing-up years, made her home his home, fed and cared for him, watched over him when he was sick, sent him to school, shared the joys and traumas of his childhood, rushed him to the emergency room at 3:00 A.M., helped him with his homework, and endured his friends and other eccentricities—may also have a black hole in the heart when not only the child starts searching, but the birth parent too. That black hole is where *her* peace of mind is supposed to be, but it is filled with doubts: Will there be a new match? Will that parent and my child get along better than we do? What is the real reason for this search? Is it something that I have not done well enough? Amazing, how providence or something keeps sending fresh ammunition for mothers to turn upon themselves.

How can the adoptive parent *not* feel hurt and insecure and inadequate and even afraid when other people's guilts and anxieties start nibbling away at her family? I don't believe it when a natural parent says ever so sincerely, "I want to meet her and see the face that maybe looks like mine, but there is nothing for you to worry about. You have done a wonderful job and you have no reason to be frightened. I think you'll just feel closer to the child."

Maybe. But isn't the self-indulgence of the birth mother's search a threat to a family she did not create? I've heard searching children say they do not want to wreck their mothers' lives, biological and adoptive, but I really haven't heard that concern expressed so clearly or even at all by the searching mothers. "You have no reason to worry."

But *you*, birth mothers, feel anxiety and guilt. *We* have reason to worry that you may mess up your child's life—again—and his parents' too.

With the undermining of the adoptive family—for that is the way some of us see it—has come a sense of diminution. What we have is not the real thing, but an imitation.

Not so, says Ronnie Diamond, assistant director of the Spence-Chapin family service agency. "Adoption is just another way of being a family. Being an adoptive family simply means that you came together in a different way than if your children had been born to you. It isn't better or worse—just different. And different is no big deal.

"But it is true that adoptive parents have special problems in regard to guilt. I find they struggle with a sense of entitlement. Are they entitled to the child? Or have they taken it away from someone who really loved and wanted it, but for some reason couldn't keep it? So there's guilt about depriving the birth mother of the child, and then perhaps not being the best possible replacement.

"One way entitlement is expressed is in a desire to make up for the child's loss of the biological parents by showering him with goodies, by not saying no, by not making the child unhappy. I think as parents we all want to protect our children from hurt, and adoptive parents tend to do that even more so. They feel they must not hurt the child any more than he has already been hurt by being given up. They only want to be nice. They don't set any limits; they will not discipline. And they wind up with a horrible, terrible child, because children have to have limits. They wind up with a child they don't like.

"What often happens at this point is that the parent blames the child's genes and starts fantasizing about sending the kid back to its birth parents. This is very similar to what happens with biological families. When a kid starts to act up, it's very common for a parent to say to the other, 'He's just like you, he's just like *your* side of the family.' And very often a divorced mother will think, 'God, my kid is being really awful—I'm going to send him to live with his father.' So this is not all that different from the fantasy in adoption, that you can send him back where he came from. But part of the adoptive mother's fantasy is that maybe the birth mother can do a better job than she can. It's her sense of inadequacy and shame that's showing.

"But it still boils down to a question of entitlement, of not knowing how to claim the child as one's own.

"Now, how do you claim someone? How do you make someone feel he's part of the family? You give him rules, and you enforce them. One way to make a child know he's an outsider is to let him know there aren't any rules for him. So the kid never finds out where and how he can make his own place in the family.

"One mother who came to us for help had been letting her child get more and more out of hand because she couldn't sort out her relationship with him. Was she entitled to him, or wasn't she? She gave him no consistent structure, no rules, no limits, no discipline. She didn't even want to withhold his allowance, because she wasn't the earner in the family. 'What did I do wrong?' she kept asking. She was feeling guilty all the time. There was a sense that if the child had been hers biologically, it would have been different and she wouldn't have gone wrong. And also that the child might have done better with a different mother.

"This mother, I believe, had a problem of self-image *before* the adoption. The child may have had no problem at all, except with an insecure mother and an unstructured home. Any kid can have that kind of problem. Our feeling at the agency is that, with adoptive families, mental health professionals have really not been on target. We've seen so many cases where a family has gone for treatment, and as soon as it has been identified that a child is adopted, that is pinpointed as the root of all problems. The real root of the problem often lies elsewhere.

Adoption is certainly a significant factor, but it's very rarely the core of the family difficulties. It's such an easy answer, and it's almost always only a small part of the truth. The larger part is that every kid needs structure and rules and discipline to show him that he has a secure place as part of the family."

It was while Jon was away at Hyde and I was supposedly getting to know my daughter that Buffy's insecurity and rage began to show. I'd long since realized how important a sense of family was to her, that her gathering of a circle of friends around her and her enjoyment of family celebrations such as birthdays, Christmas, Thanksgiving, New Year's Eve, and the Fourth of July was just a little more intense than that of most kids. Fourteen at the time, my lovely daughter—*mine*— seemed outwardly happy for the most part, but when she got angry she increasingly used her biological mother as a threat and a weapon against me: "I don't need you. I'll run away and find her. She's much better than you are—I know she is!"

So now she was going to run away. She didn't want my help in finding her real mother. She wanted to do it herself. Rightly or wrongly, I felt she was turning her rage against her birth mother against me.

I can see the Buffy of this stage as full of anger, becoming manipulative and evasive, alternating excessive displays of affection with outbursts of destructive rage. Every once in a while I'd still hear, *"Why didn't she keep me?"* and then again I was turned into the villain. I could see that she was adding nuggets to her hate book and I wondered what they were, but she hid her grimy little notebook well. Sometimes *I* felt like running away and having a little chat with the young woman who had given her up, but I could recognize this as a foolish fantasy. I was sure—no, I was not sure, but I thought it likely—that Buffy and I would ride it out.

But dealing with our different insecurities was hard, and sometimes I wondered if she and I had what it took. Maybe my adopted child, once apparently so placid and content but now a seething mass of teenaged hormones and bottled-up anger, already had too many strikes against her. And maybe I wasn't up to it. But, by *God*, she was being infuriating.

One day she pushed me just a touch too far. She loved to do the grocery shopping and she was very good at it, but she had a tendency to keep a little too much of the change for herself. This time she kept too much, and I made some comments about stealing. In return she said some awful things to me.

That was it. Misappropriation of the household money, followed by a foul-mouthed attack on me. I was really angry. But for once I didn't shout.

"You've just used up your allowance," I said coolly. "And you can't go out for a week. You're going to start learning that you can't get away with this kind of behavior, and you're going to learn it right here at home."

For a moment her expression was an odd mixture of stunned and sullen. Then she immediately got on the telephone and called all her friends, one after the other, and said, "Guess what! I'm grounded! My mother grounded me for a week!"

There was such delight in her voice that I wished I'd done it before, for her sake as well as mine.

I realized that she was telling me two things. One was that she was thrilled to be treated like all the other kids she knew, who were constantly having privileges taken away from them and, of course, bitching about it. And the other was that I had finally laid down the law and shown her that we did have rules and discipline in our family, that there were boundaries she was expected not to cross.

She had some limits at last.

CHAPTER THIRTEEN

# A Story of Three Dolls

THE letter and its enclosure took me back through the years, to a time when Jonny was little and was trying in his own way to deal with the impending loss of his father. Death is a difficult concept for a nine-year-old to grasp, but he had come to understand that we were going to be alone and sad for a time, and maybe quite a long time.

I thought of Jon, away in his boot camp of a school, and remembered as I read the document that my boy had had the right stuff when he was scarcely more than a baby. I had no reason to believe he didn't still have it. And it was not too much to hope that Buffy had it too. Maybe I even had some of it myself.

Dr. Norman Garmezy, a psychiatrist studying what he calls "invulnerable" or "stress-resistant" children, had sent me, at my request, a copy of a lecture he had delivered to the American Psychological Association. In his paper he had quoted an incident from *Widow*, using it as an example of what he described as "mastery in the faces of stress."

Jonny, in the bathtub, had been musing about how things would be for us when daddy died. I had answered him as best I could and then asked him what he would do.

He'd considered for a moment and then said what I thought was an incredible thing: "I'm a very active person. And if I start doing things"—and here he had used a strange and wonderful word for a little boy—"if I start doing things, I'll be my joyful self again."

219

It was an extraordinary thing for him to have said. His joyful self, at nine years old. The memory brought a sting to my eyes.

Dr. Garmezy had been taken with Jon, too, but not in a sentimental way.

"This," he observed in his lecture, "is what I mean by the term 'invulnerability.' Not children or adults who are super-heroes, but rather people who, in the face of great stress, seek ways to cope with it and in doing so retain mastery and control over their lives. Jonny perceived the need to resume his charac-teristic pattern of activity rather than to remain immobilized by the profound loss he was shortly to suffer. It is an 'incredi-ble' thing, as Ms. Caine notes, this great wisdom of a young child who does have the attributes that he must now utilize in the face of an overwhelming adversity."

I don't know that Jon's wisdom or characteristic pattern of activity over the last few years would have earned praise from Dr. Garmezy, but the point was well taken and cheered me enormously. Jon's instincts had been right. And the way he was hanging in at Hyde encouraged me to think that he might be one of the resilient ones—another term used by Garmezy and others in his field.

There were, I learned, a number of similar investigations under way, many of them held under the umbrella of the Na-tional Institutes of Mental Health. I wondered if these studies had concentrated on children facing loss by death in the fam-ily. I wondered, too, if there was a special ingredient in a child's life conditions or personality that made him resistant to stress. And so I undertook an informal study of my own.

My first question was easily answered. The answer to the second was a long time in coming, and inconclusive when it came.

Loss is only one form of the stresses studied, I found out, and not always the most painful one. Dr. Garmezy has pointed out that, when he first used the term "invulnerability" in re-gard to youngsters under stress, it was not in the context of adaptation to bereavement, "but rather in terms of the achievements of inner-city black children." And these children function—or sometimes malfunction—under a multiplicity of stresses, some extremely severe.

I discovered that researchers had begun their investigations with what they called "high-risk children" or "children at risk." I hoped that mine did not fit into this category. Most do not. Yet the questions and findings of the researchers are of concern to every parent, to every mother who torments herself for her children's torments.

"Children at risk" are those who are in danger of being scarred for life of lengthy exposure to any few of an incredible galaxy of stressful conditions and preconditions: genetic factors; birth complications or premature birth; organic damage; illness; overcrowding in the family unit; extreme poverty and deprivation; abuse; neglect; prolonged physical pain; divorce, job change, or death in the family; trauma of accident or criminal attack; attendance at inferior schools; consignment to foster homes; loss of caring adults; parental criminality; bizarre treatment by parents in the throes of problems ranging from marital discord to paranoid schizophrenia.

It is rare, as investigators point out, to find only one of these factors threatening a child, and common to find families in which risk factors are clustered. Where only one risk factor is evident, children apparently function effectively. But children experiencing two or more such onslaughts upon their developing selves are likely to demonstrate some form of disturbance.

The initial focus of the dozen or so major studies relating to Dr. Norman Garmezy's work was to develop techniques for risk appraisal of children with one or more psychotic—usually schizophrenic—parents, the purpose being to isolate signs of potential breakdown in these children and prevent such occurrences.

An interesting by-product of the research began to surface.

Some children of psychotic parents were seen to have become morbidly and inextricably involved in the parental psychosis and were acting out in a variety of destructive ways. This was not surprising. But other children, often in the same family, were observed to avoid such involvement and seemed to be surmounting almost overwhelming circumstances. According to Dr. Cynthia Janes, a psychologist at Washington University, most high-risk children "do better than you'd expect. They may not be the happiest children in the world, but they turn out more or less fine."

Why some, and not the others?

How much better than the others? In what way?

Now the questions started getting difficult to answer.

Dr. E. James Anthony, a psychiatrist at the Washington School of Medicine and director of the Edison Child Development Center in St. Louis, has spent almost twenty years investigating how children experience their parents' psychoses, how the parental disorder directly affects their lives, and how children deal with the family situation. His research reveals a wide disparity in the responses of various children at risk.

He began to see some children who were seemingly "more immune" than others. They were not just okay, not just "more or less fine," not just doing better than expected. They were flourishing, as if their family circumstances did not touch them at all. Or else touched them in such a way as to impel them to superior achievement. Some researchers started calling these unusually stress-resistant children "superkids."

Dr. Anthony tells of one youngster who was part of what he describes as "one of the most disorganized, chaotic, relentlessly pressuring situations I have ever seen."

There were three boys in the family. The father was a chronic alcoholic. "One of the mean ones," says Dr. Anthony. "A fighting drunk. And he beat up the mother and the children and he destroyed the furniture and was impossible day after day." The mother was a masochist who accepted her husband's abuse as a part of life, and could give neither moral nor physical support to the boys.

The two younger boys were listless, defeated children, sad in a way that little boys should never be. They had given up altogether. But the oldest boy, according to Anthony, "seemed to go from strength to strength." He was cheerful, apparently poised and capable, competent in many ways, and doing very well in school. Somehow, he had managed to distance himself from what was going on at home and preserve his separate self as a healthy being.

Another family investigated by Dr. Anthony revealed a pattern of adult schizophrenia casting its shadow upon the younger generation—not necessarily in terms of transmitting the disease, because about 90 percent of the children of schizophrenics will not develop the disorder themselves, but certainly in terms of the disordered environment created.

Three adults in the family cited were subject to schizophrenic attacks, including the father of several at-risk children. The father, when not hospitalized for "florid paranoid schizophrenia," turned the home into a fortress barricaded against invasion and coerced the family members into taking his homemade course in weapons training and keeping armed watch against the nameless enemy, which apparently included the entire rest of the world.

When Dr. Anthony's researchers were permitted to interview the children, they found themselves in a bizarre environment of secrecy and suspicion, which no one, family members and investigators alike, was allowed to enter or leave without an examination of his credentials. A child who went out shopping would be closely interrogated on his return in case he was someone else in disguise. One child complained bitterly that he even had to report before going to the bathroom, and presumably afterward as well.

"The oldest boy," reports Anthony, "was a wary, suspicious person who treated the interview like a third-degree examination. He was very reluctant to give any information and even asked for a lawyer to be present so that he would not incriminate himself. He examined the forms used in the research very carefully and declared that he was not going to give 'evidence.' He insisted that his father had lots of enemies and that it was always necessary to take proper precautions."

The second child, on the other hand, was not involved in her father's scenario, although acutely aware of it and obviously distressed by it. She told the research team that she thought her father was a very sick man and expressed the fear that if he came home to stay instead of remaining at the hospital "he would make us all sick like him." She felt frightened when he was around, she said, not so much of him as of the hair-raising plots he spun.

The youngest boy expressed an even healthier attitude. In sharp contrast to the older brother, he was, Dr. Anthony says, "cheerful, amiable, and disbelieving. He saw the whole regime as an interference with his liberty to play freely with his peers."

His own little world and his own ego were more real and important to him than the stressful and chaotic world of his family. He knew the difference, although he could not always separate himself physically from the chaos that surrounded him. In his mind, he was not part of it.

As Dr. Anthony points out, the capacity to distance oneself is a marvelous survival technique. And I am interested in survival techniques. Jon and Buffy and I each have our own, as most people do to a greater or lesser degree.

But for the high-risk, invulnerable children, the technique is exceptionally finely honed. Despite the most stressful life patterns imaginable, they don't break down. They actually seem to thrive. According to available studies, they excel academically and take on early leadership roles such as that of class president. They have jobs outside of school hours, they are popular and bright, and generally succeed where we would have expected them to fail.

The discovery of the superkids has led psychologists to new questions and a search for new definitions. Since the main thrust of their investigations is to develop preventive and therapeutic procedures for children at risk, the researchers' priority has been to find a solution in the high-risk children who appear to be invulnerable to stress or highly resilient in the face of it. Dr. Garmezy feels that he and his colleagues will not be able to tell why one child breaks down, or figure out how to prevent that breakdown, until much more is found out about why other children do not break down under similar conditions of extreme pressure. Find out what makes some children apparently invulnerable, he says, and you are on the way to finding out how to help others who are less resilient.

Intervention and therapy are beyond my scope, but as a parent with unanswered questions I am fascinated by the psychologists' attempts to determine what factors there are in the lives or personalities of the superkids that distinguish them from the vulnerables. Dr. Anthony figures that the vulnerable child lacks the ability to create distance between himself and the damaging parent. That child becomes closely entangled with the stress situation and feels all the guilt, fear, shame, and resentment of the impaired adult—plus his own, for being, as he might think, the cause of his family problems. According to Dr. Anthony, the sheer competence of the resilient child, his ability to manage the psychotic experience, is the factor lacking in the vulnerable one.

All right, but what exactly is the nature of that competence, and how does the child come by it? How is it that one kid may develop normally in spite of immersion in the subculture psychosis, in spite of what appears to be total neglect and constant exposure to irrationality, whereas another kid does not?

I found that not all the votes were in by a long, long way, but among the obvious factors suggested were innate intelligence, problem-solving ability, persistence in the face of heavy odds, hidden strengths of the family itself, substitute parents

outside the immediate family circle—like Buffy and her surrogate mothers, I couldn't help thinking—chronological position
in the family, and the selectivity with which parents deal with
their different children. And there are other elements. In fact,
there are so many, both external and internal, that Dr. Garmezy's provisional judgment is that we don't really know anything yet about the nature of the stress-resistant child or how
he got that way.

Probably, I began to think, there isn't just one secret ingredient, or just one explanation.

And yet, James Anthony feels he has found some sort of key
and is willing to offer a partial and preliminary definition of
what it is that invulnerable children have and vulnerable children don't: "a sort of self-protective ego, depending upon, and
caring for, itself."

There again is that theme of separation and aloneness.

The idea of a child having to make his way to healthy adulthood on the strength of his own ego alone is a rather sad one.
Dr. Anthony has also found it so. He compares the experiences
of some extremely high-risk, apparently invulnerable children
to those of youngsters who have been through cataclysmic
events such as earthquakes or the bombing of Hiroshima or
other major natural or man-made catastrophes, and he suggests
that invulnerable children may be paying a price after all. Sur-
vivors in both the home-stress and the disaster groups, he says,
"have this extraordinary equanimity. But the feeling one gets is
that they've placed a psychological distance between themselves and the disaster."

That distance, the crucial element in the child's salvation,
may ultimately be a mixed blessing. The children, as they
grow, carry the distancing mechanism over into interpersonal
relationships, making if difficult for them to be warm and loving or to establish an intimate relationship with others.

Difficult, but not necessarily impossible.

Dr. Anthony refers to the invulnerables as "these splendid

children" and feels that study of them will reveal much of value to all youngsters under stress. There *is* a special something that has yet to be defined. He illustrates the complex, elusive quality of the resilient kids with the parable of the three dolls.

One is made of glass, the second of plastic, and the third of steel. Each is hit by a hammer. The glass doll breaks. The plastic doll is scarred. But the third, the steel doll, gives off a fine, metallic sound.

"It's that sound," says Dr. Anthony, "that we're all trying to investigate."

In the past, it seems to me, virtually all studies attempting to identify the probable causes of adult criminality or psychosis have started with the disturbed adult and worked backward through the subject's history in an attempt to uncover a child at risk. More often than not, investigators find what they expect: a broken home, unloving and even abusive parents, an environment of poverty, deprivation, and violence. Thus scarred for life in childhood, the adolescent or adult turns to deviant behavior.

Undoubtedly, many and perhaps most troubled and troublemaking adults are products of such backgrounds. But studies concentrating on today's pathological cases and tracking them back to their roots bypass the fact that most children experience some discord, stress, and trauma in the course of growing up, ranging from illness or the effects of financial insecurity to the loss of one parent or the behavioral peculiarities of another, and that the majority of these children—as well as many of the high-risk group—grow up to be competent, fully functioning, and even high-achieving adults.

Studies starting with children and following them into adulthood present a different and more realistic picture to parents like myself who wonder, usually in the small hours of the morning, how their kids are likely to turn out. One such investigation has been reported by Arlene Skolnick of the University of California's Institute of Human Development. The study was conducted at the institute under the direction of Jean McFarlane. According to Dr. Skolnick, "Approximately two hundred children were studied intensively from infancy through adolescence, and then were seen again at age thirty. The researchers predicted that children from troubled homes would be troubled adults and, conversely, that those who had had happy, successful childhoods would be happy adults. They were wrong in two-thirds of their predictions. Not only had they overestimated the traumatic effects of stressful family situations, but even more surprisingly, they also had not anticipated that many of those who grew up under the best circumstances would turn out to be unhappy, strained, or immature adults (a pattern that seemed especially strong for boys who had been athletic leaders and girls who had been beautiful and popular in high school)."

Bright hopes are not infrequently dashed. Children of a good family, comfortable surroundings, apparently stable and affectionate parents who offer their offspring all they seem to need to grow up mentally, physically, and psychologically healthy don't always make it. We have all known or heard of families whose well-nurtured, privileged children have gone off the track. Too much affection, perhaps, of a cloying kind. Too much ease in a material sense, and not enough openly loving care. Too much pressure to satisfy parental expectations, a sort of desperation to match family standards that cannot and perhaps should not be met. Impossible expectations of the self, based on the accomplishments of others. A wayward gene. Damaging peer pressure to try out drugs and little crimes of daring, burgeoning into drug abuse and bigger crimes. A small core of vulnerability in the child, an unidentified unhappiness that bursts to the surface in the form of suicidal drug abuse or murderous attack upon a public figure. Or what?

Why does a child who seems to have everything going for him become an adult misfit?

I'm sure there isn't any one answer. But Dr. Skolnick offers a suggestion that may account for some delinquencies: "Controllable stress may be better for a child's ego development than good things that happen without any effort on the child's part. Self-esteem and a sense of competence may not depend on whether we experience good or bad events, but rather on whether we perceive some control over what happens to us."

There is, in other words, something in the child that directs his perception of events and influences his reactions. If he feels he has a measure of control, his reaction is healthy. But if there is no challenge, no stress for him to control, there is no occasion for him to rise to and no way to temper his steel. And his ego may ultimately suffer.

Another recent study has focused on the effects of common stresses on American families and the origins of disorders in children growing up in a stable environment. The project involved the "normal" community of Martha's Vineyard, an island five miles off the coast of Cape Cod with more than nine thousand permanent residents. Researchers scrutinizing the lives of four hundred children over the course of several years attempted to identify the roots of psychiatric problems in children of various ages and define the stresses that are most damaging to them.

Preliminary findings offer the unsurprising conclusions that the most prevalent stress-producing factors are financial worries, followed by housing, employment, marriage, and health problems, all of which have a filter-down effect upon the children. And all of these, of course, are very common problems in most communities.

According to Dr. Felton Earls, chief investigator for the project, the factors most closely associated with behavioral difficulties in the children studied are marital discord and parental psychiatric disorders, clinical depression ranking high on the list of such disorders. Children thus affected, Dr. Earls suggests, may suffer from low self-esteem in later years and have difficulties in their relationships with peers and parents.

Low self-esteem? I've heard this mentioned before. And not only by Dr. Skolnick, but at Hyde.

A more hopeful note, I thought, was struck by the discovery that chronic, continual stress appeared to be a significant factor in the development of behavioral and psychiatric problems in the Martha's Vineyard children. Observed Dr. Earls, "This suggests that one bad year at an early age will not necessarily produce later problems in children."

To all parents who fear the effects of one or even a few wounding experiences scattered throughout the growing-up years, or one bad session, such as that brought about by a temporary upheaval in the family or its circumstances, there is hope in Dr. Earls's observation.

There is even more hope in the study's findings relating to families experiencing a high number of stressful events. Some had children exhibiting no behavior problems whatsoever, no matter how many difficulties endured by the parents or the children themselves. This suggested to the investigators that the parents had somehow managed to shield their children from the effects of family problems—or that the children had been able to make their own successful adaptations to stress.

There it was again, that adaptive, coping element of "those splendid children." The Martha's Vineyard study had not been undertaken for the purpose of finding adaptable or resilient or stress-resistant youngsters. Yet, as other investigations had done before, it had nonetheless found them.

The investigations continue. Both Garmezy and Anthony, pioneers in the field, believe that more attention should be paid to the invulnerable ones who appear to love well, work well, play well, and expect well of other people, themselves, and their own future. A proper study of these children, Anthony says, "may eventually furnish us with the critical answers to problems of prevention, since they have to prevent a disorder in themselves by their acquisition of competence and coping skills."

And that's what fascinates me. As a parent of almost-grown children I am not especially geared to preventing disorders in toddlers or teenagers. But I am looking for answers, explanations, perhaps even reassurances. I keep thinking, what saves some kids, and not others? What does it mean, what does it take, what does it cost to be invulnerable? What coping mechanisms are employed by the survivor kids? Where and how do they find them? Even a simple definition of the word *invulnerable*, in connection with a child at risk, eludes me.

The trouble with the word *invulnerable* is that it suggests something rocklike or armor-clad, quite the opposite of resilient. Several researchers have indicated that pain and suffering in childhood may have a hardening, steeling effect on some children, making them impervious to later pain and capable of overcoming life's obstacles by ignoring them. "But," says Dr. Arlene Skolnick, "the ability to cope does not mean that the child doesn't suffer. One woman, who successfully overcame a childhood marked by the death of her beloved but alcoholic and abusive father, and rejection by her mother and stepmother, put it this way: 'We suffer, but we don't let it destroy us.' "

In an attempt to pinpoint the coping mechanisms or protective factors in the lives of children at risk, today's investigators are examining the youngsters in terms of their relationships within and outside the family, their social and academic activities, and their sense of self or self-esteem—which factors, if positive, are taken as outward evidence of an as-yet unrecognized inner resource that permits a child to overcome adverse circumstances.

Definitive results are by no means in, but the latest findings indicate that many forms of support, both internal and external, have been utilized by high-risk children in a variety of situations. The fine metallic sound that fascinates Dr. Anthony may be a harmony of several different instruments.

Some researchers have come up with an internal factor they

describe as an "adaptable temperament" in the more stress-resistant children, as distinct from the "difficult temperaments" of others, which keeps them from being scapegoated by abusive parents and spares them being devastated by insults to their sense of self. Many others continue to cite high intelligence and creative ability as major internal protective elements, which allow the child to gain self-esteem and a sense of competence from activities outside the family.

Then there are the environmental protective factors.

One may be a psychologically healthy and loving parent or other close relative with whom the child may form a bond. Another might be the positive qualities of the disordered parent: the affection, supervision, and sense of structure imparted in spite of the illness. Yet another may be the family's social network, whose members may be able to provide the child with opportunities for normal activities outside the family. Some children find alternative sources of support among their own siblings or peers; some find it in a teacher, a school, a sport, a hobby, or even a pet.

There are many such external elements that may not be readily apparent to the outsider but may serve as a lifeline for endangered children.

And yet the environmental factors, even if several are available to youngsters at risk, do not constitute an adequate explanation of invulnerability or resilience or stress resistance, or whatever the special component may be called. Many children have a healthy sibling or uncle or grandparent within reach, or an understanding teacher or a peer group or a team, but do not make that reach, whereas others do.

Perhaps the solution to the puzzle of what makes up a superkid lies not in any single special quality he may have, but in what qualities the vulnerable children lack; and perhaps it will be found that several elements work together to permit the functioning of the invulnerable child.

Certain recurring themes appear in the studies of children

who have managed to cope: a close and affectionate relationship with a healthy adult or with peers, giving the child a normal model and an acquaintanceship with the real world outside his disordered home; and high intelligence and creative talent, which not only permit the child to reach out for gratification and support not present in his home life, but permit him to achieve recognition and satisfaction in his own right.

Thus it appears that children at risk need—like all children—to feel loved, capable, and respected. With these ingredients available to him even in small quantities, plus an innate capacity to make something of them, the child is able to build up a healthy regard for himself.

Self-esteem. A sense of competence, at least of adequacy; a personal identity.

Maybe that's what the basic, magic ingredient is: a sense of self, a sturdy ego, giving off a fine metallic—perhaps even a musical—sound.

I know that the studies of Anthony, Garmezy, and others go far beyond the needs and interest of most parents, and I do not mean to trivialize them by applying their findings to my own experience. Nor distort them, because although I have my faults, I am not a psychotic parent. Nothing in the experience of my family, other than our bereavement, can compare with the life experiences of the high-risk children who may or may not show themselves to be invulnerable. But I have been a troubled mother and a very worried one, and I take great heart in what these researchers are saying.

Their message to me is that, in this mother-blaming culture, it is not mother who is primarily to blame for what her children become—or what may become of her children. She is a major element in their lives, but she is not the only one. Other elements exist within the children themselves. We still don't know very much about these secret ingredients. We don't know why some children rise above their environment to become superkids, or why others distance themselves from decent, caring parents to become antisocial and destructive.

"In fact," says psychiatrist Ronee Herrmann, "we really need to know a great deal more than we do about human development. There are so many variables involved. We don't know what influences individuals as they develop, we don't know why they have certain views of the world, or why they have certain reaction patterns. We talk about genetics, constitution, environment. But we don't know how these things come together to make something that's greater than the sum of their parts. Why certain children react in a certain way, why certain things are traumatic to one child and not to another— we still have no idea."

Complicating all our ignorance—although I do believe we may be on the verge of some illumination—is the awkward fact that we don't know how children interpret parental actions and directives. What do they make of our behavior? Do they see as we see, understand what we want them to understand? For the most part we don't know what our children's perceptions are, any more than they know what ours are. I don't know how one conveys a perception.

We all observe with different eyes and think with different minds. Adults, like children, like to think that we are in control of circumstances. To a limited degree, we are. To a larger degree, we are not.

In sum, it is rare for either mothers or fathers to shape their children to their ends, or cast the deciding vote as to what they will become.

However my children turn out, I am not going to duck responsibility. But I'm not going to feel that I have to take the rap alone.

No mother should. Not even when it's credit that's being handed out.

CHAPTER FOURTEEN

# Mothers' Lives and Mothers' Voices

INEVITABLY, I ask myself, do I have vulnerable or invulnerable children? Have I been wallowing luxuriantly, needlessly, in guilt?

The answer to the first question is: who knows? To the second, a resounding yes.

We're not out of the woods yet, and perhaps we never will be, altogether. But my kids continue to surprise me.

My son, Jon, is laboring away diligently through Hyde. My daughter Buffy is at home, grumbling to me about her homework and to her friends about me.

Jon. He is more than laboring. He is doing real work, academic work, and his grades have improved incredibly. I even see A's on his report cards, more and more with each semester. He hasn't been on the chain gang for ages. I feel that *I* have, because the Hyde experience for me is something unprecedented in my life and continues to be, at times, absolutely awful.

I have been to monthly seminars, Learning Center meetings, annual retreats. They tried to make me appear in the parents' annual musical play, and naturally I refused. The vignettes were enough. More public than that I could not get. Besides, the music was awful. Adolescent and derivative. I, who love serious music, I who listen to Buxtehude and Tele-

235

mann, I who live for literature, opera, and theater—*I* associate myself with a fifth-rate musical comedy? Dress up in a silly costume? Ha! Not a chance.

That was the first year. Next year, I watched with something like envy. Year after? Somehow I wound up as assistant director, plus doing a little toe tapping and soft-shoe.

Meanwhile, Jon was hitting the dean's list. When we were together we behaved like civilized human beings. I felt that I was loosening up and coming to terms with life. A kind of togetherness movement was beginning to roll and it seemed to me that I had become part of it just by showing up. Something about the Hyde connection was helping both Jon and me. I felt close to some of the parents, actually fond of them, always glad to be with them; glad to be done with lonely secrecy.

Between Hyde on the one hand and my research on The Meaning of Mother Guilt According to the Experts on the other, I had come to realize that I used to go to people for their credentials rather than for their humanity or common sense. Now, I felt, I was open to new ideas and new ways of doing things.

Jon came home for an occasional weekend, checked out some of his old friends, and came in late, unstoned. One Saturday he repaired, impeccably, the door panels he'd kicked in two years earlier. Something obstinate in me had refused to hire someone to do it, and now the job was done. Invisible mending, I called it. Thank you, and about time.

"I'm a good workman, Mom," was all Jon had to say.

Buffy and Jon . . . Another time, Jon cleaned the refrigerator. Buffy flew into a rage. I was bewildered. She never defrosted it; why shouldn't he? He hadn't done it right! He hadn't cleaned up properly! There were pools of water all over the place that he hadn't wiped up! He was a mess! They had a nice little pre-Hyde fight.

Apart from that, Buffy was elaborately bored with anything having to do with her brother and his triumphs at school. As he rounded into normality she was becoming increasingly rebellious, manipulative, and untidy around the house. Her homework was sliding. She changed schools, and her grades, never spectacular, dropped alarmingly. I could see no signs of homework at all. She liked the kids at her new school and brought them around to smear popcorn butter and fudge around the kitchen—without, naturally, cleaning any of the pots and pans—but I never saw her doing any lessons with them. When she called them on the phone she didn't talk about math problems or botany projects. She talked about when they'd be old enough—in about three months, according to her—to go to Xenon or Studio 54.

With incredible lack of tact, considering how much I thought I had learned, I asked if she might also like to go to Hyde. After all, it seemed to be very good for Jon and he would be graduating soon . . .

Buffy hit the ceiling. Go to Hyde? Was I crazy, to suggest that she go to that dumb place where Jon was? Wasn't she supposed to have a life of her own? Was she supposed to track along behind him forever? Couldn't she have the run of the household for a change? Wasn't she allowed to have some fun in school, just once in a while? Was I never going to stop complaining about her friends?

Okay, okay. Stay where you are, do your schoolwork, keep your friends—but clean up, or you'll get grounded.

Once, in a calmer mood, we talked about Myra, who had told Buffy she could go out and find her real mother.

"How did you feel when she told you that?" I asked my child.

Her answer surprised me.

"Happy," said Buffy. "Happy because I knew then that if I wanted to—not that I definitely would—I could go out and find her. It's like a fear in the heart, in the heart of everyone who is adopted, I think. I've always had the fear that she's going to come back and get me. Sometimes it's good, other times it's bad. Sometimes I think, Please come back and get me! Rescue me from the bad mother who's always screaming, always worried about making a living, always nagging at me. And then at other times, when Jon isn't here and you're not going on about how wonderful he is, I think, What luxury, having my own mom to myself."

That got to me. What luxury for a kid, to have her own mom to herself!

For me, it was also sometimes good and sometimes bad. It was good when Buffy and I were being cuddly and affectionate, and talking as mother to child or as woman to woman. And good when she told me she was too chicken to experiment with drugs, and I could see that, chicken or not, she wasn't playing dangerous games with out-of-control substances. I wanted her to be scared of them, and she was.

It was good when, oblivious to her own casual attitude toward the work ethic, she took me to task for what she considered my inefficient work habits. I was unaware that she'd privately been comparing me with her friend Megan's mother, Charlotte, who, through the years, has battled valiantly to establish herself as a first-class literary agent. Buffy had watched her very carefully and knew that Charlotte was up at six and working diligently.

In a long talk with me one day, Buffy said, "No wonder we don't have any money. You read too much. You knit too much. You have no routine. You get up early; why don't you use your time better? Now, take Charlotte . . ."

I had to laugh. She was so earnest. And so right.

"She's up every morning. She's dressed right away. Her files are in order. She's organized. Why can't you organize, too?" She paused for a critical look at me before issuing her instructions: "You've got to work, really work."

It was not so good when she was being deliberately argumentative, antagonistic, and downright mean. Much of the time, everything I did or didn't do was wrong. My life was too precarious. No one should live that way. I should get a regular job in an office. I should spend less time talking on the phone to my friends. I should work days and stay home evenings and weekends.

In vain, I pointed out that my telephone conversations were part of my work and that some of my workshops could only be scheduled for evenings and weekends. I reminded her that when I was home, which was most of the time, she wasn't, and that I would welcome a chance to see *her* doing some work.

She did not study. She stopped messing up the kitchen and, instead, stayed out late with her friends, no longer at Chess City but at discos instead. She was disco mad, clothes mad, more streetwise for her age than I thought she should be. I was no longer the wicked witch of the West Side but Mommy Dearest, so described with a curl of the lip and something like a gleam of hatred in the luminous brown eyes.

But these, I figured, are the terrible teens. I've been through one siege; I can get through another. And for all the hassles between Buffy and me she knows that, this time around, I am here for her—perhaps even more than she wants me to be. Terrible as she is, I think she's smart and funny. I find I like adolescents, when they're not completely off the wall, because one day they're grown-up and the next they're not and they're very much like me.

By this time in my odyssey I no longer believed my kids' traumas were extraordinary or that I was scarring them for life. Far more conscientious parents than I, as I had seen at Hyde, had far worse trouble with their children. And far less competent parents, as I had learned from the high-risk studies, had virtually trouble-free children. What the kids become is not just up to me. It's up to a whole lot of influences, including the stuff that is in themselves.

My burden of self-indulgent guilt was beginning to dissolve. I had progressed from a resentful caretaker to a loving mother—hot-tempered, sharp-tongued, possibly emotionally and certainly verbally abusive, but on the whole quite . . .

Ah, well. Change comes slowly.

I know hasty words can be damaging, but I also know that what I do is more important than what I say. What I have started to do is show my kids I love them by making it clear that I care about their behavior and what becomes of them. Buffy, like Jon, will simply have to stay within bounds or face the consequences.

And, at this point, I think both my kids are getting the idea.

I had long since given up my old, ineffectual method of disciplining them: let the kids get away with whatever it was for as long as I could stand it, and then explode into screams and slaps and threats of deprivation.

Also my other tactic: talk things out.

Listen to them, yes. Be receptive and understanding. But try to be rational at all times? Forget it. Your carefully reasoned points get lost in the talking-out process. Children are diabolically skilled at digressing from the matter at issue and diverting your complaint into their complaint. This must be nipped in the bud, and very firmly. Talk is nothing. Action is all. When you tell them you're going to lock them out if they're not in by twelve, *do it.* You don't have to win arguments. You have authority, and you must exercise it.

Toughness doesn't work? Sure it does. Rules are essential. You are not operating a Holiday Inn with paying guests. You are running a home that should be comfortable for everyone in it, not geared to the whims of the youngsters at anyone else's expense. It is your responsibility as an adult to maintain discipline and enforce simple rules without resorting to tedious explanation. You can have the grace to change your mind when you see that you have made a mistake, but you are not going to make any points for yourself or your kids if you are putty in their hands. There are times when it is essential to lay down the law, whether you like it or not.

I was making these dramatic revelations to myself while on a lecture tour that took me, over the course of time, from Palm

Springs to Battle Creek, from Forest Hills to Salt Lake City, from Memphis to Denver to Cleveland and a number of other places. Often I was given the choice of staying in a hotel or with a family, and I always chose the family. I liked being with other parents and their children. I felt in touch with them on many levels, in a way I would never have considered possible in my days as an ineffectual young mother.

At a postlecture discussion about hindsight—all the things we mothers would do differently if we could do it all over again—I suddenly remembered the young mothers in the park and the sandbox seminars from which I had remained aloof because the women bored me. And all these years later, after going through the wringer at Hyde and talking to women all over the country, I finally grasped the value of such meetings. Or, at least, the potential value.

Those young women had a support system going for them. They were not growing up in isolation, alone with their fears and convinced of the exclusivity of their problems with their children, as are so many young mothers. I could see now that it was useful for them to exchange observations about their kids and their foibles and their pediatricians and their nursery schools and their teachers. They had the comfort of each other's company and similar experiences. I could also see that there were things between the lines that were not being said, feelings that were unexpressed. The words said one thing, unemotionally. The body language and the tone often said another. I can see them and I can hear them, from way back through the years, and I know that they were glossing over the frustrations and anxieties that almost every mother has.

They also had that tendency to be competitive, that my-kid-is-in-the-99-percentile syndrome. One young woman in the postlecture discussion group brought the typical park scene back to me as vividly as if it had been yesterday.

"You sit there and listen, and you think that all the other people are doing a better job," she said. "All the other children are *brilliant.* Your first instinct is, 'I'm raising an idiot!' I used to sit so meekly and come home and tell Bob, 'Something's wrong with our kid—and it's *us.* That *moron* has a brilliant child.' Until after a while I realized what this was all about. All of them were raising their own idiots and playing 'can you top this?' It's all a game!"

General laughter. A voice in the background: "But we were sharing."

First mother: "Well, you don't share with 'can you top this?' "

Right. You compete. But if you leave the game playing to the kids in the sandbox, you have an ideal opportunity to say, "I'm terribly worried about Tommy. Look at him. He's listless. He won't play with the others. He sits on his sister's face. He bites the mailman. He screams until midnight." Or whatever the problem is.

Women are surprising. They may not always be able to help themselves as individuals, but they can turn all their objectivity and sympathy to helping others who need help. Get them going in a discussion, and out comes a little horde of similar experiences, worries, and suggestions. Something rings a bell. The mother knows her child better than anyone, but she's been so worried that she's missed a signal, overlooked some commonsensical approach. *You mean you made that same mistake? You mean your kid did that same disgusting, scary thing? You mean there's something can be done about it, apart from penal servitude? Thank God!*

I talked to women who felt they had made bad mistakes and others who said to each other, "Hey, look. If you were so bad, would you be worrying? Sure, you can think of things you would have done differently. But you also have to say, 'I did the very best I could at that time, so I forgive myself.' Whatever your past sins were, you're finally letting yourself out of prison."

To myself I thought, these women already know what I went to my friendly experts to find out.

Fascinated by this belated insight, I developed a questionnaire designed to elicit from mothers what they felt about motherhood, how they felt about themselves as mothers, what frustrations and difficulties they had had. As time went by I turned the questionnaires into an interviewing tool, because there wasn't room enough on the pages for everything the mothers had to say. Talking was better. But in my initial, informal poll of about three hundred mothers, ranging in age from twenty-one to fifty and over, only about 5 percent indicated that motherhood, for them, had been a dream come true. The rest suggested that it was okay to wonderful, and yet . . .

"I am afraid of what I'll do if he keeps on crying all the time." "I was programmed to be a mother and now I wonder if I wouldn't have been better off working." "I had no preparation and I'm scared of doing it all wrong." "I have a bicultural marriage and the world's most beautiful baby, but I'm afraid she's going to suffer." "I love my child, but I'm bored at home and I miss the excitement of my job." "I had to go back to work because I was going crazy doing cooking, cleaning, housework, and all that stuff I've never been any good at." "I miss the companionship of adults." "I feel terribly guilty, but I know I must get out of the house." "I lose my temper and feel like a monster." "I slap these little helpless things and I could kill myself." "I worry endlessly about what they're doing, and what I'm doing to them." "I lose patience!"

"I thought raising children was like baking a cake. You put in certain ingredients and then, after twenty-one years, you get the expected result. It doesn't work so easily. I did not get the expected result."

A Long Island mother compared raising children with gardening: "You never know when you plant something how it's going to come up." She nourished her little seedlings, gave them a nice environment, fed, watered, and fertilized them, protected them from weeds and squirrels and deer, and gave them her constant concern. "And you look at them when they come up, and the cutworms are demolishing the whole lot or they're covered with some obscure fungus—something beyond your control, but it must be something you did or didn't do because *you* were the one who was raising them.

"Same with kids. You've read the books, followed the directions on the packet. You think you're exposing them to the right environment and all the best that the twentieth century can offer—and then something goes wrong."

This mother has two daughters and two sons, one of whom is gay. He is attractive and extremely intelligent but afraid to assert himself, too insecure to leave his undemanding, dead-end job to look for something that will give him more satisfaction in terms of money, prestige, and pleasure; he has few friends, other than the young man he lives with, and feels ill at ease with most of his family and their friends.

"Jeffrey hates me," his mother says flatly. "I think basically he's disappointed in himself and he's turned it on me. I also think he was disappointed in his father and afraid of him, and that's been turned on me." His father, she adds, is not usually a frightening person, but he has something of a dual personality: coolly intellectual on the one side, subject to occasional violent rages on the other. Both boys have found it difficult to identify with him; Jeffrey ultimately found it impossible.

"I do think his father's behavior is a big factor, which we have tended to ignore," his mother says, "although I've always seen Jeff's problems as a reflection on me because I should have known there was something wrong. I love him very much and think him wonderful in many ways. But in some other ways, he's strange. And I thought his strangeness—his *wimpiness*, I can't help saying—was an indication of my shortcomings. I took it personally. I was very unhappy about it. And I still am, because he's so unhappy and dissatisfied with himself. I've blamed myself, and maybe it *is* my fault."

She pauses, her expression indicating quite clearly that she still blames herself.

"I've been searching my brain and my heart for the last three years, ever since he moved in with his friend, thinking, what could I have done differently? And I can't think of it. Except maybe being more aware of his needs as he was growing up. But it's very hard to get a little kid to talk about his needs. There are things that are beyond your control. I didn't know what was going on in school. I didn't have feedback at that time. Your kid doesn't tell you that the others are jumping on him and calling him a sissy. I never knew how miserable he was until one day his sisters came home from school and said, 'Hey, Mom, the kids in Jeffrey's class were ganging up on him in the gym today.' "

She changed his school. He went on to the prep school and the college of his choice. His grades were excellent. He did graduate work in Europe. He came back and could not decide what he wanted to do with his life. He hasn't yet. He is still unhappy.

"He's going nowhere. He has a mass of problems, unresolved. I just wish he were happy, but his whole life seems so drab and awful. I keep thinking I must have failed somewhere, somehow. Why didn't I know more about him? Why did I let his life go off the track? What did I do wrong?"

I met a high-powered young salesman not too long ago. He casually asked me what I was working on and I, as casually, told him. He was enormously interested.

"When I told my mother I was gay," he said, "she was appalled and asked, 'What did I do wrong?' Fathers never say that. The fathers blame the mothers. 'You made him a mama's boy. You made a fag out of him.' But that's what all the mothers say: 'What did I do wrong?' "

More discussions on the road. I ask the mothers what has hurt them the most. Some speak openly. Some draw me aside when discussions end. I feel like an intruder, exacerbating their pain, but—unlike the mothers of earlier times—they do not seem to mind others knowing about their agony. And possibly finding some comfort in it.

Their tales are sometimes familiar: a boy was a drug addict, a girl an alcoholic; a boy delinquent, a girl promiscuous; a son cruised the streets at night, a daughter was living on a bean-sprout farm with people who wore rags around their heads; a teenager was a dropout and a runaway; a child was alternately hyperactive and withdrawn, talked little, couldn't read or write, had a father who said angrily, "There's nothing wrong with my son! Don't tell me there's anything wrong with him!" A child who was institutionalized for life. An adoptive mother who could not honestly blame herself for her teenager's incorrigible behavior because she'd adopted him when he was twelve and already extremely troubled. But she's deeply distressed because she can't stand the boy and yet cannot let him go. He has been rejected twice already.

And some tales are too terrible to contemplate.

A twenty-year-old son is in a home for the severely retarded and the estranged father is drinking his troubles away.

A baby was brain-damaged at birth. Or was it before birth, because of something the mother did? Or in the days or weeks following? She will never know.

Somebody was supposed to have closed the window and kept an eye on the toddler, who crawled out and fell six stories to land, miraculously, on the front-entrance canopy. It was days before the parents knew whether he would live or die, and sometimes it seems he never fully recovered.

The eighteen-month-old in her high chair was fussing with her supper. A tired, exasperated mother said, "You're going to sit there till you eat your food," and left the kitchen to do something in another room. When she came back moments later, the child had choked to death. Oh, God, the guilt!

The teenaged daughter was a dwarf. Bright, active, witty, well liked, but a dwarf. Mother loved her, but hated the fact that her child was a dwarf and hated herself for hating it.

A child who had committed suicide.

In 1983, six thousand teenagers killed themselves. I cannot speculate on the reasons why there is something like an epidemic of suicides among young people today; I only know it is so. The experts, appalled, have no explanations beyond saying that no single reason *ever* suffices; the causes of any youngster's suicide are enormously complex. I have seen the face of the mother of a suicide victim; I have read the anguished words and seen the faces of other mothers in the newspapers, looked at them on the television news. For the loving, uncomprehending parent, there can scarcely be a greater pain.

What could we have done to prevent it? Why? *Why?*

In a less somber vein, I ask the mothers I meet, "Do you feel that you are mothering as you yourselves were mothered? Do you think this is effective mothering? Or do you do and say things that you swore you never would?"

These questions usually elicit rueful laughter. Again and again the mothers say, "Oh, *I* was going to be so much better! I was never going to whack my kid, least of all in anger. I was never going to say some of the things she said. But now I keep hearing my mother's voice coming out of me!"

Saying what sort of things?

Oh . . .

"Wait till your father gets home."

"Stop crying or I'll give you something to cry about."

"You do that just to be mean; you're bad."

"You're making me hate you."

"When you're my age you'll understand."

"Look it up in the dictionary."

"I've forgotten more than you'll ever know."

"How many times do I have to tell you . . . ?"

"Because I'm the mommy, that's why."

One young woman confessed to a serious case of "matrophobia." As she described it, "It's a fear of being like my mother, of mothering like my mother. It's a failure of the separation thing. The separation was never complete or successful. It's a fear of being absorbed in her again. One of the funniest experiences I ever had as a mother was watching a film a producer friend had made on natural childbirth. Suddenly the film goes on rewind, and everything goes backward, and the baby goes right back into the mother. And that, for me, is matrophobia. It's just getting lost in her all over again. It's in a sense a kind of death for me."

Another, in her early forties, said that one of her ambitions had been to be completely unlike her mother. "I thought I was beautifully prepared to be a good mother. I could do more for my children because I was better educated, I knew books, I knew good music, I wasn't so stressed. But my family was undemonstrative and so am I. I can't hug and kiss the kids. My mother didn't do it, and it's totally alien to me. Demonstrations of affection embarrass me. I just can't do it for my kids. To me, to have physical contact was reserved for men, sex. It never spilled over to anyone else. So, in the end, I'd picked up my mother's most negative trait."

But even a negative sometimes contains something positive. "My images of my mother," said a high-powered female executive, "are as a very powerful negative role model. She didn't mother. She didn't encourage our aptitudes. She had a lot of card parties. She was self-absorbed and immature. I wanted my boys to grow up happier than we did, and more content with themselves. My mother had a bromide for everything. But she had one great quality: she was very, very consistent, as was her own mother, even in her bromides. There were rules that were made out of glass, made to be broken; rules made out of wood, that might or might not be broken; and rules that were made out of iron, that were not to be broken. My mother's no meant no. My mother's maybe meant maybe. My mother's yes meant yes. My sister and I learned this early, and I've done this with my boys. It was a nice, fundamental thing to know."

I must say that a surprising number of young women, particularly those who live outside the great eastern metropolitan centers, show a great deal of warmth and respect for their mothers. I should not be surprised, I suppose, but as I recall my sandbox days, the mothers were always complaining about their mothers. Now I find a different, more tolerant attitude emerging, and I'm not quite sure why this is. Greater understanding, more resilience, a readiness to forgive? Or less need to blame?

Still, most mothers who speak up about their mothers have at least a few criticisms to make. Something was said or done over a period of time that hurt. Seeing herself in her own kid, she wants to spare today's child the stings and slights she suffered. Bearing little animus, she wants to be a better mother than her mother was. It is easier for her to simply blame her mother than to make her own effort to change, and yet she consciously tries to be different. She is taking action.

I have found that those who make the greatest effort to be as unlike their mothers as possible are those who have the strongest reason: they were the victims of abuse. Not of the most violent physical kind, but of freqent slappings, whacks with rulers, deprivation punishments, hysterical tirades; vicious, hateful words and threats alternating with periods of cold neglect.

These parents are not perpetuating a pattern of abuse.

Invariably, they have said to me, "Having the children was the greatest thing that ever happened to me. They have changed my life completely. I can't treat them the way I was treated."

Yes, they get angry at times, but they stop and ask themselves, "Am I losing my temper over something that really has nothing to do with them, just something to do with the way my mother was with me? Do I have to extend my anger to everything he's ever done or said, just because he's knocked his milk over five times today? Do I have to tell him he's bad and stupid because I don't like what he just did?"

A number of college-educated mothers have told me how

they consciously, deliberately, try to eliminate certain behavior patterns they feel they have inherited, and how at the same time they try not to take a second crack at childhood through their children.

Luz is different. I think she may be invulnerable. So maybe she's living her life through her children. Who cares?

Luz, late thirties, was born in Puerto Rico, orphaned at two, and brought up in Brooklyn by an aunt she called mother. Luz was the only child in the house. Her baby sister, Rosa, was brought up by a couple with three children of their own.

Rosa was lucky. Luz was not.

"I loved my mother to no end," says Luz, "but she was so strict! She disciplined, physically and mentally and everything. Even when I was older. If I came home late from school, or five minutes late from the job because of the bus or some crazy thing, she'd start whacking. She'd whack my face with her hand open, fingers curved like claws, and she'd whack me and scratch me with the nails. Sometimes I think now, going back, that she wasn't well in her mind. She couldn't have been. Because I know she loved me. I know she did."

Luz has two boys, seven and five, bright-eyed, demanding, enormously energetic. She talks about her "mother," thinks of them. "She never cuddled me or hugged me. I just felt she did love me. But if I ever went to her in a loving way, she'd say, 'Oh, get outa here—stop that faking!' I loved her very much. You want to know, how could I? That was all I had to love, you know? There's a lot of love in me, and that was all I had to love. I think that's why, now, I just *have* to have my husband and my stepkids and my four cats and my own two kids. If we could afford it, I think I'd have five kids. You understand? I just have all that love in me that didn't have anyplace to go. There's more I can give. There's more."

I ask, "Did you ever say to yourself, 'When I'm a mother, I'm not going to be like her.' "

"I never thought about it then. I probably didn't even think

I'd get married. *Now* I go back and think, I can never be like that. Not because of the way she treated me, but because I just don't think I could. Know what I mean? It's not in me. I don't think I could."

Still, there must be something she deliberately does differently.

There isn't. Not deliberately. She just does everything differently, for the very good reason that now she can do what she wants to do.

"I don't stay home. I'm always out with the kids. You'll never catch me in the summertime. If you can't catch me in the wintertime, you'll never catch me in the summertime. Especially now that I like to drive. I am like a free bird. And I go with my kids to the end of the world. Well, Brooklyn and Long Island! They tell me about Chuck E. Cheese. Yesterday I went to Chuck E. Cheese. Ate there, played the machines. I take them to pottery classes, take Eric to chess, take them to soccer, take them anyplace where there's something new going on. I enjoy it. I want to do it. And I think it's because I never had it. A lot of people don't understand that. They say, "But how can you spend all your time like that? You're dedicating yourself just for your kids, you're not going to be compensated.'

"I don't want to be compensated. This is it. Right now, with them, *I am living*. Doing what I didn't, years ago, when I was a kid. I'm having a ball. And people can't believe this. I have fun. I enjoy it. They ask, 'How could you?' But I do. This is my real life. This is how I'm happy."

# CHAPTER FIFTEEN

# We Are Here for the Mothers

SUSAN would be the one in the small red station wagon, she told me over the phone, and she'd have her two-year-old boy with her. They would be looking out for me at the Westbury Railroad Station at ten next Wednesday morning.

By a couple of minutes past ten I was scanning the station parking lot for a little red wagon, a young woman, and a small boy. There were several such groups, but only one mother seemed to be peering around for a stranger.

Identifications made, we drove to the Westbury Mothers' Center, which, Susan told me, used rented meeting rooms in the United Methodist Church. The steering committee was due to meet upstairs to discuss such business as the fund-raising art auction, the annual dinner and fashion show, the forthcoming workshops on such topics as "Sibling Rivalry and Behavioral Problems" and "Role Expectations in Parenthood: Who's Got It Worst?," the Puppets Workshop, the Children's Craft Fair and Carnival, and several other activities, while the children played or napped in other rooms under the supervision of paid but motherly caretakers whom the children adored.

"It sounds like an ideal setup," I observed.

"It's something special," said Susan. "This is not a well-knit neighborhood in the sense that we know many of our neighbors—most are older people—or meet other mothers while strolling down the street to do the shopping. You don't do that in station wagons. It's hard to get to know other parents, and it can be very lonely. I don't know what we'd do without the Mothers' Center. It's a nursery school, a play group, a discussion group, a social club—everything. It's an integral part of our lives."

It is also a part of a movement that is sweeping the nation: self-help for mothers.

We drew up near the church. Other small station wagons were parking nearby, and mothers and little children were piling out and greeting each other. They looked like members of one huge family gathering for a picnic, except that the daddies weren't there. The daddies were at work. But one item on the day's agenda would be to begin planning for a Couples Night, on which occasion—according to my informants—the fathers would tell each other and everyone else who might care to listen what a tough time they were having, working all day and coming home to find that the clothes they had dropped on the floor the night before had not yet been hung up.

Laughter, fading into the interior of the church's community center. I saw the babies being settled into the nursery and the toddlers heading for their indoor sandbox, a vast toy chest and a variety of sticky art projects; and then I went upstairs with the mothers. It was my first personal encounter with a mothers' support group. No such thing existed in my sandbox days.

The 1980s are a difficult time for young women facing choices about their future. I suspect the nineties will be no easier. This is a revolutionary time for women, and revolutions disrupt and tear apart before they put together something new and better.

Today's experienced mothers, those who came out of school or college in the fifties or sixties, have a unique perspective.

We were the last to be exhorted to go on to bigger and better things, to dabble in a career for a year or two or a few, then become the loyal wife of some fine man and the mother of his children. We were flashed a glimpse of a future beyond a part-time job and settled down, vaguely uneasy. The housewife-mother-partner role was being filled and often very well filled indeed, but were not some talents underutilized and some minds going to waste? And why did we have that sense of non-professionalism in the job of motherhood? We had always heard it was woman's most glorious role. Now, it appeared, it was her only one; and it seemed to be nothing.

Then came the great wave of the women's movement. Within the span of a single generation, there has been a surge of energy and enormous change.

Women think and talk about this all over the country.

The impact is greater in the cities than in the heartland, and makes itself felt in fits and starts, but nonetheless it is apparent everywhere. A message is going the rounds: you don't have to be just a mother. You *ought* to be more than a mother. See yourself as you can be: you are siren, wife, entrepreneur in your three-piece suit, gourmet cook and financial whiz, jogger and tennis player, and gracious winner of Trivial Pursuit. You are running for Congress and your children adore you. So does your old man.

Sure. There may be nineteen such women in the United States. Forty-eight? One hundred and five? So what? What about the real people?

A fifty-year-old Pennsylvania mother of five, including one daughter recently married, one about to be, and one in college, observed that facing life as a young woman in her day was hard enough, but is now absolutely bewildering.

"Most of us," she says, "were programmed to either have a career or get married and have kids, and most of us did what we were programmed to do. But my mother used to tell me stuff like, 'Be a gynecologist, be a lawyer.' And on the other hand, 'Stay home and have children!' She was very modern in that she felt women should have careers, but she never had sorted out in her own mind how you're supposed to do it. Well, hey! We haven't either.

"Women today are getting worse mixed signals that ever before. They're being *brainwashed* into: yes, you can be president of IBM at thirty-two and raise a couple of kids as well. Sure, you can do everything, and you'd better get out there and do it. Or else: you can stay home and raise your kids, and then you can go back to work. Yeah, really. You stay home for ten or fifteen years, and you're out of whatever high-tech thing is going on. How are you going to catch up?

"Look, there've always been extraordinary people doing lots of things and doing them in different ways. But the fact that they do them doesn't mean that you or I can do them. I think people ignore reality a lot. They're telling girls now, 'You can have it all!' *And of course it isn't true.* What you have is a maze of signals to sort out and live with. How can you have a professional career and be a successful wife and mother and homemaker without some of the wires coming undone in your brain? You can only do it if you are a superperson. And then if one aspect of all that fails, *something* has to give. And I suspect that, right now, it's the kids, because we haven't got the answers yet.

"I think it's very important to tell young women on the eve of college, 'Don't let them confuse you with all these different signals. Just decide what it is that you are inclined toward, and go along with your inclinations. Don't listen to everybody else.' And that's very tough to do, because all the options can be made to sound so attractive!

"But that of course is the core of this problem: to be a woman is to face life with mixed messages, and it's never been easy to sort them out."

I myself have mixed feelings about the mixed messages.

If there is one legacy of the early feminist movement I regret, it is the perception that still lingers among some women who have chosen to stay at home and rear their children that theirs is a lesser role than that of their working sisters. Most women who find themselves juggling the demands of their jobs and their obligations to their children, their husbands, and their households find their lives a very difficult balancing act indeed and acknowledge this. But though few still subscribe to the simplistic absolutes of twenty years ago that said for a woman to work was good, to stay at home to care for her family bad, many stay-at-home women across the country still feel they are put down by their working sisters. Truly, all they have to do is be themselves, doing as individuals all the things they do best.

The great value of the women's movement has been to demonstrate the versatility of women and the many options available to them. To show women that the world is as much theirs as it is anyone's. That they can make their own choices. To jolt them into a new openness. To let them know that there is nothing wrong with craving strength and admitting weakness and talking to each other about problems that might be solved together.

In large part because of that new awareness, something refreshing and exciting is sweeping the country. Women are talking to each other about all the mixed signals they are receiving and the conflicts they are enduring while trying simultaneously to be good mothers, contribute to the family income, and live up to their full potential as people.

On recent tours I have been astounded to learn how many mothers are openly admitting their fears and inadequacies and are prepared to tackle them. Not all, though. Most of the older mothers I talk to—today's grandmothers and great-grandmothers—are reluctant to concede that their child-rearing days were anything but rosy and their children anything but perfect.

"If you could do it over, what would you do differently?" I ask. "Nothing!" "Have you ever felt that you might have had unreasonably high expectations of your children?" "Never. They have exceeded my every hope." Or such glowing reviews as,"I am eighty-one years old and every moment was absolute bliss."

Many of today's young mothers have a decent reticence, too, but they are not ashamed of seeking help when they need it. And more and more of them are finding it through their peers, either informally or, more lately, in organized groups. On a swing through the Midwest I met only one mother under thirty-five who did not readily admit to a need for the company and counsel of other mothers. "Support? Never needed any. I had faith in myself." She is divorced, works, has four children. Two are high achievers; two are delinquent. Faith is not always enough.

On the other hand, there was one mother in the fifty-plus category whose ten children—yes, ten!—are all comfortably making their way in the world, who said rather ruefully, "The rest of us were born twenty years too soon."

Many of us feel that way. There never was such a time of opportunity for women. We have discovered an old bandwagon, leapt on it, and turned it into something new. It is called "self-help."

I used to say that everyone and every group has a champion but moms. Nobody speaks up for us, nobody lobbies for us, nobody lends an ear or a shoulder when mothers need help.

Within the last few years I have discovered that I myself have been behind the times. There are plenty of people who speak up for mom and offer help in enormously practical ways. These people are mothers. There *are* groups, and indeed lobbies, for troubled parents: for mothers with universal problems, with aches of loneliness and frustration, with lives splintered by terrible tragedy.

Such groups have long been with us, and now they are proliferating. In the beginning they were for the few. Now they are for the many: *Mothers Matter. Tough Love. Single Parents*

*Resource   Center.   Compassionate   Friends.   S.O.S.   for Women's Rights, Inc. Parents of Suicides. Parents Anonymous. Parents of Murdered Children. Widowed Persons Service. Adoptive Parents Support Group. Parents of Dwarf Children.* Hundreds of them. Informal self-help groups that start meeting in living rooms or church basements when one person in need realizes that others have similar needs. Small groups that develop into larger ones with organized programs and facilities for classes, social activities, discussions of problems, and supervised playrooms and nap rooms.

"The concept of self-help has always been with us," says Frances J. Dory, executive director of the New York City Self-Help Clearing House, which publishes a directory of more than 350 organizations.* "When I was growing up in rural Long Island, the volunteer fire department was the center of life in the community. As kids we had to grab brooms and buckets and chase the fire trucks and help put out the fires. Everybody pitched in. You knew that if something happened in your house these same people were going to come and help you. When my father was ill and had to be cared for at home, there wasn't anything he needed that the people in the fire department didn't bring to him. All my father had to say was, 'I need,' and it came."

These very rich experiences of her childhood have convinced Fran Dory of the value of community cooperation.

"I don't believe that the way to make it in life is to go out and get an education and then choose a career and *be* it. I think that experience, and sharing experience, is *the* most important and valid resource and knowledge base that we have in this world. It has got to be uplifted and cannot become second-

* It is obviously impossible to include the entire list of self-help organizations within the body of the text, but information about a particular group may be obtained from: The National Self-Help Clearing House, Graduate School and University Center of the City University of New York, 33 West 42nd Street, Room 1227, New York, NY 10036.

ary to what people like to call more scientific or more organized information bases."

Of course, things aren't what they used to be. They never are. In past decades, many and perhaps most of us had the feeling that there was always somewhere and someone to go to when we needed help. But that has become much less true as jobs move many young people away from their families or older family members retire to better climates. Fran Dory points out that schools, churches, and families are no longer the sources of support they used to be. All are in a state of change. Self-help groups are the new resource, and a very healthy one. Parents' groups exist in numbers impossible to contemplate a decade ago, when they first began to appear here and there in widely scattered communities—and not always to the acclaim of all concerned. Today's groups have a built-in sense of purpose and success. They are made up of people who have reasons to come together and share, and know how to do it effectively.

How does an organization such as the Clearing House help to start such a group?

Dory tells me, "Someone calls us up and says, 'This is my situation and I would like to know if there is someone else in the same situation.' If the answer is yes, we give them that person's name and number, and we encourage them to call and talk and get together and share—and do all those good things.

"Then what is most challenging for us is when people call and say, 'I want to talk to someone'—and we don't have anyone for them to talk to. So we have to help them find people, and that's when we begin the process of outreach, which is kind of incredible. People are searching, and we are trying to help them connect."

Women whose husbands were health nuts and dropped dead while jogging. Mothers who have had multiple births. Women in their late thirties and early forties with their first child. Interracial couples. "No one is dealing with the problems of interracial children," says Dory. "These children do not appear in literature, in children's books, hence there is nothing to validate their existence." There are all kinds of reasons for mothers to get together, and they can't always easily find people with their kinds of problems.

"A lot of our parent groups start out with mothers of young babies. Part of the phenomenon is that there are no longer many women at home and around the neighborhood, and people need to find some equivalent of the playground groups we used to have. So the mothers call us up and tell us what they are looking for: this is where I live, this is my background, these are the kinds of people I would like to talk to. More and more, people are wanting to sit down and talk with each other in small groups. Oddly enough, they don't always want to talk with their next-door neighbor or the mothers in the playground, because they need a certain level of anonymity. If they are feeling uncertain, it is more comfortable to talk with new people who are going through the same problems at the same time. It's different from friendship."

Dory tells me about a wonderful mothers' group in Ridgewood, Queens: women without station wagons.

"They meet once a week at a church, and they bring all their kids. They sit around and they talk, because they are feeling that they are not a part of the eighties. This group was organized by a woman who felt that being a housewife and mother was pretty important, and she sort of thought that other women did too. She advertised in local papers and on supermarket bulletin boards and invited people who thought the way she did to come to this church on Thursday morning at ten o'clock.

"About forty mothers and all their kids showed up—nursing mothers, and mothers with little preschool kids—all women who didn't work, who were at home, whose husbands were blue-collar workers. That wasn't *them* on the soap operas and that wasn't them on the six o'clock news. They weren't like that. They just didn't know where they were. And they sat around and talked about how good it was to be with their kids. They needed to say that to each other, because the world was saying about them, 'God, look at all those women sitting around living off their husbands!' "

At this point they suddenly got the signal that they were onto something larger than life and they didn't know what to do with it. They called the Clearing House. Fran Dory went out to Ridgewood to tell the mothers more about self-help and how to get organized.

She spent a couple of weeks with them, for the most part making practical suggestions about obtaining a reasonably quiet place in which to meet, where the adults could be in one room and the kids in another with a couple of the mothers taking turns, and how to keep the group going with fund raisers such as pot-luck suppers and other events.

Another of Fran Dory's favorite groups is the Sisterhood of Black Single Mothers in Brooklyn, of which she herself—a divorced mother—is a long-time member.

It was started about ten years ago on the basis of shared baby sitting and clothes swapping by a woman named Daphne Busby. Now the women have an office in which to meet, but Daphne began it in her house.

"These black women," says Dory, "are concerned about their image. They don't like the fact that when Mia Farrow goes out and has a baby without benefit of marriage, that's a love child, and when they have it, it's an illegitimate child. They are concerned about what's going out on the media. They are concerned about relationships with men.

"They are a fascinating group of women. Some of them are on welfare, and some of them are corporate executives. They all share the experience of being single mothers, and somehow make it all come together. The sisterhood has become a very important group. It has funding now and serves as a model for others; it demonstrates the strength of black mothers. At the crossroads of history and opportunity, Daphne Busby was right there. She herself is a model of strength. People ask her about the problems of broken homes.

" 'Broken?' she says. 'My home works. Something that is broken doesn't work.' "

"What about women who feel they need professional help?" I ask. "Can the groups help them?"

"More and more mothers," replies Dory, "are being told or made to feel that, if things aren't right, they need to go into counseling. When they mention this, I ask them if they have ever thought of talking to another group of parents. This, by the way, usually means mothers, because 75 percent of self-helpers are women. And these women say, 'Is it all right, just to talk to other parents? Isn't there a professional there? I mean, how do I know that what they're saying is right?'

"I tell them, 'You know, if something is really wrong, people aren't going to sit there and say it's okay, don't worry about it. They're going to say that you really need help. And if you hear that often enough, you'll seek out some other kinds of help, and they'll help you do that. In the meantime, why don't you just try to see what other people have done in the same situation?' Women are so relieved to hear this."

Yet they are still reluctant to follow their own instincts.

"Then I say to them, 'Hey, look, take back a piece of your life. Give yourself the power. Express a little bit of your own power. Tell yourself, *I can do this.* That's what you need to know. Once you make that decision, you know that you're not going to lose control in the parenting situation. You are in the empowering position. It takes feeling it just one time to know how it feels to be powerful. And if you feel powerful once, you never want to feel powerless again.' So that's what we've got to get these folks to do in groups, so they won't spend so much of their time and energy wondering about who is giving them permission to do this."

*    *    *

More trips around the country, more meetings with organized mothers.

*Cleveland suburbs, Marilyn Fenton:*

"Our co-op started in an interesting way. Several of us, all
pregnant and due within a few weeks of each other, met in our
Lamaze class. Three of us became very close friends.

"When the kids were about a month or two months old we
decided to get together once a week at each one's house in turn
for a kind of kaffeeklatsch and just talk about what was going
on and how the children were progressing. So the three of us
started, and within a couple of months we were joined by four
other women who'd also had children within the same month
or two. This worked out beautifully. It was nice to look at each
other's children and see how they were growing.

"Our first playgroup started when the babies were just a few
months old and ended when they turned three and entered
nursery school. When the children were small, all the mothers
stayed with them. We had coffee and watched the children
play. We could also help each other out when we felt there was
a problem. One child's foot was turning in. Did you notice it?
What can be done about it? One of the little girls was not
talking at two and a half and we encouraged her mother to take
her to a speech therapist. It turned out that she did need help.
She had speech lessons twice a week for a year or two.

"It was a terrific support group. We all knew each other, and
we felt free to ask questions. 'What would you do if your child
kept waking up? Would you let him cry it out?' ' I don't know
how to handle this. What would *you* do?' And we could always
call each other if we had a problem. This was very helpful to
us, because we weren't getting advice from our mothers, who
had raised children twenty or more years ago. And of course
things have changed, and attitudes have changed, and it was
nice for a group of peers to see if we were all doing it the same
way. Sometimes we might feel that another mother was too

strict, or too lenient, but at least we got the viewpoints, and no one felt threatened, and that was excellent.

"As the children got older, we would leave four mothers with the seven children and the other three mothers would have a morning or afternoon free for themselves. We had a chart, and we rotated in and out. The mothers who stayed were responsible for the children and for snacks.

"Then it progressed even further. We turned the group into a baby-sitting co-op. There was no money involved; the co-op worked on a point system. Each mother would get two points for every half hour of baby-sitting, with extra points for lunch, dinner or weekend baby-sitting, and she could collect those points in baby-sitting time due to her. This worked beautifully and got us all through the nursery school years, after which the kids started off to real school and we had our days free anyway.

"The co-op has been a lifesaver. Mothers need to get out, and it is so hard to find sitters during the day and so expensive. Sometimes when you ask your own mother or mother-in-law to sit for you, you've got to have a really good reason. They'll sit for you if you are going to the doctor, but they don't want to sit for you if you feel like going out to lunch. There aren't too many young mothers who will give themselves the luxury of a whole afternoon off, or lunch downtown with their husbands, or tennis, or art classes. The cost is so high. So our co-op has been wonderful, for the children as well as for us.

"One of the women in our group was a diabetic, and her child was born with cerebral palsy. At first she was not sure if she could stay in the group because it was very hard for her to see children the same age as her child who were walking and doing things that her child couldn't do. She didn't know if he would ever be able to walk.

" 'I don't know if I can stay,' she said. 'My child is eleven months old and your children are eleven months old. Your children are all starting to walk, and my child might be sitting in his infant seat forever.' But she liked us. She needed and wanted the support. We encouraged her to stay in the group. She felt that, besides the classes he was taking with children like himself, he should be with normal children. So she stayed, and we were really glad she did. Her son has done so beautifully.

"He is walking now and going to a school where there is a good chance that he will be progressing. The support was terrific, and we were just crazy about him. The other kids loved him. They would ask why Matthew wasn't walking, and we would be very open and explain that Matthew had an illness and we didn't know why he wouldn't walk or when he'd be able to. And the kids just accepted it. If a child is part of the group and they grow up together, they accept him.

"The backgrounds of the people in the group varied widely. We had librarians, we had schoolteachers, and a couple of the girls hadn't been to college, but everyone blended beautifully. Quite a few of our mothers worked part time, and others went back to full time. One of the librarians went back to work when her kids were six and three, and one went to law school.

"Now that my little girl has started going to kindergarten I've stopped using the co-op, but we're all still friends. It's been an extended family in the best sense. We used to have picnics on Sundays so that the fathers could meet, and we all became friends—the fathers and mothers and the children. It was a lovely way to do things.

"But what was best was the way the mothers could say to each other, 'See you Monday,' and know that we'd all be there. And the way the kids would walk right in the door. Toddlers are afraid to go with strangers, but we were all so close and such good friends that there never was a problem of fear. They were more like brothers and sisters.

"It was a special group."

*Rockford, Illinois. Janice Gustavson:*
"We went to the library to do research on mothers' groups

and we used someone else's previous experience with a baby-sitting co-op, since our reason for being was to get help with baby-sitting. We felt we needed guidelines.

"Originally we had a bridge group, and the co-op grew out of it. It started at my house, with eight of us who had small children. None of us was working outside the home at that time. My little girl was four months old. We decided that everyone would bring their kids. All of them were under three years old. So we brought in playpens and infant seats and set them up and tried to play bridge and have lunch.

"But the oldest kid, a three-year-old, unlocked the door somehow, got out of the house, and wandered around the neighborhood. A very nice residential neighborhood, but—! We had to go searching for her. Finally we found her on the next block sitting on the sidewalk petting a dog. Everyone thought this was peculiar because there we were, all supposedly watching the childen, yet one escaped. So we decided to set up a baby-sitting co-op, which worked on the point system: one point per hour for baby sitting, an extra point for feeding children, an extra point for taking them to school or some other place, and so on.

"One of the things we decided was really important was to have a medical release form. If a child got sick at your house and you couldn't get hold of the mother, we wanted authorization to get treatment. So we made up a form on which we put the child's name, the mother's name and address, and the sitter's name and address, the name of a witness to our signatures, and the doctor's name, address, and telephone number. Everyone agreed it was a good idea to have the forms. We still do, even though nobody has needed one in the six years we've been in existence. I keep knocking on wood that it will never be necessary to use them."

*Westbury, Long Island:*
First thing on the day's agenda was the Steering Committee meeting. About fifteen mothers were gathered around the

table. The children, downstairs, were divided into two groups: infants in one room, napping and crawling about; toddlers and other preschoolers in another, playing with an amazing variety of inventive toys. Two motherly child-care professionals were in charge in each room, fully responsible for their small clients, but ready to take any one to mother should the request be made.

The business of the day was slightly edited for my benefit, because I'd said I'd like to hear the mothers talking about their needs and feelings rather than sit in on the planning arrangements for the fall festival and other upcoming events; but as things turned out I got a sense both of the committee's work and of the mothers' feelings about why they were there and what they were getting out of it.

One of the first things I discovered is that the Westbury Mothers' Center is not one of a kind, but one of a chain coming under the heading of the Mothers' Center Development Project, sponsored by the Family Service Association of Nassau County, Inc. It is not a local phenomenon; there are two dozen mothers' centers in various parts of the country, from Long Island to South Carolina, from Missouri to Florida; and project coordinators offer free consultation service to all groups and individuals interested in starting a mothers' center in their own community. Requests for information have come from almost every state and from several foreign countries. The centers are family-oriented community programs run by the mothers in cooperation with carefully selected health care and child-rearing specialists. Each mothers' center sets up its own program according to the needs of the members and of the community.

"We are nonhierarchical and nonjudgmental," one member told me as the mothers settled into their folding chairs and started comparing notes on the previous week's activities. "Which means we don't have any bosses and we can all say what we please without somebody saying, 'You feed him all that sugar? He stays up so late? That's terrible!'"

Almost imperceptibly, the nonbossy, nonjudgmental, but thoroughly competent coordinator got the meeting going by noting the items to be discussed and introducing me. From the children's rooms below there were occasional whoops and hollers of joy or anger, but not a mother turned a hair.

Brief business first: the last fund raiser had collected a satisfactory amount of money, but it was to be hoped that the art auction would do even better. Any more pictures available for contribution? The group planning the fashion show was to meet next Thursday at the local Chinese restaurant. Those desiring a little wine with lunch would have to bring their own. Couples Night was scheduled, as all knew, for the Saturday after next. More main dishes were needed. Anyone else want to bring a hot dish? Okay, Wednesday afternoon is the sibling rivalry workshop. Anyone here interested? A question: "Is someone going to come and talk about it?" Answer: "Yes, if anybody's going to show up. Please, all of you interested, give your names to Debbie."

My turn next. I looked around at this group of women in their twenties and early thirties, perhaps one or two a little older, and thought how involved and articulate they all were. I dropped in a comment about my inadequacies as a mother, a question about their feelings, and the ball was rolling.

"My baby was six weeks old. I'm on the couch, in my nightgown, crying. In six weeks, I'd never been out of my nightgown. I was nursing him and I was crying. My mother was there, and I said to her, 'I don't know what's wrong with me. I can't stand it. I feel like I really hate this baby, hate this house, can't do anything, don't want to do anything!' Well, at that point I knew I had to go someplace and get help. I'd heard of the mothers' center when I was fund raising for a charity. I came here, and it's been my support and my life. I wonder how many women out there have that same feeling and are not coming to the center."

I wondered, too, and one of the founding mothers answered,

"Oh, I think there's probably a good many. It doesn't appeal to everybody, and anyway they don't know what it's all about. There's actually something of a negative feeling on the outside about mothers' centers.

"Whenever I have a discussion with people about it, the first reaction is, 'What's the matter? What do you have to talk about? Something wrong with your household?' It's like going to a psychiatrist, especially with the last generation. When I discussed this with my mother-in-law in the beginning—not now, she's very gung-ho about it, but before—she said, 'Why do you have to talk about what's going on in her house or your house? What's wrong that you need to discuss or need the support of something more than our everyday environment?' And you get that resistance from a lot of women who are not ready yet. They feel that going into this thing for themselves is like admitting that they need to work through something that might be a problem, but they're not willing to admit there is a problem. They'd rather go out to a junior gym or a swimming program with their little one. They're not troubled. Everything is good. They *say*. But they're not doing anything for themselves. Everything is for their kids."

Said a very young but clearly competent woman, who has been listening while making up lists and addressing envelopes, "It's too much, all this baby gym-and-swim stuff. Current concerns seem to be to produce the perfect child. Parents will pay for anything for their kids. But mothers find it difficult to spend on themselves, even at a mother center. The business of serving the children is getting outrageous. Our focus is on the mothers. The children are also well taken care of and there's no need to worry about them. There's so much competition out there for things for children, *we* are here for the mothers."

Another added, "We want self-respect and self-esteem. We benefit from being with each other, and bringing in outside people who run workshops and give us information on prenatal and postnatal care and midwifery and things like that. And the children benefit so much from the socializing—from us being with each other, and them being with each other, and them being able to come in and see us if they want to."

Coincidentally, the door opened and a woman came in holding a weepy toddler by the hand.

"He just had to see you for a moment, Janet," said the woman, letting the little one run to his mother.

Janet reached for him, all the mothers made welcoming sounds, and the meeting went on. Soon the small one was wreathed in smiles, and a few minutes later his mother took him back to the playroom. He had touched base with his mom and now he was okay.

"My son *loves* to come here," said another young woman. "This is like his home. Everybody knows him. He walks in, and everybody greets him by name. Plus we, the mothers, have made friends. I feel more comfortable with the people at the center than anyone I've met since leaving my job. It isn't all that easy to make new friends. A lot of us move into neighborhoods with no other kids, and you don't meet other young mothers. You've got to! Get in the car! Meet! Save your sanity!"

Chuckles. Seriousness. The conversation turned to doctors, primarily gynecologists and obstetricians, and their attitude toward their patients. More often than not, it was noted, these doctors were men. I was a little surprised to learn that most of the young women felt that the doctor-patient relationship was still seriously wanting. They had felt demeaned, pushed around, dictated to, brushed aside, intimidated. But now!

But now that they are talking to each other, they are free to express their opinions, make referrals, shop around, ask questions, demand answers. In meetings of prenatal and other groups, there are blunt exchanges of information about various doctors, the obstetrical units of local hospitals, the quality of the birth experience and nursing care, and all factors bearing upon the best interests of mother and child. "You don't have to be dictated to by your ob-gyn. If you don't like him, leave him. And tell us why. Mother centers offer a sense of advocacy. We're free to discuss our doctors. We're free to say, 'Yes, I can make a choice.' The doctor doesn't have to be the authority figure. *We* are the authority figures, and we're hiring their help."

Tough talk! But, yes, we have to be firm and make our needs and wishes known. Having a baby is supposed to be a glorious experience, and there's no reason why some stranger or a bunch of strangers should turn it into an ordeal. These are our bodies, our lives, our babies.

More business: items, including birthday notices, are requested for the newsletter. The design for the new brochure has been completed and is circulated. There is brief talk about starting a grandmothers' group, but so far there are only two interested grandmothers. Table that one. An extremely attractive mother in her mid-twenties reports on her experience with the Exploring Nature group of the Fun at One program for preschoolers. She and six lively little kids had gone on a nature walk in the vicinity of the mothers' center. "We went out to find spring, and we found it, and put it into bags." Smiling, she shows little baggies of pale green sprigs and leaves and tiny blossoms, slightly wilted now, but evocative, endearing.

Time for lunch. A mother goes to the local deli to pick up sandwiches and we adjourn to the toddlers' playroom. While working my way through my BLT, courtesy of the center, I have a word with Stella, the only single mother in the group. She is in her mid to late forties. The child of her long-dissolved marriage is twenty-six years old, the only positive result of a series of attempts and miscarriages; her baby, twenty-six months old, the unexpected but delightful product of a brief liaison with a runaway father.

He is a perfect little physical specimen, bright-eyed and alert, endlessly active and into everything. "I sometimes feel overwhelmed," said Stella. "He's a joy, but so hyper, so destructive. But what's been hardest for me about having him is that I lost practically all my friends. They just dropped me when I decided to keep him. Some people I thought were my friends gave me a baby shower, and at the shower they told me I ought to give him away. I said I wouldn't, and they never spoke to me again. I lost my job, too. They told me they didn't want me back after the baby was born. Nobody in my age group wanted anything to do with me, nor anyone with little kids. And then I came here. You get feedback from others, and nobody's being judgmental."

A little boy romped over to her from the sandbox and snuggled into her lap. They exchanged conspiratorial smiles.

"We try to have a normal life," said Stella. "He loves it here. First day I came here, I stood in the doorway for a moment and then turned away. I didn't have the guts to come in. Then Ruth came over and grabbed me. 'Try it, try it!' she said. 'It's not a life sentence.' So I tried it. I thought they'd look down on me, but they didn't. They've made life possible. They've even made it good."

After lunch I attached myself to the postnatal discussion group. Eight or nine young mothers were sitting in a semicircle, three of them accompanied by babies who periodically made off with each other's toys or sought the safety of a motherly lap. Others of these mothers' children—napping newborns or older children—were in the downstairs rooms.

The afternoon's discussion was incredibly wide-ranging and, for all its diversion into humor and various observations on current books and theater, confirmed virtually all my findings about motherhood today. Lack of preparation, and consequent self-blame, was a dominant theme.

"Nobody tells you what to expect! One day I got so uptight and furious with the kid fussing and not eating that I poured his cereal over his head. I felt terrible about it. How could I do a thing like that?"

Easily!

Everybody else is an expert: "Your mother and your mother-in-law are the main guilt inducers. Everyone was trying to tell me how to hold him, how long to leave him in his crib, how to do this or that, until finally I managed to shut them out and do what I wanted to do."

Weariness: "It never ends. As long as I'm up, there are things I could and should be doing." "The naps are such a relief. Even if I'm mopping the floor they're a relief, because she's not on my mind." "My biggest surprise—and my husband's—was that it takes *all day* to take care of one baby."

Shame: "My son hits people! Ever since the new baby came, he punches people. I think, my God, what will they think— that I abuse him?" And: "I feel like *nothing*. We mothers play a really important role in society, and yet we don't feel we're doing a professional job. *Any* job."

Old familiar concerns, mixed up with newer ones: "I wasn't ready. I never felt prepared. I was the youngest of all my family. When I worked, it was on Wall Street with career-oriented single people. They didn't know anything about kids. Now I don't know whether I should pursue a career or not. Shouldn't I? Am I not a total person? I'd like to go back to work, and I want a second child. My husband says, 'Do whatever you want to do, as long as you are happy.' But it's still a mother's job, taking care of the children, whether you work or not."

This is the biggest issue confronting and conflicting many young mothers of today: to pursue a career, to be a full-time homemaker, or to try to do both. They know it's hard. Like my fifty-year-old friend, mother of five, they know that something is likely to slip between the cracks, and they're very much concerned that it's going to be either the kids or themselves.

I noted many signs of worry and frustration. One mother had taught for six years and made a good salary. Now she had to ask *him* for money and felt guilty about buying things for herself. She also felt guilty about just wanting to go back to work, never mind actually going. Another had been a workaholic who had worked her way up through a banking firm for ten years, quit to have a baby, opted to stay home with her, and is still turning down fabulous job offers from her previous company and others as well. The baby is the most important thing in her life, but the young woman feels just as guilty about not working as she would about not staying home.

And there was one young woman, the mother of three, who didn't want to work, who liked being at home, and whose husband wanted her there. She was very content in her role. "I feel I'm old-fashioned. My husband is a good provider. There are other things to do besides go back to work." The only drawback was that other people say to her, "Oh, it's all right for *you. You* can afford to stay home." Which makes her feel somehow incomplete, overprivileged, and rather guilty.

Not fair! Why shouldn't she be able to enjoy being "just a mother"?

"Yes, well, the women's movement presumably gave us choices. You want to stay home and you can afford it, then that's what you should be doing. But you worry about losing your skills. What happens if you eventually *have* to go back to work? You've been left behind. You don't want to start back in some low-level job if you've been a stockbroker or a lab technician. And you lose your accreditation after a while. How are you going to keep up with your licenses, catch up with all that's new in your field?"

Another new concern: the high divorce rate, and the even higher skip rate. Perhaps the word *liberation* has been too loosely interpreted in some quarters. But in the opinion of these young women, there is an increasing tendency among youngish husbands to drop their wives and families and run.

"We know nice couples; they're our friends and neighbors. They seem settled and happy and they enjoy their kids. Then boom! The man just walks out. He leaves her flat, and she's not working. We have to think of this as a possibility."

And they do. Almost every one of those young mothers

knew of a case of a man abandoning his wife and kids for greener pastures or another woman. This is nothing new in the long history of marriage, but what does seem to be new is its frequency and its pervasiveness through all classes. Women who believe they have a happy home and marriage are seriously discussing what they will be able to do if a husband just takes off one day and leaves a wife with kids, a mortgage, and earning skills rusted out by years of absence from the job market.

I got the impression that these young women would be able to cope with such an event. Even if, as individuals, they couldn't handle it, they had each other. I sensed that the support was very strong. As one said, "We're like family, except that we're even less threatening."

I also got the very strong impression that these mothers, who shared so many of the concerns I had found in myself and in other women, were neither helpless nor anxious. They do have self-doubts and fears. They do worry that their mistakes will harm their children. But they do their worrying among friends with similar problems, and they find enormous relief in the realization that their experiences are not unique and that other women are happy to help them.

And they laugh at the idea of trying to be perfect mothers trying to raise perfect kids.

"The hell with all that self-blame and perfection stuff," one said inelegantly, wiping her child's orange juice off her own face. "We've seen that, with all our differences, we're pretty much alike. It's good enough to be a good enough mother. You don't have to go out of your way to be wonderful. There's no point putting expectations too high. How can you do better than create an emotionally healthy environment for your kid? A good enough mother is one who feels comfortable with herself and what she is doing."

And a quiet one said unexpectedly, "You can only do the best you can, and there's no use hitting yourself for everything.

If you have some good ideas and do some things right, you have to give yourself credit for them and not think about all the things you're not going to be able to do. Anyway, it's pretty hard to influence a kid one way or another. And usually," she added sagely, "they don't turn out too badly in the end."

I begin to think I have arrived someplace.

# CHAPTER SIXTEEN

# Here Comes the Tiger

"USUALLY they don't turn out too badly in the end."

How did she know? She only had one small girl and a little boy who stuck his fingers in people's eyes.

But I've heard that same thing said over and over again by mothers whose children are now grown. They have been desperately worried by what they perceive as their own mistakes; watched their kids grow up through destructive toddlerhood into the maniacal teens, observing their excesses and sullenness and abrupt departures with troubled eyes; endured their demands, their bad-mouthing, their hatred, their terrifying adventures on the highways and experiments with life until one day . . . I have seen many a surviving mother going around wearing a look of dazed disbelief that she had brought up a bunch of brain-damaged hoodlums.

Irene, for one. All four of her kids, three girls and a boy, were at Woodstock. All four were either school or college dropouts, and dropouts from home as well. There were days, nights, sometimes weeks when she had no idea where they all were. One girl joined a commune in Southern California, found it too boring, and went up into the mountains to shack up in a tepee with a goatherd.

But Irene kept the lines of communication open. Sometimes they wrote to her; sometimes they called. She never lectured them or hectored them. Wherever they were, they always came home for Christmas. Then they started coming home more often. Eventually they came home and stayed for a while, finished school, put on their white collars, went to work, got married, had children.

Second daughter, Peg, now has two little girls of her own. She looks forward, with apprehension, to the time when they'll be coming home late at night or not at all and she'll be listening for the sound of wheels in the driveway or a police siren.

"How could you bear it, Mom?" she says. "How could you bear not knowing where we were?"

"How could I bear knowing you were living in a tepee with a goatherd?" asks Irene.

Slightly more typical is the experience of Gina, whose two conventional daughters—loved their dad, tried their best to raise mother so she'd be fit to be taken out in public—are now beginning their careers. "In my thirties," says Gina, "I knew I would make some terrible mistake that would ruin my children's lives. Now I know I did make mistakes and the children turned out to be fine—just different. Neither is a musician or a dancer. I have a stock trader and a P.R. person. After all those years of music and ballet!"

Expectations can be a real trap. Why should our children be what we want them to be? Gina's pleased with the way her kids turned out. So is Irene.

I myself have a sense of wonder and gratitude.

It may be too early for me to say how things have turned out for me and my kids, because I like to think we're all still learning and changing. But let's just pause and have a look.

Jon became an academic triumph at Hyde, after which he stayed an extra year to participate in a leadership program and graduated with honors. The boy who had set a national standard for clownish and disreputable clothes requested a suit for his graduation ceremony. I wondered what he might consider appropriate. I asked a male friend to go shopping with him so that my son, unrehearsed and impractical as he was in the ways of haute couture, would not get something too awful.

The friend reported back that Jon had gone unerringly to the Giorgio Armani suits. They were magnificently tailored and of really splendid quality. I was very amused, and a little taken aback. Jon said, "I know it's extravagant, but I like this suit and it's good quality." I let him buy it. I figured that if I amortized the money that I might have spent on clothes for him over the years, I was still coming out ahead. And I was pleased that he thought enough of himself to want to look good at graduation. Also he pointed out, reasonably enough, that he could wear the dark blue jacket with other trousers. It meant a whole new wardrobe for him. If he were to get any other trousers.

He looked splendid when he graduated.

It was a scene to make a family's heart swell with pride, a fitting climax to years of effort—with one reservation. Jon made a superb graduation speech in which he gave his father full credit for his being there. His father, who had died years before and had never heard of Hyde! But his father's spirit was in Maine, Jon said, and that's why he was there. After my three years of agony with the rest of the Hyde parents I felt somewhat slighted—I mean, I actually felt stabbed—but I understood that Jon needed to say what he'd said about Martin. Afterward, in private and with no prompting, he put his arm around me and said, "I know that you're really the one who made this possible."

I personally thought the school had saved his life. When I made this observation to Jon he gave me a look that was cynical, amazed, contemptuous, and I don't quite know what else. Among other things, he said, "It wasn't just Hyde that turned me around. I was ready, that's all. I wasn't before." "I figured that you wanted me to go down the drain, and I said to myself, I'll show you." "Deep down, I always liked to learn things." "I was pretty young before, having a lot of fun hanging out. None of the kids my age were thinking about the future. But I've always been a pretty ambitious person. I knew that I could be really good at whatever I did." "It just shows I can do something when I put my mind to it."

Fine. It got better. He chose an excellent college in New York State and he's on the dean's list. The little boy who loved the dinosaurs at the Museum of Natural History and the junk peddlers in the park is now captivated by rocks and stalactites. When he comes home for occasional weekends and vacation days he brings stones with him and enthusiastically points out their separate, wholly different beauties. And they are truly beautiful. So is his enthusiasm. Soon he will be a qualified and practicing geologist.

He is also a fanatic about conservation, drilled into him at the Hyde School. For a while, his self-righteousness was hard to live with. He lectured Buffy and me about turning off lights and not letting the water run. He believed, and I think still does, that all we need for a bath is a puddle in the bottom of the tub. He counts toilet flushes. But he also does repairs around the apartment and his house painting is excellent.

Jon still doesn't think he owes his transformation to the Hyde School. If it hadn't been that experience it would have been something else, and he would have found it. Maybe he's right. I do know that the old-fashioned virtues of hard work and responsibility that the school taught in those days, its pioneer days, became a part of his being. There was no truck with "fulfillment," or self-indulgence. What you could do for others, as well as what you could do for yourself—that was important.

I know nothing about Hyde today. I just know that when my son was there it was run by idealistic, energetic young men whose courage and passionate convictions communicated themselves to parents and kids alike. They offered an opportunity for change to all those who were ignited by their enthusiasm. I am convinced that, in its time, it was the salvation of youngsters like Jon.

My daughter, Elizabeth (sometimes Liz but no longer

Buffy), now nineteen, thinks so too. She talks of Hyde as having "turned Jon around." But its great advantage, in her opinion, is that it took him away, and the last thing in the world she wanted to do was to follow him there and be just his little sister, as she had been for so much of her life.

"That was *my* time," she said afterward, "and I took advantage of it so I could be with you. That was when we finally did get close."

We did. And we are very close now. Close enough so that Elizabeth is very open and direct about what she has on her mind. We talked recently, without her old anger, about Jon and Hyde, Jon and jealousy, Jon and favoritism, Jon and gifts.

"I was jealous of Jonny ever since I can remember," she tells me. "You *know* he was the one who always got more valuable gifts. Yet he always thought *I* was the spoiled brat and got whatever I wanted. I guess kids are always measuring—who gets more love, more money, better presents. I did get better presents as I got older. I watched my big brother and I learned from him how to get the things I wanted.

"At least I never got hand-me-downs," she adds. "A lot of my friends always got hand-me-downs. It's a good thing I'm a girl, because if I'd been a boy I *would* have gotten hand-me-downs, and then I would really have a bad case of jealousy. I had a bad enough case as it was."

(I could just see her, my clothes-conscious, elegantly fashionable child, in Jon's hand-me-downs. A ragpicker would have refused them.)

"I'm not always jealous now," Elizabeth reflects. "Just sometimes. Jon feels the same way I do, I am sure. He may not be honest about it, but he is always going to resent the fact that I was home getting close to you while he was up at boarding school. He went away and we just got closer and closer."

I am interested in this repeated theme of closeness. It is obviously something that is of primary importance to her, and we finally achieved it. Very often, mothers and daughters never do. And that is human too. The love may be there, and usually is, but they just don't match.

Buffy and I—I can't seem to get used to Elizabeth—Elizabeth and I share a great deal. We do a lot of girl things together. We both like glamor, and care how we look; we buy makeup and try it out on each other. We celebrate holidays, birthdays, Sundays, and other days with a great deal of enthusiasm. Our daily schedules seldom coincide, yet we try to eat together as often as possible. We talk constantly, but not necessarily consistently. I chide her about a bad habit; she says she got it from me. Then why, I ask, didn't she pick up the habit of reading? Because, she answers, she knew I wanted to her to.

Her old destructiveness is gone. Her room is always neat. She plans menus because she likes to know what she's going to be eating. She loves order. Hates mess. "Mom! Can't you keep the kitchen counters clean?"

There she goes, raising mother.

She is not yet sure what her future will be, but she has decided to try out a variety of jobs before plunging into the rest of her education. At this admittedly fleeting moment she is a trainee in a publishing firm. Will she major in English? I doubt it. Too much reading. Will she be an MBA? A horse trainer? A veterinarian? A fashion designer? Her world is wide open, and she surveys its possibilities with wonder and enthusiasm. Right now she would like to be a psychologist. It would be ironic to have an expert in the family, but I want her to do what she wants to do. (As Harry Truman once said, the best thing you can do for your child is find out what he wants to do and encourage him to do it.) "I am really interested in psychology," she says. "I enjoy people. I love working with them, and not being stuck alone. And I've always been the one my friends call to discuss their problems with. I want to know more about why people do the things they do and feel the way they feel."

She would also like to get married, keep working, earn a

good living, maintain her independence, and bring up her kids to be independent too. Did she get *that* from me?

Not long ago, when we were exchanging confidences, I asked my daughter to tell me about her hate book. In fact, I tried to cajole her into letting me have a look at it. Not a chance. She wrote me something instead:

*Buffy's Hate Book* enabled me to get out my feelings at the very moment. During a fight a lot of nasty things are said, and whether they are meant or not, I'm hurt. The Book keeps track of what you've called me, or thrown into my face. For instance, if you said you hadn't wanted me, I'd write that down, and I'd be able to keep track of how many times you've said it to me. Somehow this would convince me that you meant what you said. You always taught me to write my feelings down, so I guess that is how I started it. I used to write down, along with what you said, something to verify why you said it. That's what the Buffy Book is all about.

So she's been counting insults as well as gifts.

We still have mother-daughter hassles that I know very well are childish and avoidable. A while ago we went out for dinner, since neither of us felt like cooking. I wanted to sit near the window, she wanted to sit in the back of the restaurant. We began to argue, I clutching at her arm to steer her to the window seats. And then suddenly Minerva or Jove or whoever was observing us at the moment threw a thunderbolt right at me and in a flash I saw the ridiculous power struggle I was having with my daughter. She was my kid and I wanted her to do what I wanted her to do. Why? Because I'm the mommy, that's why. I looked at her tense little face. "I'll flip you for it," I said and smiled at her as I dug out a coin. A great big smile spread over her face. She was delighted. We flipped. My "heads" won, but she didn't care. I had treated her like a person, a friend, a dinner companion.

It was a very, very small thing, but somehow a revelation, and it was a breakthrough in our relationship.

I remembered Leah Schaefer telling me that, usually, mothers are waiting for their daughters to change and the daughters are waiting for their mothers to change. Well, it is up to the older, more responsible individual to make the first move, whether it be toward a new firmness or a healthier sense of give-and-take. I was being a mother when it was only necessary for me to be a slightly more flexible person. So I made a little change, and so did my daughter.

And, as Leah says, it is never too late to change.

"I believe," she says, "that there is no time in life when people stop growing, including—and perhaps especially—in their relationships with their children. When your children are little you have a lot of power over them. As they get older you lose your power. They want to please their peers more than they want to please you. But that changes also. The capacity to change any relationship, and to continue to grow in it, is there forever."

You can change, but you cannot control the world. You cannot spare your children from all hurt. One of the hardest things about being a mother is to go through all your old rejections, to relive your childhood pains and disappointments through your child. The twin difficulty is to avoid trying to turn your child into what you wanted to be.

Leah again: "There's one thing I always wanted to create with my daughter, which I don't think I am going to be able to do. I always wanted to be confidante and pals with my mother. I have three brothers. I'm the only girl. I wanted to confide in my mother, talk to her, be chums with her and all that. It took me a long time to realize that that was not the way my mother was. I used to think that there was something wrong with me, why she wasn't that way. It took me a long time to realize that that was not a part of her nature.

"Nevertheless, I keep trying to do things with and about my daughter, where she'll be a certain way toward me, and she isn't. I've come to realize that the things I needed in my childhood that made me look for them in my mother—my daughter isn't like that either. For one thing, I was a loner when I was a child; my daughter has tons of friends. She belongs to a crowd at school. I wore hand-me-downs; she wears beautiful clothes. My daughter is good-looking; I felt unattractive. You get the picture. So there were things I needed in life that she doesn't. And I can't arrange to have certain things with her in life, at least not at this moment, because we don't want the same thing."

Which makes a mother feel bad. But not nearly as bad as lacking self-esteem, not listening to one's own instincts, failing to shop around for practical professional advice, not being assertive when you know you know better than other people, not taking action—*not doing* what is worth trying to do.

I can't count the number of times I've heard mothers play the sad games of "I shouldn't have let them . . . I should have known . . . I should have said . . ." But it cheers me enormously to think of the case of Marvelle Colby and her son, Eric, who has a learning disability that might have destroyed him if he and Marvelle had not been such a terrific team.

Eric is twenty, and he cannot read. Nevertheless, he is in his third year at Carnegie Mellon, one of the toughest colleges in the United States, and doing very well. How could this be? Because he is ingenious and intelligent, and his mother is a tiger.

"Let me give you some idea of the dimensions of the problem," says Marvelle. "In the English part of the Achievement Test, the top score is 100. Eric got *nine* when he was in high school. I'd known since he was two or three that he had a problem. As he grew up, other people—including his father—said that he was stupid. In grade school they called him stupid, and they put him in the stupid room. But I knew that, even though there was something wrong, he was a bright, adorable, precious child. He was six when his problem was diagnosed as 'minimal brain dysfunction' by a pediatric neurologist in Florida, where we were living at the time.

" 'Well, that's the diagnosis,' he said.

"And I said, 'Fine, what's the prescription?'

"He said, 'There isn't any. We don't know what to do.'

"And that's when I started my fourteen-year search for answers. But I don't consider Eric's problem a disability. It is a difference. We don't know how to teach these children because they learn differently. And obviously they can learn, or Eric would not be in college. We have overcome so much—but it hasn't been easy."

Marvelle describes their efforts in a book coauthored by Charles Straughn, *Lovejoy's College Guide for the Learning Disabled Student.* The gist is this: "What has become clear to me over the years is that parents must fight for their children, and when school authorities are negative or hostile toward their efforts, they must not let it bother them. Parents must go on and push for what their child needs—keep trying, keep doing everything they can. *They must advocate.*

"Six months to a year after Eric graduated from high school, I met the director of his school in the street. He said he had something to tell me. And that was that Eric had never used his handicap as an excuse when he couldn't do something. He thought that was terrific. 'And by the way,' he said, 'there's something else. When you came to the school to talk about Eric, the woman at the switchboard would let people know that the tiger was there. Behind my back—at least, they thought it was behind my back—they said, Here comes the tiger! And I'm telling you this as a compliment.'

"I'd had no idea of this. All the time Eric was in school, I was sure I was annoying everybody, that they didn't want me there. You don't have to have a thick skin, not to feel uncomfortable. But despite that, you can see when you are successful that it was all right to have done it.

"You always have to arm yourself with questions and with facts. If you are not a fighter, it is hard for you to attack. You must attack in a different way. You have to learn a lot. You have to learn not to accept everything the school is telling you, or believe that what people are telling you is gospel. Instead, do some investigating. Find out if there are other ways, other methods. Be your own lawyer. Be your own defense. That's a different kind of fighting. It's not being loud and aggressive. It's being smart.

"Above all, you must believe in yourself, believe in your child, and get for your child what is rightfully your child's. All children have a right to free and appropriate education. Parents have to become more actively involved, because the schools don't know everything about what is appropriate and what is not.

"In Eric's Dade County school, they tested all the children and Eric tested out as gifted. A friend on the staff called me, off the record, and told me, 'This is the word. Eric did very well, but they are not going to put him in the gifted program because he is learning disabled.' I knew people on the school board and I protested. I just talked to everybody, and they told me nothing could be done. 'Then I'll go to Tallahassee, I'll go to the governor, I will insist!' And finally they told me that they didn't know how to count Eric—label him, that is.

"I said, 'Isn't it possible that you can have LD and be gifted as well?' Because the definition of LD is that you must be of at least average intelligence and even above average intelligence, otherwise you would be retarded. I then said, 'Why don't you use Eric as a test case and put him in both programs, and then look and see if there aren't any more like him?' And after Eric, they realized that there were more like him, and they set up an LD-gifted program.

"But there were times when I almost stopped. I told the school principal, a good friend of mine, that I couldn't go on, I felt like such an idiot. Everyone said I was a crazy mother. But the principal said to me, 'You have to go on. Because who else is going to do it? If you are seriously concerned about your child, you just have to do this. And if you stick to it, you will succeed.' "

288 WHAT DID I DO WRONG?

And she did.

There are ways in which Eric helps himself by using recordings for the blind and a computer with a spelling software package, as well as doing his homework with a girl friend at school. There is every indication that he will be a very successful graduate in engineering.

He is determined to do well. And it all started with his mother, the tiger.

Only Pollyanna would suggest that all mothers and sons are capable of working their way through this kind of problem, which is not only academically, but psychologically and socially disabling. And sometimes terminally depressing. But effort, action, and determination go a long, long way. There should be no room for guilt if you have tried your damndest.

Still, guilt being a part of the human condition, we are not yet through with it. As analyst Edith Gould points out, most people who have rageful feelings toward others feel guilty about those feelings. Mothers often feel resentful and even hurtful toward their children, but they translate their anger into guilt "because the guilt is more allowable."

The fact is that there is a place for anger in mothers. Being angry is part of being human. And being angry with children doesn't destroy them. Mothers can have rousing battles with their kids and work things out. Mothers can be both loving and not loving at various times.

"The problem is," says Gould, "that mothers think they have to be loving all the time, and their anger frightens them. Men are allowed much more aggression. If women get excited and angry and start to express their anger, they are often viewed by men as hysterical. When men get excited and angry, it is almost enhancing to their masculinity."

(Are we more beautiful when we are guilty?)

Furthermore, we can't seem to forgive ourselves.

But we must.

Edith Gould elaborates: "Mothers must know that they have room for error. They have to give themselves more of a margin. But mothers fear that once they've made a mistake, it's carved in granite. They always go back to it.

"Once you've made a mistake, every trouble that the child has can be ascribed to that single original mistake. I've been talking to a mother who thinks she made a terminal error when her child was six weeks old. The little girl was very colicky and the mother couldn't stand the crying. So she put the baby in her carriage, wheeled the carriage into a room in the back of the house, closed the door, and locked it. She left her there for about forty minutes, still yelling.

"When she couldn't bear the guilt any longer she went back into the room and the child was naturally purple with crying. The mother felt terrible. Now I grant this is not the best thing to do with a six-week-old baby. However, other experiences in that child's life surely have ameliorated the effects of that episode. But the mother has never forgotten it. It's like her scarlet letter. The child is doing well. She's a happy and successful teenager. But once in a while she gets depressed or anxious, as we all do. And when she does, the mother—very psychologically aware—immediately goes back to the time she let the child cry herself purple in the back room. So this woman has a sense of herself as being an emotionally toxic mother in spite of the objective reality."

Now how could a smart woman have prevented the buildup of such guilt, such unreasonable guilt?

By not being alone with it. By talking to other mothers.

Every mother has done something similar. Every mother flips once in a while, makes wrong moves and faulty decisions; every mother says ill-chosen, hurtful things. And it helps mothers to be aware of the experiences of others—and see how other people's children are romping sturdily through life in spite of those supposedly horrendous mistakes. Thus the importance of the groups. They can save a mother's sanity.

Do we really have a chance to erase our errors? Do we have second chances throughout a child's development? I asked this of Elaine Heffner, author of *Mothering* and a specialist in family counseling, and she said emphatically, "You not only have second chances, you have a hundred thousand chances!" You learn, your children learn; each interaction is part of a learning process. If something does not work out well the first time, try again. Your child is doing that all the time. So should you. The interaction, the testing out, is not going to damage either of you.

And kids are much less fragile than we think. Many mothers try too hard to spare their children unhappiness and frustration. It isn't by avoiding these feelings that we and our children grow and mature. It's by living with them and learning to deal with them that we become able to function in society. The real goal of child rearing, as Heffner says, is "to teach your child how to live in the world. The art of mothering is the art of living, of imparting a personal value system." And that is a continuing process, providing countless chances.

Feel guilt, by all means. Recognize it. Talk about it. And realize that your guilt has little, if any, basis in reality. If none, get rid of it. If some, make reparation.

Is reparation possible? Sure it is. It's as possible and necessary as discipline. Virginia Pomeranz points out that any psychological damage you might inflict upon your child if you should happen to let your anger get out of control can be greatly reduced if you are open and honest with the child. "If you feel you've carried on too badly you can apologize afterward. You can say you were troubled and tired. You can tell your child you know he didn't deserve what you said. He'll forgive you. Children are the most forgiving creatures if you are honest with them. It's so much better to apologize for being hard on a kid than to let it go to save your pride. It's simply aggravating the child's situation.

"It is basically your asking for their forgiveness and understanding that enables them to cope with their own mistakes and to realize that if you are not infallible, they certainly are not required to be. So that if they make a mistake, they can be more forgiving of themselves—just as you can."

As for discipline, it is not to be confused with punishment. Discipline involves teaching children what is acceptable behavior and what is not. It means teaching them the rules of life. And for this, you'll need all your hundred thousand chances.

In Virginia's view, a lot of the friction between mothers and children is caused by the mothers expecting their kids to do everything they are told to do in exactly the way mother tells them to do it. "Control is some mothers' idea of doing it right." But if the child is a normal child, he's got his own ideas of how he wants to do it. "And it may not be such a terrible way of doing it, even if it's totally different from mother's way. Back off. Let him explore. Let him try it his way, if it's not going to be hurtful or infringe on other people's rights. Be patient and let him make his own discoveries. Loosen the reins a little. Be flexible."

This does not mean that a child's bad behavior should change a mother's no to yes. "But as soon as the child can talk, you really have to listen. And every now and then you've got to bend and say, 'Okay, let's do it your way, you convinced me.' If everything you say is by fiat, if you don't let the kid win occasionally, there's no point in him talking to you at all. But if you've enabled the kid to take some control of his life through listening to him, there's a percentage for him in talking to you. He thinks, maybe I can get the old girl to change her mind if I present a valid case. Which is a lot better than having him stomp to his room and slam the door."

Dr. Pomeranz suggests that there is a way for youngsters to prepare for parenthood and know in advance such astounding facts as that their newborn babies will have bowed legs, which will ultimately straighten out. Schools are going to have to be of more help, but if they can teach sex education—which they do—they can also give courses in child development and family life.

"I think it would be not a bad idea," she says, "for kids as young as thirteen or fourteen, boys as well as girls, to study early childhood development and family relationships. Let them observe little kids in a nursery school setup, so they can deal with them when they are not in a position of full responsibility; so that they can say to someone in authority, 'Why is this kid throwing things? Why is he refusing to put on his coat?' And so that they can talk to young parents about the realities of parenthood and learn something directly from them. If people were exposed to babies and small children, so that they felt comfortable with them when suddenly they were on their own, it wouldn't be quite so overwhelming."

There are also child-care and parenting books. Masses of them. More than ever before. Presenting many different opinions requiring evaluation. By all means read them, and evaluate. Believe what makes sense to you. "An understanding of a child's development needs," says T. Berry Brazelton, the distinguished pediatrician who is chief of the child development unit at Boston's Children's Hospital, "can help parents relax and allow the child's own drive toward health to take over."

As of now, we still have such great gaps in our knowledge of child development that we don't really know *how crucial* it is for a mother to be close to her child for *how long* to ensure his healthy development. A few months? A year? Three years? Five? More? The question has become almost academic. Most women *must* work. Over half of the women in this country have to work for either financial or psychological reasons. More than two-thirds of today's mothers are working women. Economic necessity drives the majority of them into the job market. "It is not really possible," says Dr. Brazelton, "to make them choose anymore between staying home and working."

This means, says Brazelton, that mothers and children need backup and support from fathers and employers—and a day-care system far better than we know it today, for which a nationwide program is needed.

Women often ask Dr. Brazelton, "When will I be able to go back to work without hurting the baby?"

Again, there is no absolute answer. It varies from mother to mother and child to child. But Brazelton believes that loving, qualitative mother care within the first few months of birth is enough to equip the child to handle the working hours of separation from his mother; and that at least four months should be nationally mandated as paid maternity leave. Most important is that the working parent should not feel torn and guilty about leaving her baby. It she does, her child will likely be tense and miserable too.

The truth is that today's mothers are doubly blessed in that they cannot afford the pain of guilt as they go out to earn the rent money, yet they can look to role models who have paved their way for them. It used to be hard, even bizarre, for a woman to be a college professor, lawyer, architect, surgeon, airline pilot, corporate executive, or politician as well as a mother. Now it is much easier. The trail has been blazed.

Daughters today look at their mothers and their mothers' friends and at women in the headlines, and they see assertive women, women of self-esteem, happy women—mothers who value work in all fields of endeavor. Sons today see mothers achieving in areas that used to be exclusive to men, and they see them as self-assured and unafraid. As they come to adulthood, their attitude will be different from that of their fathers. The change is already well under way. The "male chauvinist pig" of the heady days of liberation is already an anachronism, an artifact. He may not know it, but he is. We are closing in on a new concept of Mother's Day. This time is our time.

"The next generation of young women will start from a different place—a more confident place—about what it means to be a women," says Betty Friedan. "To be sure, they may face a new set of problems, but there won't be that automatic shrinking away, that sense of being something less. I believe that women will enjoy better mental health and more political power and will relish both their careers and their motherhood. Their sense of possibilities will be lovely."

Oh, yes, it will be lovely!

Our changing revolutionary times are scary but wonderful and exciting. Mother blaming and mother hatred have been developmental stages, similar to the development of our children. To our children, we started out as omnipotent and wonderful; we then acquired some kind of fungus and became horrible; time wrought its magic, and we became whole. Fathers and other factors were seen as having some influence upon our children's lives.

So go the notions attendant upon motherhood as seen by our culture. Mother was toppled off her pedestal to be denounced as a jerk. Then she was observed to pick herself up, dust herself off, and storm the barricades, at which time she was seen to be a person of formidable talents. We have reached another developmental stage, and an inspiring one. Fathers as well as mothers, whole families, schools, the church, the media, the neighbors, the genes, and a whole galaxy of previously underrated elements have been seen to be among the ingredients that used to spell *mother.*

We are looking at a picture in which the father has an increasingly prominent role, and in which the extended family—in its various forms—is coming back into its own.

I see this as part of the process of evolution, a leap toward the future. And this, in turn, is a phase of the revolution that is both complicating and transforming our lives as women and as mothers.

Let us seize this revolutionary moment for the sake of our children, their fathers, and ourselves.

Not so long ago, Jon came home for a weekend and Elizabeth gave him a warm hello. To my astonishment, they gave each other a big hug and a kiss. It would be all right if he called her Liz, she said, but there's to be no more Buffy.

Fine. Everybody was happy.

We got along like a family: warm, caring, laughing, raising our voices, squabbling, never actually screaming or coming to blows. It was wonderful, almost too good to be true. I looked at my two loved ones benignly. If they had turned out bad, I thought, critics would have attributed their flaws to childhood trauma and the unfortunate effects of my haphazard child-rearing methods. If they triumph noticeably, as they seem well on their way to doing—please, kids! for your mother's sake!—it will be said that they were shaped and strengthened by adversity.

But I had a hand in it too. I am still not looking for praise or blame, but I don't think my kids are the terrific, funny, and outgoing people they are "in spite of me." I believe, and I gather they believe, that I have not been the terrible mother I used to think I was. Sure, I've rocked them around a little. I have been afraid, and I have undoubtedly made a lot of mistakes. But I have loved them and I do love them. I have taken action for them, been honest with them, and they know that I will go to bat for them any time it's necessary.

They are stable, sane, witty, wonderful, ambitious in what seems to me a very healthy way, generally considerate of other people, and sometimes utterly exasperating. All this, not just in spite of me, but partly because of me.

Obviously, I didn't do everything wrong. Are my kids maladjusted? No. Ill prepared for life? No. Unhappy? No. Jealous? Hardly at all. Ignorant, friendless, resentful, self-pitying? No. Lively, alert, attractive, interested in the world and people around them? Yes. Capable of laughter and forgiveness? Yes. I think they're okay.

I look at them and I look back on all the things I thought I did wrong (and some things I *know* I did wrong) and see two individuals. Not two products. I alone did not make them what they are today. I am not solely responsible for what they have become, and for what will yet become of them. They have taken over much of the responsibility themselves. And a little bit of luck hasn't hurt us.

We look at each other. I don't know exactly what they're thinking, but for a change I do know exactly what is in my mind. Why should I ask myself, "What did I do wrong?" *Is* something wrong? Are these, my offspring, worthless messes? Indeed not. Maybe somewhere in my heart or mind I have had a blueprint for what my kids were supposed to be, and perhaps they haven't turned out the way I thought they would. They've turned out to be real people, their own selves, not the product of my imaginings.

I am so happy with them as they are.

My happiness gives me the freedom to search myself and ask—just as other mothers should—not, "What did I do wrong?" but "What did I do right?"